Fifth Edition

A Pocket Style Manual

Diana Hacker

Contributing Authors

Nancy Sommers
Tom Jehn
Jane Rosenzweig

Harvard University

Contributing ESL Specialist

Marcy Carbajal Van Horn

Santa Fe Community College

Clarity

Grammar

Punctuation and Mechanics

Research

MLA, APA, *Chicago*

Usage/Grammatical Terms

Bedford/St. Martin's   Boston ◆ New York

For Bedford/St. Martin's

Executive Editor: Michelle M. Clark
Development Editors: Mara Weible and Barbara G. Flanagan
Senior Production Editor: Anne Noonan
Senior Production Supervisor: Nancy Myers
Senior Marketing Manager: John Swanson
Assistant Production Editor: Katherine Caruana
Editorial Assistant: Alicia Young
Copyeditor: Linda B. McLatchie
Text Design: Claire Seng-Niemoeller
Cover Design: Donna Lee Dennison
Composition: Matrix Publishing Services
Printing and Binding: Quad/Graphics Leominster

President: Joan E. Feinberg
Editorial Director: Denise B. Wydra
Editor in Chief: Karen S. Henry
Director of Marketing: Karen Melton Soeltz
Director of Editing, Design, and Production: Marcia Cohen
Managing Editor: Elizabeth M. Schaaf

Library of Congress Control Number: 2009902511

Manufactured in the United States of America.

4   3   2   1

e   d

For information, write: Bedford/St. Martin's, 75 Arlington Street,
Boston, MA 02116   (617-399-4000)

ISBN-10: 0-312-66480-X
ISBN-13: 978-0-312-66480-0

Acknowledgments

Louise Bogan, excerpt from "Women," from *The Blue Estuaries: Poems
    1923–1968.* Copyright © 1968 by Louise Bogan. Reprinted with
    the permission of Farrar, Straus & Giroux, LLC.
EBSCO Information Services, various screen shots. Reprinted with
    the permission of EBSCO Information Services.

How to Use This Book

A Pocket Style Manual is a quick reference for writers and researchers. As a writer, you can turn to it for advice on revising sentences for clarity, grammar, punctuation, and mechanics. As a researcher, you can refer to its tips on finding and evaluating sources and to its color-coded sections on writing MLA, APA, and *Chicago* papers.

Here are the book's reference features.

The brief or detailed contents The brief table of contents inside the front cover will usually send you close to the information you're looking for. Occasionally you may want to consult the more detailed contents inside the back cover.

The index If you aren't sure which topic to choose in one of the tables of contents, turn to the index at the back of the book. For example, you may not realize that the choice between *is* and *are* is a matter of subject-verb agreement. In that case, simply look up "*is* vs. *are*" in the index, and you will be directed to the pages you need.

Research sources For advice on posing a research question and on finding and evaluating sources, turn to sections 25–27.

MLA, APA, and Chicago papers Color-coded sections—orange for MLA, green for APA, and brown for *Chicago*—keep you focused on the type of research paper you are writing. Each section gives discipline-specific advice on supporting a thesis, avoiding plagiarism, and integrating and documenting sources. Directories to the documentation models are easy to find. Just look for the first of the pages marked with a color band.

The glossaries When in doubt about the correct use of commonly confused or misused words (such as *affect* and *effect*), consult section 44, the glossary of usage. For brief definitions of grammatical terms such as *subordinate clause* and *participial phrase,* turn to section 45.

On the Web boxes On the Web boxes in the book direct you to exercises, model papers, and other resources on the companion Web site.

A Pocket Style Manual is meant to be consulted as the need arises. Keep it on your desk—right next to your mouse pad—or tuck it into your backpack or jacket pocket and carry it with you as a ready reference.

How to Use the Companion Web Site

The Web site for *A Pocket Style Manual* offers an extensive collection of carefully developed writing and research help—the largest and best collection available on the Web. Visit <**dianahacker.com/pocket**> to begin exploring the resources listed below and more.

Exercises   Practice online with nearly twelve hundred interactive grammar and research exercise items with immediate feedback. Unique research exercises will help you integrate sources and avoid plagiarism in MLA, APA, and *Chicago* papers.

Model papers   Model research essays in MLA, APA, *Chicago,* and CSE styles provide cross-curricular guidance in writing and formatting a variety of documents.

Research and Documentation Online   Find guidelines and models for documenting sources in more than thirty academic disciplines.

Language Debates   If you're wondering about whether to use *lie* or *lay, that* or *which,* and so on, check out these mini-essays on controversial topics of grammar and usage.

ESL help   New Web-based help designed for ESL and multilingual writers includes charts and study help, sample papers, and exercises.

Resources for writers and tutors   Make the most of your writing center sessions with these revision checklists, tips, and helpsheets for common writing, grammar, and research problems.

Interactive tutorials   Developed with visual learners in mind, these tutorials illustrate real-world student writing situations. Watch as students learn to integrate sources, navigate campus ESL resources, work with paraphrase and summary, and talk about peer review.

Clarity

1 Tighten wordy sentences.

Long sentences are not necessarily wordy, nor are short sentences always concise. A sentence is wordy if its meaning can be conveyed in fewer words.

1a Redundancies

Redundancies such as *cooperate together*, *basic essentials*, and *true fact* are a common source of wordiness. There is no need to say the same thing twice.

▶ Daniel ~~is employed~~ *works* at a software company ~~working~~

as a marketing assistant.

Modifiers are redundant when their meanings are suggested by other words in the sentence.

▶ Sylvia ~~very hurriedly~~ scribbled her name and

phone number on the back of a greasy napkin.

1b Empty or inflated phrases

An empty word or phrase can be cut with little or no loss of meaning. An inflated phrase can be reduced to a word or two.

▶ ~~In my opinion,~~ *O*ur current immigration policy is

misguided on several counts.

▶ We will file the appropriate forms ~~in the event that~~ *if*

we cannot meet the deadline.

INFLATED	CONCISE
along the lines of	like
at the present time	now, currently
because of the fact that	because
by means of	by
due to the fact that	because
for the reason that	because
in order to	to
in spite of the fact that	although, though

INFLATED	CONCISE
in the event that	if
until such time as	until

1c Needlessly complex structures

In a rough draft, sentence structures are often more complex than they need to be.

► ~~There is~~ A̲nother DVD ~~that~~ tells the story of Charles Darwin and introduces the theory of evolution.

► ~~It is imperative that~~ A̲ll police officers *must* follow strict procedures when apprehending a suspect.

► The CEO claimed that because of volatile market conditions she could not ~~make an~~ estimate ~~of~~ the company's future profits.

ON THE WEB > dianahacker.com/pocket > Grammar exercises > Clarity > E-ex 1–1 to 1–3

2 Prefer active verbs.

As a rule, active verbs express meaning more vigorously than their duller counterparts—forms of the verb *be* or verbs in the passive voice. Forms of *be* (*be, am, is, are, was, were, being, been*) lack vigor because they convey no action. Passive verbs lack strength because their subjects receive the action instead of doing it.

Forms of *be* and passive verbs have legitimate uses, but if an active verb can convey your meaning as well, use it.

BE VERB	A surge of power *was* responsible for the destruction of the coolant pumps.
PASSIVE	The coolant pumps *were destroyed* by a surge of power.
ACTIVE	A surge of power *destroyed* the coolant pumps.

2a When to replace *be* verbs

Not every *be* verb needs replacing. The forms of *be* (*be, am, is, are, was, were, being, been*) work well when you want to link a subject to a noun that clearly renames it or to a vivid adjective that describes it: *Advertising is legalized lying. Great intellects are skeptical.*

If a *be* verb makes a sentence needlessly wordy, however, consider replacing it. Often a phrase following the verb will contain a word (such as *violation*) that suggests a more vigorous, active alternative (*violate*).

▶ Burying nuclear waste in Antarctica would ~~be in~~ *violate* ~~violation of~~ an international treaty.

▶ When Rosa Parks ~~was resistant to~~ *resisted* giving up her seat on the bus, she became a civil rights hero.

NOTE: When used as helping verbs with present participles to express ongoing action, *be* verbs are fine: *She was swimming when the whistle blew.* (See 11b.)

2b When to replace passive verbs

In the active voice, the subject of the sentence does the action; in the passive, the subject receives the action.

ACTIVE   The committee *reached* a decision.

PASSIVE   A decision *was reached* by the committee.

In passive sentences, the actor (in this case *committee*) frequently disappears from the sentence: *A decision was reached.*

In most cases, you will want to emphasize the actor, so you should use the active voice. To replace a passive verb with an active alternative, make the actor the subject of the sentence.

▶ *Lightning struck the transformer.* ~~The transformer was struck by lightning.~~

▶ *The settlers stripped the land of timber before realizing* ~~The land was stripped of timber before the settlers~~ ~~realized~~ the consequences of their actions.

The passive voice is appropriate when you wish to emphasize the receiver of the action or to minimize the importance of the actor. In the following sentence, for example, the writer wished to focus on the tobacco plants, not on the people spraying them: *As the time for harvest approaches, the tobacco plants are sprayed with a chemical to retard the growth of suckers.*

NOTE: Scientific writing often uses the passive voice to emphasize the experiment or the process: *The solution was heated to the boiling point and then reduced in volume by 50 percent.*

ON THE WEB > dianahacker.com/pocket > Language Debates >
Passive voice

ON THE WEB > dianahacker.com/pocket > Grammar exercises >
Clarity > E-ex 2–1 to 2–3

---

3 Balance parallel ideas.

If two or more ideas are parallel, they should be expressed in parallel grammatical form.

> A kiss can be a comma, a question mark, or an exclamation point.   —Mistinguett
>
> This novel is not to be tossed lightly aside, but to be hurled with great force.   —Dorothy Parker

3a Items in a series

Balance all items in a series by presenting them in parallel grammatical form.

▶ Cross-training involves a variety of exercises,
such as running, swimming, and weights.
                                        lifting

▶ Children who study music also learn confidence,
coordination, and ~~they are creative.~~
                          creativity.

▶   **After assuring us that he was sober, Sam drove**

   down the middle of the road, ran one red light,
       went through
   and ^ two stop signs.

3b Paired ideas

When pairing ideas, underscore their connection by expressing them in similar grammatical form. Paired ideas are usually connected in one of three ways: (1) with a co-ordinating conjunction such as *and*, *but*, or *or*; (2) with a pair of correlative conjunctions such as *either . . . or*, *neither . . . nor*, *not only . . . but also*, or *whether . . . or*; or (3) with a word introducing a comparison, usually *than* or *as*.

▶   **Many states are reducing property taxes for home**
                    extending
   owners and ~~extend~~ ^ financial aid in the form of tax

   credits to renters.

The coordinating conjunction *and* connects two *-ing* verb forms: *reducing . . . extending.*

▶   **Thomas Edison was not only a prolific inventor**

   but also ~~was~~ a successful entrepreneur.

The correlative conjunction *not only . . . but also* connects two noun phrases: *a prolific inventor* and *a successful entrepreneur.*

                           to ground
▶   **It is easier to speak in abstractions than ~~grounding~~**
                                  ^

   one's thoughts in reality.

The comparative term *than* links two infinitive phrases: *to speak . . . to ground.*

NOTE: Repeat function words such as prepositions (*by*, *to*) and subordinating conjunctions (*that*, *because*, *when*) to make parallel ideas easier to grasp.

▶   **Online merchants are motivated to mark down**

   prices when sales slump before a major holiday
       when
   or ^ the competition offers new discounts.

ON THE WEB > dianahacker.com/pocket > Grammar exercises > Clarity > E-ex 3–1 to 3–3

4 Add needed words.

Do not omit words necessary for grammatical or logical completeness. Readers need to see at a glance how the parts of a sentence are connected.

4a Words in compound structures

In compound structures, words are often omitted for economy: *Tom is a man who means what he says and* [*who*] *says what he means.* Such omissions are acceptable as long as the omitted word is common to both parts of the compound structure.

If the shorter version defies grammar or idiom because an omitted word is not common to both parts of the structure, the word must be put back in.

▶ Some of the regulars are acquaintances whom we
  who
  see at work or live in our community.
  ^

  The word *who* must be included because *whom live in our community* is not grammatically correct.

▶ *accepted*
  Mayor Davis never has and never will accept a bribe.
  ^

  Has . . . accept is not grammatically correct.

▶ *in*
  Many South Pacific tribes still believe and live by
  ^

  ancient laws.

  Believe . . . by is not idiomatic English.

4b The word *that*

Add the word *that* if there is any danger of misreading without it.

▶ *that*
  Looking out the family room window, Sara saw her
  ^

  favorite tree, which she had climbed so often as

  a child, was gone.

  Sara didn't see the tree; she saw that the tree was gone.

4c Words in comparisons

Comparisons should be between items that are alike. To compare unlike items is illogical and distracting.

▶ The women entering VMI can expect haircuts as
  those of
  short as the male cadets.
         ^

  Haircuts must be compared with haircuts, not with cadets.

Comparisons should be complete enough so that readers will understand what is being compared.

INCOMPLETE   Brand X is less salty.

COMPLETE   Brand X is less salty than Brand Y.

Also, comparisons should leave no ambiguity about meaning. In the following sentence, two interpretations are possible.

AMBIGUOUS   Kai helped me more than my roommate.

CLEAR   Kai helped me more than *he helped* my roommate.

CLEAR   Kai helped me more than my roommate *did*.

ON THE WEB > dianahacker.com/pocket > Grammar exercises >
Clarity > E-ex 4–1 and 4–2

5 Eliminate confusing shifts.

5a Shifts in point of view

The point of view of a piece of writing is the perspective from which it is written: first person (*I* or *we*), second person (*you*), or third person (*he, she, it, one,* or *they*). Writers who are having difficulty settling on an appropriate point of view sometimes shift confusingly from one to another. The solution is to choose a suitable perspective and then stay with it.

▶ Our class practiced rescuing a victim trapped in a
                                    We   *our*
  wrecked car. ~~You~~ were graded on ~~your~~ speed
     our   ^   ^
  and ~~your~~ skill.
          ^

▶ *You need*
~~One needs~~ a password and a credit card number to
    ^
access this database. You will be billed at an

hourly rate.

Shifts from the third-person singular to the third-person plural are especially common. (See also 12a.)

▶ *Artists are*
~~The artist is~~ often seen as a threat to society,
    ^
especially when they refuse to conform to

conventional standards of taste.

NOTE: The *I* (or *we*) point of view, which emphasizes the writer, is a good choice for writing based primarily on personal experience. The *you* point of view, which emphasizes the reader, works well for giving advice or explaining how to do something. The third-person point of view, which emphasizes the subject, is appropriate in most academic and professional writing.

5b Shifts in tense

Consistent verb tenses clearly establish the time of the actions being described. When a passage begins in one tense and then shifts without warning and for no reason to another, readers are distracted and confused.

▶ There was no way I could fight the current and
                                              jumped
win. Just as I was losing hope, a stranger ~~jumps~~
                         swam   ^
off a passing boat and ~~swims~~ toward me.
                          ^

Writers often shift verb tenses when writing about literature. The literary convention is to describe fictional events consistently in the present tense. (See p. 30.)

▶ The scarlet letter is a punishment placed on
                                              is
Hester's breast by the community, and yet it ~~was~~
                                               ^
an imaginative product of Hester's own needlework.

ON THE WEB > dianahacker.com/pocket > Grammar exercises >
Clarity > E-ex 5–1 to 5–4

6 Untangle mixed constructions.

A mixed construction contains sentence parts that do not sensibly fit together. The mismatch may be a matter of grammar or of logic.

6a Mixed grammar

You should not begin with one grammatical plan and then switch without warning to another.

▶ ~~For~~ *M*ost drivers who have a blood alcohol concentration of .05 percent increase their risk of causing an accident.

The prepositional phrase beginning with *For* cannot serve as the subject of the verb *increase*. The revision makes *drivers* the subject.

▶ Although the United States is one of the wealthiest nations in the world, ~~but~~ more than twelve million of our children live in poverty.

The *Although* clause is subordinate, so it cannot be linked to an independent clause with the coordinating conjunction *but*.

6b Illogical connections

A sentence's subject and verb should make sense together.

▶ Under the revised plan, the elderly ~~who now receive a double personal exemption,~~ *the double personal exemption for* will be abolished.

The exemption, not the elderly, will be abolished.

▶ Social workers decided that ~~Tiffany's welfare~~ *Tiffany* would not be safe living with her mother.

Tiffany, not her welfare, would not be safe.

6c *is when*, *is where*, and *reason . . . is because* constructions

In formal English, many readers object to *is when*, *is where*, and *reason . . . is because* constructions on either logical or grammatical grounds.

▶   Anorexia nervosa is ~~where people,~~ *a disorder suffered by people who,* believing they are too fat, diet to the point of starvation.

Anorexia nervosa is a disorder, not a place.

▶   ~~The reason~~ I was late ~~is~~ because my motorcycle broke down.

> **ON THE WEB > dianahacker.com/pocket >** Grammar exercises > Clarity > E-ex 6–1 and 6–2

7   Repair misplaced and dangling modifiers.

Modifiers should point clearly to the words they modify. As a rule, related words should be kept together.

7a   Misplaced words

The most commonly misplaced words are limiting modifiers such as *only*, *even*, *almost*, *nearly*, and *just*. They should appear in front of a verb only if they modify the verb. If they limit the meaning of some other word in the sentence, they should be placed in front of that word.

▶   Lasers ~~only~~ destroy *only* the target, leaving the surrounding healthy tissue intact.

▶   I couldn't ~~even~~ save *even* a dollar out of my paycheck.

When the limiting modifier *not* is misplaced, the sentence usually suggests a meaning the writer did not intend.

▶   In 1860, all black southerners *not* were ~~not~~ slaves.

The original sentence means that no black southerners were slaves. The revision makes the writer's real meaning clear.

7b Misplaced phrases and clauses

Although phrases and clauses can appear at some distance from the words they modify, make sure your meaning is clear. When phrases or clauses are oddly placed, absurd misreadings can result.

▶ *On the walls*
  ~~There~~ are many pictures of comedians who have

  performed at Gavin's~~.~~ ~~on the walls.~~

  The comedians weren't performing on the walls; the pictures were on the walls.

▶ *150-pound,*
  The robber was described as a six-foot-tall man

  with a mustache~~.~~ ~~weighing 150 pounds.~~

  The robber, not the mustache, weighed 150 pounds.

7c Dangling modifiers

A dangling modifier fails to refer logically to any word in the sentence. Dangling modifiers are usually introductory word groups (such as participial phrases) that suggest but do not name an actor. When a sentence opens with such a modifier, readers expect the subject of the following clause to name the actor. If it doesn't, the modifier dangles.

DANGLING   Upon entering the doctor's office, a skeleton caught my attention.

This sentence suggests—absurdly—that the skeleton entered the doctor's office.

To repair a dangling modifier, you can revise the sentence in one of two ways:

1. Name the actor immediately following the introductory modifier or
2. name the actor in the modifier.

▶   *I noticed*
  Upon entering the doctor's office, a skeleton~~.~~

  ~~caught my attention.~~

▶ *As I entered*
  ~~Upon entering~~ the doctor's office, a skeleton

  caught my attention.

A dangling modifier cannot be repaired simply by moving it: *A skeleton caught my attention upon entering the doctor's office.* The sentence still suggests that the skeleton entered the doctor's office.

▶ Encouraged by the mayor's new economic initiative, renovation ~~has begun~~ *business owners have begun* in many of the storefronts in Dock Square.

Renovation wasn't encouraged; the business owners were.

▶ After completing seminary training, ~~women's~~ *women were often denied* access to the priesthood~~, was often denied.~~

The women (not their access to the priesthood) complete the training. The writer has revised the sentence by making *women* (not *women's access*) the subject.

ON THE WEB > dianahacker.com/pocket > Language Debates > Dangling modifiers

7d Split infinitives

An infinitive consists of *to* plus a verb: *to think, to dance.* When a modifier appears between its two parts, an infinitive is said to be "split": *to carefully balance.* If a split infinitive is awkward, move the modifier to another position in the sentence.

▶ Cardiologists encourage their patients to ~~more carefully~~ watch their cholesterol levels *more carefully.*

Attempts to avoid split infinitives sometimes result in awkward sentences. When alternative phrasing sounds unnatural, most experts allow—and even encourage—splitting the infinitive. *We decided to actually enforce the law* is a natural construction in English. *We decided actually to enforce the law* is not.

ON THE WEB > dianahacker.com/pocket > Language Debates > Split infinitives

ON THE WEB > dianahacker.com/pocket > Grammar exercises > Clarity > E-ex 7–1 to 7–4

8   Provide some variety.

When a rough draft is filled with too many same-sounding sentences, try to inject some variety—as long as you can do so without sacrificing clarity or ease of reading.

8a   Combining choppy sentences

If a series of short sentences sounds choppy, consider combining sentences. Look for opportunities to tuck some of your ideas into subordinate clauses. A subordinate clause, which contains a subject and a verb, begins with a word such as *after, although, because, before, if, since, that, unless, until, when, where, which,* or *who.* (See p. 248.)

▶   The executive committee was made up of super-

           who

    stars. ~~They~~ fought for leadership instead of

    addressing the company's problems.

▶   *because we*

    We keep our use of insecticides to a minimum.

    ~~We~~ are concerned about the environment.

Also look for opportunities to tuck some of your ideas into phrases, word groups that lack subjects or verbs (or both).

▶   The Chesapeake and Ohio Canal, ~~is~~ a 184-mile

    waterway constructed in the 1800s. ~~It~~ was a major

    source of transportation for goods during the Civil War.

    Enveloped

▶   ~~Sister Consilio was enveloped~~ in a black robe with

                                    Sister Consilio

    only her face and hands visible. ~~She~~ was an

    imposing figure.

At times it makes sense to combine short sentences by joining them with *and, but,* or *or.*

▶   *and*

    Shore houses were flooded up to the first floor.

    Brant's Lighthouse was swallowed by the sea.

TIP: Most of the time, you should avoid stringing a series of sentences together with *and*, *but*, or *or*. For sentence variety, place some of the ideas in subordinate clauses or phrases.

▶ *When my*
~~My~~ uncle noticed the frightened look on my face,
^

~~and~~ he told me that the dentures in the glass were

not real teeth.

▶ These particles, ~~are~~ known as "stealth liposomes,"
^

~~and they~~ can hide in the body for a long time

without detection.

8b Varying sentence openings

Most sentences in English begin with the subject, move to the verb, and continue to an object, with modifiers tucked in along the way or put at the end. For the most part, such sentences are fine. Put too many of them in a row, however, and they become monotonous.

Words, phrases, or clauses modifying the verb can often be inserted ahead of the subject.

▶ *Eventually a*
~~A~~ few drops of sap ~~eventually~~ began to trickle into
^

the pail.

▶ *Just as we were heading to work, the*
~~The~~ earthquake rumbled throughout the valley. ~~just~~
^   ^

~~as we were heading to work.~~

Participial phrases (beginning with verb forms such as *driving* or *exhausted*) can frequently be moved to the beginning of a sentence without loss of clarity.

▶   *D*
~~The university,~~ discouraged by the researchers'
^
                              the university
apparent lack of progress, nearly withdrew funding
^

for the prize-winning experiments.

NOTE: In a sentence that begins with a participial phrase, the subject of the sentence must name the person or thing being described. If it doesn't, the phrase dangles. (See 7c.)

ON THE WEB > dianahacker.com/pocket > Grammar exercises >
Clarity > E-ex 8–1 and 8–2

9 Find an appropriate voice.

An appropriate voice is one that suits your subject, en-
gages your audience, and conforms to the conventions of
the genre in which you are writing. When in doubt about
the conventions of a particular genre—lab reports, informal essays, research papers, business memos, and so on—
look at models written by experts in the field.

In the academic, professional, and business worlds,
four kinds of language are generally considered inappropriate: jargon, which sounds too pretentious; clichés,
which are overused and predictable; slang, which sounds
too casual; and sexist or biased language, which offends
many readers.

9a Jargon

Jargon is specialized language used among members of a
trade, profession, or group. Use jargon only when readers
will be familiar with it; even then, use it only when plain
English will not do as well.

JARGON For years, the indigenous body politic of South
Africa attempted to negotiate legal enfranchise-
ment without result.

REVISED For years, the indigenous people of South Africa
negotiated in vain for the right to vote.

Broadly defined, jargon includes puffed-up language
designed more to impress readers than to inform them.
Common examples in business, government, higher education, and the military are given in the following list,
with plain English translations in parentheses.

commence (begin)   indicator (sign)
components (parts)   input (advice)
endeavor (try)   optimal (best)
exit (leave)   parameters (boundaries, limits)
facilitate (help)   prior to (before)
factor (consideration, cause) prioritize (set priorities)
finalize (finish)   utilize (use)
impact (v.) (affect)   viable (workable)

Sentences filled with jargon are hard to read, and they are often wordy as well.

▶ If managers ~~have adequate input from~~ *listen to* subordi-
   nates, they can ~~effectuate more visible~~ *make better* decisions.

▶ All ~~employees functioning in the capacity of~~ work-
   study students ~~are required to give evidence of~~ *must prove that they are*
   ~~current enrollment.~~ *currently enrolled.*

9b Clichés

The pioneer who first announced that he had "slept like a log" no doubt amused his companions with a fresh and unlikely comparison. Today, however, that comparison is a cliché, a saying that has lost its dazzle from overuse.

In your writing, do not rely heavily on clichés. To see just how predictable clichés are, put your hand over the right-hand column below and then finish the phrases given on the left.

cool as a	cucumber
beat around	the bush
busy as a	bee, beaver
crystal	clear
light as a	feather
like a bull	in a china shop
playing with	fire
nutty as a	fruitcake
selling like	hotcakes
water under the	bridge
white as a	sheet, ghost
avoid clichés like the	plague

The cure for clichés is frequently simple: Just delete them. When this won't work, try adding some element of surprise. One student who had written that she had butterflies in her stomach revised her cliché like this:

> If all of the action in my stomach is caused by butterflies, there must be a horde of them, with horseshoes on.

The image of butterflies wearing horseshoes is fresh and unlikely, not dully predictable like the original cliché.

ON THE WEB > **dianahacker.com/pocket** > Language Debates > Clichés

9c Slang

Slang is an informal and sometimes private vocabulary that expresses the solidarity of a group such as teenagers, rock musicians, or soccer fans. Although it does have a certain vitality, slang is a code that not everyone understands, and it is too informal for most written work.

▶   The new governor is ~~an out of the box~~ *a creative* thinker.

9d Sexist language

Sexist language is language that stereotypes or demeans women or men. Such language arises from stereotypical thinking, from traditional pronoun use, and from words used to refer indefinitely to both sexes.

Stereotypical thinking.   In your writing, avoid referring to any one profession as exclusively male or exclusively female (such as referring to nurses in general as females). Also avoid using different conventions when identifying women and men (such as giving a woman's marital status but not a man's).

▶   All executives' ~~wives~~ *spouses* are invited to the picnic.

▶   Boris Stotsky, attorney, and ~~Mrs.~~ Cynthia Jones, ~~mother of three,~~ *graphic designer,* are running for city council.

The pronouns he *and* him.   Traditionally, *he*, *him*, and *his* were used to refer indefinitely to persons of either sex: *A journalist is stimulated by his deadline*. You can avoid such usage in one of three ways: substitute a pair of pronouns (*he* or *she*, *his* or *her*); reword in the plural; or revise the sentence to avoid the problem.

▶   A journalist is stimulated by his *or her* deadline.

▶   ~~A journalist is~~ *Journalists are* stimulated by ~~his deadline.~~ *their deadlines.*

▶ A journalist is stimulated by ~~his~~ *a* deadline.

man *words*.   Like *he* and *his*, the nouns *man* and *men* and related words were once used indefinitely to refer to persons of either sex. Use gender-neutral terms instead.

INAPPROPRIATE	APPROPRIATE
chairman	chairperson, chair
congressman	representative, legislator
fireman	firefighter
mailman	mail carrier, postal worker
mankind	people, humans
to man	to operate, to staff
weatherman	meteorologist, forecaster
workman	worker, laborer

ON THE WEB > dianahacker.com/pocket > Language Debates > Sexist language

9e Offensive language

Obviously it is impolite to use offensive terms such as *Polack* or *redneck*, but offensive language can take more subtle forms. When describing groups of people, choose names that the groups currently use to describe themselves.

▶ North Dakota takes its name from the ~~Indian~~ *Sioux* word meaning "friend" or "ally."

▶ Many ~~Oriental~~ *Asian* immigrants have recently settled in our small town.

Avoid stereotyping a person or a group even if you believe your generalization to be positive.

▶ It was no surprise that Greer, ~~a Chinese American,~~ *an excellent math and science student,* was selected for the honors chemistry program.

ON THE WEB > dianahacker.com/pocket > Grammar exercises > Clarity > E-ex 9–1 to 9–3

Grammar

10 Make subjects and verbs agree.

In the present tense, verbs agree with their subjects in number (singular or plural) and in person (first, second, or third). The present-tense ending *-s* is used on a verb if its subject is third-person singular; otherwise the verb takes no ending. Consider, for example, the present-tense forms of the verb *give*:

	SINGULAR	PLURAL
FIRST PERSON	I give	we give
SECOND PERSON	you give	you give
THIRD PERSON	he/she/it gives	they give
	Yolanda gives	parents give

The verb *be* varies from this pattern; unlike any other verb, it has special forms in *both* the present and the past tense.

PRESENT-TENSE FORMS OF *BE*		PAST-TENSE FORMS OF *BE*	
I am	we are	I was	we were
you are	you are	you were	you were
he/she/it is	they are	he/she/it was	they were

Problems with subject-verb agreement tend to arise in certain tricky contexts, which are detailed in this section.

10a Words between subject and verb

Word groups often come between the subject and the verb. Such word groups, usually modifying the subject, may contain a noun that at first appears to be the subject. By mentally stripping away such modifiers, you can isolate the noun that is in fact the subject.

The *samples* on the tray in the lab *need* testing.

▶ High levels of air pollution damages the

respiratory tract.

The subject is *levels*, not *pollution*.

▶ The slaughter of pandas for their pelts ~~have~~ has

caused the panda population to decline drastically.

The subject is *slaughter*, not *pandas* or *pelts*.

NOTE: Phrases beginning with the prepositions *as well as, in addition to, accompanied by, together with,* and *along with* do not make a singular subject plural: *The governor as well as his aide was* [not *were*] *indicted.*

10b Subjects joined with *and*

Compound subjects joined with *and* are nearly always plural.

▶ Jill's natural ability and her desire to help others
have
~~has~~ led to a career in the ministry.

EXCEPTION: If the parts of the subject form a single unit, however, you may treat the subject as singular: *Bacon and eggs is always on the menu.*

10c Subjects joined with *or* or *nor*

With compound subjects joined with *or* or *nor*, make the verb agree with the part of the subject nearer to the verb.

▶ If an infant or a child *is* ~~are~~ having difficulty breathing,

seek medical attention immediately.

▶ Neither the lab assistant nor the students *were* ~~was~~ able

to download the program.

10d Indefinite pronouns such as *someone*

Indefinite pronouns refer to nonspecific persons or things. The following indefinite pronouns are singular: *anybody, anyone, anything, each, either, everybody, everyone, everything, neither, nobody, no one, somebody, someone, something.*

▶ Nearly everyone on the panel *favors* ~~favor~~ the new budget.

▶ Each of the furrows *has* ~~have~~ been seeded.

A few indefinite pronouns (*all, any, none, some*) may be singular or plural depending on the noun or pronoun they refer to: *Some of the lemonade has disappeared. Some of the rocks were slippery. None of his advice makes sense. None of the eggs were broken.*

ON THE WEB > dianahacker.com/pocket > Language Debates > *none*

10e Collective nouns such as *jury*

Collective nouns such as *jury, committee, club, audience, crowd, class, troop, family,* and *couple* name a class or a group. In American English, collective nouns are usually treated as singular: They emphasize the group as a unit.

▶   The board of trustees ~~meet~~ *meets* in Denver on the first
   Tuesday of each month.

Occasionally, to draw attention to the individual members of the group, a collective noun may be treated as plural: *The class are debating among themselves.* Many writers prefer to add a clearly plural noun such as *members*: *The members of the class are debating among themselves.*

NOTE: In general, when fractions or units of measurement are used with a singular noun, treat them as singular; when they are used with a plural noun, treat them as plural: *Three-fourths of the pie has been eaten. One-fourth of the children were labeled "talented and gifted."*

10f Subject after verb

Verbs ordinarily follow subjects. When this normal order is reversed, it is easy to become confused.

▶   Of particular concern ~~is~~ *are* penicillin and tetracycline,
   antibiotics used to make animals more resistant
   to disease.

The subject, *penicillin and tetracycline,* is plural.

The subject always follows the verb in sentences beginning with *there is* or *there are* (or *there was* or *there were*).

▶ There ~~is~~ *are* a small aquarium and an enormous
terrarium in our biology lab.

The subject, *aquarium and terrarium,* is plural.

10g *who, which,* and *that*

Like most pronouns, the relative pronouns *who, which,*
and *that* have antecedents, nouns or pronouns to which
they refer. Relative pronouns used as subjects of subordinate clauses take verbs that agree with their antecedents.

Pick a *stock that pays* good dividends.

Constructions such as *one of the students who* (or *one of
the things that*) cause problems for writers. Do not assume
that the antecedent must be *one.* Instead, consider the
logic of the sentence.

▶ Our ability to use language is one of the things
that ~~sets~~ *set* us apart from animals.

The antecedent of *that* is *things,* not *one.* Several things set us
apart from animals.

When the word *only* comes before *one,* you are safe in
assuming that *one* is the antecedent of the relative pronoun.

▶ SEACON is the only one of our war games that
~~emphasize~~ *emphasizes* scientific and technical issues.

The antecedent of *that* is *one,* not *games.* Only one game
emphasizes scientific and technical issues.

ON THE WEB > dianahacker.com/pocket > Language Debates >
one of those who (or *that*)

10h Plural form, singular meaning

Words such as *athletics, economics, mathematics, physics,
politics, statistics, measles,* and *news* are usually singular,
despite their plural form.

▶ Politics *is* are among my mother's favorite pastimes.

EXCEPTION: Occasionally some of these words, especially *economics*, *mathematics*, *politics*, and *statistics*, have plural meanings: *Office politics often sway decisions about hiring and promotion. The economics of the building plan are prohibitive.*

10i Titles, company names, and words mentioned as words

Titles, company names, and words mentioned as words are singular.

▶ *Lost Cities* *describes* describe the discoveries of many

ancient civilizations.

▶ Delmonico Brothers *specializes* specialize in organic produce

and additive-free meats.

▶ *Controlled substances* *is* are a euphemism for illegal

drugs.

ON THE WEB > dianahacker.com/pocket > Grammar exercises > Grammar > E-ex 10–1 to 10–3

11 Be alert to other problems with verbs.

The verb is the heart of the sentence, so it is important to get it right. Section 10 deals with the problem of subject-verb agreement. This section describes a few other potential problems with verbs.

11a Irregular verbs

For all regular verbs, the past-tense and past-participle forms are the same, ending in *-ed* or *-d*, so there is no danger of confusion. This is not true, however, for irregular verbs, such as the following.

BASE FORM	PAST TENSE	PAST PARTICIPLE
begin	began	begun
fly	flew	flown
ride	rode	ridden

The past-tense form, which never has a helping verb, expresses action that occurred entirely in the past. The past participle is used with a helping verb — either with *has*, *have*, or *had* to form one of the perfect tenses or with *be*, *am*, *is*, *are*, *was*, *were*, *being*, or *been* to form the passive voice.

PAST TENSE	Last July, we *went* to Paris.
PAST PARTICIPLE	We have *gone* to Paris twice.

When you aren't sure which verb form to choose (*went* or *gone*, *began* or *begun*, and so on), consult the list that begins on page 27. Choose the past-tense form if your sentence doesn't have a helping verb; choose the past-participle form if it does.

▶ Yesterday we ~~seen~~ *saw* an unidentified flying object.

> Because there is no helping verb, the past-tense form *saw* is required.

▶ By the end of the day, the stock market had ~~fell~~ *fallen*

two hundred points.

> Because of the helping verb *had*, the past-participle form *fallen* is required.

Distinguishing between **lie** *and* **lay**. Writers often confuse the forms of *lie* (meaning "to recline or rest on a surface") with *lay* (meaning "to put or place something"). The intransitive verb *lie* does not take a direct object: *The tax forms lie on the table.* The transitive verb *lay* takes a direct object: *Please lay the tax forms on the table.*

In addition to confusing the meanings of *lie* and *lay*, writers are often unfamiliar with the standard English forms of these verbs.

BASE FORM	PAST TENSE	PAST PARTICIPLE	PRESENT PARTICIPLE
lie	lay	lain	lying
lay	laid	laid	laying

Elizabeth was so exhausted that she *lay* down for a nap.
[Past tense of *lie*, meaning "to recline"]

The prosecutor *laid* the pistol on a table close to the jurors. [Past tense of *lay*, meaning "to place"]

Letters dating from the Civil War were *lying* in the corner of the chest. [Present participle of *lie*]

The patient had *lain* in an uncomfortable position all night. [Past participle of *lie*]

ON THE WEB > dianahacker.com/pocket > Language Debates >
lie versus *lay*

Common irregular verbs

BASE FORM	PAST TENSE	PAST PARTICIPLE
arise	arose	arisen
awake	awoke, awaked	awaked, awoke
be	was, were	been
beat	beat	beaten, beat
become	became	become
begin	began	begun
bend	bent	bent
bite	bit	bitten, bit
blow	blew	blown
break	broke	broken
bring	brought	brought
build	built	built
burst	burst	burst
buy	bought	bought
catch	caught	caught
choose	chose	chosen
cling	clung	clung
come	came	come
cost	cost	cost
deal	dealt	dealt
dig	dug	dug
dive	dived, dove	dived
do	did	done
draw	drew	drawn
dream	dreamed, dreamt	dreamed, dreamt
drink	drank	drunk
drive	drove	driven
eat	ate	eaten
fall	fell	fallen
fight	fought	fought
find	found	found
fly	flew	flown

BASE FORM	PAST TENSE	PAST PARTICIPLE
forget	forgot	forgotten, forgot
freeze	froze	frozen
get	got	gotten, got
give	gave	given
go	went	gone
grow	grew	grown
hang (suspend)	hung	hung
hang (execute)	hanged	hanged
have	had	had
hear	heard	heard
hide	hid	hidden
hurt	hurt	hurt
keep	kept	kept
know	knew	known
lay (put)	laid	laid
lead	led	led
lend	lent	lent
let (allow)	let	let
lie (recline)	lay	lain
lose	lost	lost
make	made	made
prove	proved	proved, proven
read	read	read
ride	rode	ridden
ring	rang	rung
rise (get up)	rose	risen
run	ran	run
say	said	said
see	saw	seen
send	sent	sent
set (place)	set	set
shake	shook	shaken
shoot	shot	shot
shrink	shrank	shrunk, shrunken
sing	sang	sung
sink	sank	sunk
sit (be seated)	sat	sat
slay	slew	slain
sleep	slept	slept
speak	spoke	spoken
spin	spun	spun
spring	sprang	sprung
stand	stood	stood
steal	stole	stolen
sting	stung	stung
strike	struck	struck, stricken
swear	swore	sworn
swim	swam	swum

BASE FORM	PAST TENSE	PAST PARTICIPLE
swing	swung	swung
take	took	taken
teach	taught	taught
throw	threw	thrown
wake	woke, waked	waked, woken
wear	wore	worn
wring	wrung	wrung
write	wrote	written

11b Tense

Tenses indicate the time of an action in relation to the time of the speaking or writing about that action. The most common problem with tenses—shifting from one tense to another—is discussed in 5b. Other problems with tenses are detailed in this section, after the following survey of tenses.

Survey of tenses.   Tenses are classified as present, past, and future, with simple, perfect, and progressive forms for each.

The simple tenses indicate relatively simple time relations. The present tense is used primarily for actions occurring at the time of the speaking or for actions occurring regularly. The past tense is used for actions completed in the past. The future tense is used for actions that will occur in the future. In the following table, the simple tenses are given for the regular verb *walk*, the irregular verb *ride*, and the highly irregular verb *be*.

PRESENT TENSE

I	walk, ride, am	we	walk, ride, are
you	walk, ride, are	you	walk, ride, are
he/she/it	walks, rides, is	they	walk, ride, are

PAST TENSE

I	walked, rode, was	we	walked, rode, were
you	walked, rode, were	you	walked, rode, were
he/she/it	walked, rode, was	they	walked, rode, were

FUTURE TENSE

I, you, he/she/it, we, they	will walk, ride, be

A verb in one of the perfect tenses (a form of *have* plus the past participle) expresses an action that was or will be completed at the time of another action.

PRESENT PERFECT

| I, you, we, they | have walked, ridden, been |
| he/she/it | has walked, ridden, been |

PAST PERFECT

| I, you, he/she/it, we, they | had walked, ridden, been |

FUTURE PERFECT

| I, you, he/she/it, we, they | will have walked, ridden, been |

Each of the six tenses has a progressive form used to express a continuing action. A progressive verb consists of a form of *be* followed by the present participle.

PRESENT PROGRESSIVE

I	am walking, riding, being
he/she/it	is walking, riding, being
you, we, they	are walking, riding, being

PAST PROGRESSIVE

| I, he/she/it | was walking, riding, being |
| you, we, they | were walking, riding, being |

FUTURE PROGRESSIVE

| I, you, he/she/it, we, they | will be walking, riding, being |

PRESENT PERFECT PROGRESSIVE

| I, you, we, they | have been walking, riding, being |
| he/she/it | has been walking, riding, being |

PAST PERFECT PROGRESSIVE

| I, you, he/she/it, we, they | had been walking, riding, being |

FUTURE PERFECT PROGRESSIVE

| I, you, he/she/it, we, they | will have been walking, riding, being |

Special uses of the present tense.   Use the present tense when writing about literature or when expressing general truths.

▶   Don Quixote, in Cervantes's novel, ~~was~~ an idealist
                                        is
    ill suited for life in the real world.

▶   Galileo taught that the earth ~~revolved~~ around the
                                  revolves
    sun.

The past perfect tense. The past perfect tense is used for an action already completed by the time of another past action. This tense consists of a past participle preceded by *had* (*had worked, had gone*).

▶ We built our cabin forty feet above an abandoned
  had been
  quarry that ~~was~~ flooded in 1920 to create a lake.

▶ By the time dinner was served, the guest of
       had
  honor left.

11c Mood

There are three moods in English: the *indicative,* used for facts, opinions, and questions; the *imperative,* used for orders or advice; and the *subjunctive,* used for wishes, conditions contrary to fact, and requests or recommendations. Of these three moods, the subjunctive is most likely to cause problems.

Use the subjunctive mood for wishes and in *if* clauses expressing conditions contrary to fact. The subjunctive in such cases is the past-tense form of the verb; in the case of *be,* it is always *were* (not *was*), even if the subject is singular.

I wish that Jamal *drove* more slowly late at night.

If I *were* a member of Congress, I would vote for the bill.

TIP: Do not use the subjunctive mood in *if* clauses expressing conditions that exist or may exist: *If Dana passes* [not *passed*] *the swimming test, she will become a lifeguard.*

Use the subjunctive mood in *that* clauses following verbs such as *ask, insist, recommend,* and *request.* The subjunctive in such cases is the base form of the verb.

Dr. Chung insists that her students *be* on time.

We recommend that Dawson *file* form 1050 soon.

ON THE WEB > dianahacker.com/pocket > Grammar exercises > Grammar > E-ex 11–1 to 11–3

12 Use pronouns with care.

Pronouns are words that substitute for nouns: *he, it, them, her, me,* and so on. Four frequently encountered problems with pronouns are discussed in this section:

a. pronoun-antecedent agreement (singular vs. plural)
b. pronoun reference (clarity)
c. pronoun case (*I* vs. *me,* etc.)
d. pronoun case (*who* vs. *whom*)

12a Pronoun-antecedent agreement

The antecedent of a pronoun is the word the pronoun refers to. A pronoun and its antecedent agree when they are both singular or both plural.

SINGULAR The *doctor* finished *her* rounds.

PLURAL The *doctors* finished *their* rounds.

Writers are sometimes tempted to choose the plural pronoun *they* (or *their*) to refer to a singular antecedent. The temptation is greatest when the singular antecedent is an indefinite pronoun, a generic noun, or a collective noun.

Indefinite pronouns. Indefinite pronouns refer to nonspecific persons or things. Even though some of the following indefinite pronouns may seem to have plural meanings, treat them as singular in formal English: *anybody, anyone, anything, each, either, everybody, everyone, everything, neither, nobody, no one, nothing, somebody, someone, something.*

In this class *everyone* performs at *his* or *her* [not *their*] fitness level.

When *they* or *their* refers mistakenly to a singular antecedent such as *everyone,* you will usually have three options for revision:

1. Replace *they* with *he* or *she* (or *their* with *his* or *her*).
2. Make the singular antecedent plural.
3. Rewrite the sentence.

Because the *he* or *she* construction is wordy, often the second or third revision strategy is more effective.

▶ When someone has been drinking, ~~they are~~ *he or she is* more

likely to speed.

▶ When ~~someone has~~ *drivers have* been drinking, they are more

likely to speed.

▶ ~~When someone~~ *Someone who* has been drinking/ ~~they are~~ *is* more

likely to speed.

NOTE: The traditional use of *he* (or *his*) to refer to persons of either sex is now widely considered sexist. (See p. 18.)

Generic nouns.　A generic noun represents a typical member of a group, such as *a student*, or any member of a group, such as *any musician*. Although generic nouns may seem to have plural meanings, they are singular.

Every *runner* must train rigorously if *he* or *she* wants [not they *want*] to excel.

When *they* or *their* refers mistakenly to a generic noun, you will usually have the same three revision options as for indefinite pronouns.

▶ A medical student must study hard if ~~they want~~ *he or she wants* to

succeed.

▶ ~~A medical student~~ *Medical students* must study hard if they want to

succeed.

▶ A medical student must study hard ~~if they want~~ to

succeed.

Collective nouns.　Collective nouns such as *jury, committee, audience, crowd, family,* and *team* name a class or group. In American English, collective nouns are usually singular because they emphasize the group functioning as a unit.

> The planning *committee* granted *its* [not *their*]
> permission to build.

If the members of the group function individually, however, you may treat the noun as plural: *The family put their signatures on the document.* Or you might add a plural antecedent such as *members* to the sentence: *The members of the family put their signatures on the document.*

> **ON THE WEB > dianahacker.com/pocket >** Language Debates >
> Pronoun-antecedent agreement

> **ON THE WEB > dianahacker.com/pocket >** Grammar exercises >
> Grammar > E-ex 12–1 to 12–3

12b Pronoun reference

A pronoun should refer clearly to its antecedent. When it does not, it is usually because of ambiguous, implied, vague, or indefinite reference.

Ambiguous reference. Ambiguous reference occurs when the pronoun could refer to two possible antecedents.

> *The cake collapsed when Aunt Harriet put it*
> ▶ ~~When Aunt Harriet put the cake~~ on the table~~,~~ it
>
> ~~collapsed.~~

> *"You have*
> ▶ Tom told James, ~~that he had~~ won the lottery.*"*

What collapsed — the cake or the table? Who won the lottery — Tom or James? The revisions eliminate the ambiguity.

Implied reference. A pronoun must refer to a specific antecedent, not to a word that is implied but not actually stated.

> *the braids*
> ▶ After braiding Ann's hair, Sue decorated ~~them~~ with
>
> ribbons.

Vague reference of this, that, *or* which. The pronouns *this, that,* and *which* should not refer vaguely to earlier word groups or ideas. These pronouns should refer to specific antecedents. When a pronoun's reference is too vague, either replace the pronoun with a noun or supply an antecedent to which the pronoun clearly refers.

► More and more often, especially in large cities, we are finding ourselves victims of serious crimes. We learn to accept ~~this~~ *our fate* with minor complaints.

► Romeo and Juliet were both too young to have acquired much wisdom, which *a fact* accounts for their rash actions.

Indefinite reference of *they, it, or you.* The pronoun *they* should refer to a specific antecedent. Do not use *they* to refer indefinitely to persons who have not been specifically mentioned.

► *Congress* ~~They~~ shut down all government agencies for more than a month until the budget crisis was resolved.

The word *it* should not be used indefinitely in constructions such as *In the article it says that. . . .*

► *The* ~~In the~~ encyclopedia ~~it~~ states that male moths can smell female moths from several miles away.

The pronoun *you* is appropriate when the writer is addressing the reader directly: *Once you have kneaded the dough, let it rise in a warm place.* Except in informal contexts, however, the indefinite *you* (meaning "anyone in general") is inappropriate.

► Ms. Pickersgill's *Guide to Etiquette* stipulates that *guests* ~~you~~ should not arrive at a party too early or leave too late.

ON THE WEB > dianahacker.com/pocket > Language Debates > *you*

· **ON THE WEB > diana hacker.com/pocket > Grammar exercises >** Grammar > E-ex 12–4 to 12–6

12c Case of personal pronouns (*I* vs. *me*, etc.)

The personal pronouns in the following list change what is known as *case form* according to their grammatical function in a sentence. Pronouns functioning as subjects or subject complements appear in the *subjective* case; those functioning as objects appear in the *objective* case; and those showing ownership appear in the *possessive* case.

SUBJECTIVE CASE	OBJECTIVE CASE	POSSESSIVE CASE
I	me	my
we	us	our
you	you	your
he/she/it	him/her/it	his/her/its
they	them	their

For the most part, you know how to use these forms correctly, but certain structures may tempt you to choose the wrong pronoun.

Compound word groups. When a subject or an object appears as part of a compound structure, you may occasionally become confused. To test for the correct pronoun, mentally strip away all of the compound structure except the pronoun in question.

▶ While diving for pearls, Ikiko and ~~her~~ *she* found a treasure chest full of gold bars.

Ikiko and she is the subject of the verb *found.* Strip away the words *Ikiko and* to test for the correct pronoun: *she found* [not *her found*].

▶ The most traumatic experience for her father and ~~I~~ *me* occurred long after her operation.

Her father and me is the object of the preposition *for.* Strip away the words *her father and* to test for the correct pronoun: *for me* [not *for I*].

When in doubt about the correct pronoun, some writers try to evade the choice by using a reflexive pronoun such as *myself*. Using a reflexive pronoun in such situations is nonstandard.

▶ The Egyptian cab driver gave my husband and ~~myself~~ *me* some good tips on traveling in North Africa.

My husband and me is the indirect object of the verb *gave*.

ON THE WEB > **dianahacker.com/pocket** > Language Debates > *myself*

Appositives. Appositives, noun phrases that rename nouns or pronouns, have the same function as the words they rename. Problems often arise with compound appositives. To test for the correct pronoun, mentally strip away the words the appositive renames and all of the compound structure except the pronoun.

▶ The chief strategists, Dr. Bell and ~~me,~~ *I,* could not agree on a plan.

The appositive *Dr. Bell and I* renames the subject, *strategists*. Test: *I could not agree on a plan* [not *me could not agree on a plan*].

▶ The reporter interviewed only two witnesses, the shopkeeper and ~~I.~~ *me.*

The appositive *the shopkeeper and me* renames the direct object, *witnesses*. Test: *interviewed me* [not *interviewed I*].

Subject complements. Use subjective-case pronouns for subject complements, which rename or describe the subject and usually follow *be, am, is, are, was, were, being,* or *been*.

▶ During the Lindbergh trial, Bruno Hauptmann repeatedly denied that the kidnapper was ~~him.~~ *he.*

If *kidnapper was he* seems too stilted, rewrite the sentence: *During the Lindbergh trial, Bruno Hauptmann repeatedly denied that he was the kidnapper.*

We or us before a noun. When deciding whether *we* or *us* should precede a noun, choose the pronoun that would be appropriate if the noun were omitted.

▶ *We*
~~Us~~ tenants would rather fight than move.

Test: *We would rather fight* [not *Us would rather fight*].

▶ Management is short-changing ~~we~~ *us* tenants.

Test: *Management is short-changing us* [not *Management is short-changing we*].

Pronoun after *than* or *as*.   Sentence parts, usually verbs, are often omitted in comparisons beginning with *than* or *as*. To test for the correct pronoun, finish the sentence.

▶ My husband is six years older than ~~me.~~ *I.*

Test: *than I* [*am*].

▶ We respected no other candidate for city council as much as ~~she.~~ *her.*

Test: *as* [*we respected*] *her.*

Pronoun before or after an infinitive.   An infinitive is the word *to* followed by a verb. Both subjects and objects of infinitives take the objective case.

▶ Ms. Wilson asked John and ~~I~~ *me* to drive the senator and ~~she~~ *her* to the airport.

John and me is the subject and *senator and her* is the object of the infinitive *to drive.*

Pronoun or noun before a gerund.   If a pronoun modifies a gerund, use the possessive case: *my, our, your, his, her, its, their.* A gerund is a verb form ending in *-ing* that functions as a noun.

▶ The chances against ~~you~~ *your* being hit by lightning are about two million to one.

Nouns as well as pronouns may modify gerunds. To form the possessive case of a noun, use an apostrophe and *-s* (*a victim's suffering*) or just an apostrophe (*victims' suffer-ing*). (See 19a.)

▶ The old order in France paid a high price for the
aristocracy's
~~aristocracy~~ exploiting the lower classes.
  ^

ON THE WEB > dianahacker.com/pocket > Grammar exercises >
Grammar > E-ex 12–7 and 12–8

12d *who* or *whom*

Who, a subjective-case pronoun, can be used only for sub-jects and subject complements. *Whom*, an objective-case pronoun, can be used only for objects. The words *who* and *whom* appear primarily in subordinate clauses or in questions.

In subordinate clauses.   When deciding whether to use *who* or *whom* in a subordinate clause, check for the word's function within the clause.

                         whoever
▶ He tells that story to ~~whomever~~ will listen.
                           ^

Whoever is the subject of *will listen*. The entire subordinate clause *whoever will listen* is the object of the preposition *to*.

                                            whom
▶ You will work with our senior engineers, ~~who~~ you
                                             ^
will meet later.

Whom is the direct object of the verb *will meet*. This becomes clear if you restructure the clause: *you will meet whom later*.

In questions.   When deciding whether to use *who* or *whom* in a question, check for the word's function within the question.

  Who
▶ ~~Whom~~ was accused of receiving money from
  ^
the Mafia?

Who is the subject of the verb *was accused*.

  Whom
▶ ~~Who~~ did the Democratic Party nominate in 1992?
  ^

Whom is the direct object of the verb *did nominate*. This becomes clear if you restructure the question: *The Democratic Party did nominate whom in 1992?*

ON THE WEB > dianahacker.com/pocket > Language Debates >
who versus *whom*

ON THE WEB > dianahacker.com/pocket > Grammar exercises >
Grammar > E-ex 12–9 and 12–10

13 Choose adjectives and adverbs with care.

Adjectives modify nouns or pronouns; adverbs modify
verbs, adjectives, or other adverbs.

Many adverbs are formed by adding *-ly* to adjectives
(*formal, formally*). But don't assume that all words ending
in *-ly* are adverbs or that all adverbs end in *-ly*. Some adjectives end in *-ly* (*lovely, friendly*) and some adverbs don't
(*always, here*). When in doubt, consult a dictionary.

13a Adverbs

Use adverbs, not adjectives, to modify verbs, adjectives,
and adverbs. Adverbs usually answer one of these questions: When? Where? How? Why? Under what conditions? How often? To what degree?

The incorrect use of adjectives in place of adverbs to
modify verbs occurs primarily in casual or nonstandard
speech.

▶ The manager must see that the office runs
smoothly efficiently.
~~smooth~~ and ~~efficient.~~

The incorrect use of the adjective *good* in place of the
adverb *well* is especially common in casual and nonstandard speech.

▶ We were delighted that Nomo had done so ~~good~~ *well*
on the exam.

Adjectives are sometimes incorrectly used to modify
adjectives or other adverbs.

▶ In the early 1970s, chances for survival of the bald
eagle looked ~~real~~ *really* slim.

13b Adjectives

Adjectives ordinarily precede nouns, but they can also function as subject complements following linking verbs (usually a form of *be*: *be, am, is, are, was, were, being, been*). When an adjective functions as a subject complement, it describes the subject.

Justice is *blind*.

Verbs such as *smell, taste, look, appear, grow,* and *feel* may also be linking. If the word following one of these verbs describes the subject, use an adjective; if the word modifies the verb, use an adverb.

ADJECTIVE   The detective looked *cautious*.

ADVERB   The detective looked *cautiously* for the fingerprints.

Linking verbs usually suggest states of being, not actions. For example, to look *cautious* suggests the state of being cautious, whereas to look *cautiously* is to perform an action in a cautious way.

▶ Lori looked ~~well~~ *good* in her new raincoat.

▶ All of us on the debate team felt ~~badly~~ *bad* about our

    performance.

The verbs *looked* and *felt* suggest states of being, not actions, so they should be followed by adjectives.

> **ON THE WEB** > dianahacker.com/pocket > Language Debates > *bad* versus *badly*

13c Comparatives and superlatives

Most adjectives and adverbs have three forms: the positive, the comparative, and the superlative.

POSITIVE	COMPARATIVE	SUPERLATIVE
soft	softer	softest
fast	faster	fastest
careful	more careful	most careful
bad	worse	worst
good	better	best

Comparative vs. superlative.   Use the comparative to compare two things, the superlative to compare three or more.

▶ Which of these two brands of toothpaste is ~~best?~~ *better?*

▶ Hermos is the ~~more~~ *most* qualified of the three

   applicants.

Form of comparatives and superlatives.   To form comparatives and superlatives of most one- and two-syllable adjectives, use the endings *-er* and *-est*: *smooth, smoother, smoothest.* With longer adjectives, use *more* and *most* (or *less* and *least*): *exciting, more exciting, most exciting.*

   Some one-syllable adverbs take the endings *-er* and *-est* (*fast, faster, fastest*), but longer adverbs and all of those ending in *-ly* use *more* and *most* (or *less* and *least*).

Double comparatives or superlatives.   When you have added *-er* or *-est* to an adjective or an adverb, do not also use *more* or *most* (or *less* or *least*).

▶ All the polls indicated that Dewey was more *likely* ~~likelier~~ to win than Truman.

Absolute concepts.   Do not use comparatives or superlatives with absolute concepts such as *unique* or *perfect.* Either something is unique or it isn't. It is illogical to suggest that absolute concepts come in degrees.

▶ That is the most ~~unique~~ *unusual* wedding gown I have

   ever seen.

ON THE WEB > dianahacker.com/pocket > Language Debates > Absolute concepts such as *unique*

ON THE WEB > dianahacker.com/pocket > Grammar exercises > Grammar > E-ex 13–1 and 13–2

14 Repair sentence fragments.

As a rule, do not treat a piece of a sentence as if it were a sentence. When you do, you create a fragment. To be a

sentence, a word group must consist of at least one full independent clause. An independent clause has a subject
and a verb, and it either stands alone as a sentence or
could stand alone.

You can repair a fragment in one of two ways: Either
pull the fragment into a nearby sentence, punctuating
the new sentence correctly, or turn the fragment into a
sentence.

14a Fragmented clauses

A subordinate clause is patterned like a sentence, with
both a subject and a verb, but it begins with a word that
tells readers it cannot stand alone—a word such as *after*,
although, *because*, *before*, *if*, *so that*, *that*, *though*, *unless*, *until*,
when, *where*, *who*, or *which*. (For a longer list, see p. 66.)

Most fragmented clauses beg to be pulled into a sentence nearby.

▶ Patricia arrived on the island of Malta, ~~Where~~ *where*

she was to spend the summer restoring frescoes.

If a fragmented clause cannot be combined gracefully
with a nearby sentence, try rewriting it. The simplest way
to turn a fragmented clause into a sentence is to delete the
opening word or words that mark it as subordinate.

▶ Uncontrolled development is taking a deadly

toll on the environment. ~~So that in~~ *In* many parts

of the world, fragile ecosystems are collapsing.

14b Fragmented phrases

Like subordinate clauses, certain phrases are sometimes
mistaken for sentences. They are fragments if they lack a
subject, a verb, or both. Frequently a fragmented phrase
may simply be attached to a nearby sentence.

▶ The archaeologists worked slowly, ~~Examining~~ *examining* and

labeling hundreds of pottery shards.

The word group beginning with *Examining* is a verbal phrase,
not a sentence.

▶ Many adults suffer silently from agoraphobia, A ^a fear of the outside world.

A fear of the outside world is an appositive phrase, not a sentence.

▶ It has been said that there are only three indigenous American art forms/: ~~Jazz,~~ *jazz,* musical comedy, and soap operas.

Clearly the list is not a sentence. Notice how easily a colon corrects the problem. (See 18b.)

If the fragmented phrase cannot be attached to a nearby sentence, turn the phrase into a sentence. You may need to add a subject, a verb, or both.

▶ If Eric doesn't get his way, he goes into a fit of rage. For example, ~~lying~~ *he lies* on the floor screaming or ~~opening~~ *opens* the cabinet doors and then ~~slamming~~ *slams* them shut.

The writer added a subject, *he,* and substituted verbs for the verbals *lying, opening,* and *slamming.*

14c Acceptable fragments

Skilled writers occasionally use sentence fragments for emphasis. Although fragments are sometimes appropriate, writers and readers do not always agree on when they are appropriate. Therefore, you will find it safer to write in complete sentences.

ON THE WEB > dianahacker.com/pocket > Grammar exercises > Grammar > E-ex 14–1 to 14–3

15 Revise run-on sentences.

Run-on sentences are independent clauses that have not been joined correctly. An independent clause is a word group that stands alone or could stand alone as a sentence. When two or more independent clauses appear in one sentence, they must be joined in one of these ways:

- with a comma and a coordinating conjunction (*and, but, or, nor, for, so, yet*)
- with a semicolon (or occasionally a colon or a dash)

There are two types of run-on sentences. When a writer puts no mark of punctuation and no coordinating conjunction between independent clauses, the result is a *fused sentence*.

FUSED Air pollution poses risks to all humans it can be deadly for asthma sufferers.

A far more common type of run-on sentence is the *comma splice*—two or more independent clauses joined with a comma and no coordinating conjunction. In some comma splices, the comma appears alone.

COMMA Air pollution poses risks to all humans, it can be
SPLICE deadly for asthma sufferers.

In other comma splices, the comma is accompanied by a joining word that is *not* a coordinating conjunction. There are only seven coordinating conjunctions in English: *and, but, or, nor, for, so, yet.*

COMMA Air pollution poses risks to all humans, however,
SPLICE it can be deadly for asthma sufferers.

The word *however* is a conjunctive adverb, not a coordinating conjunction.

To correct a run-on sentence, you have four choices:

1. Use a comma and a coordinating conjunction.
2. Use a semicolon (or, if appropriate, a colon or a dash).
3. Make the clauses into separate sentences.
4. Restructure the sentence, perhaps by making one of the clauses subordinate.

One of these revision techniques will usually work better than the others for a particular sentence. The fourth technique, the one requiring the most extensive revision, is frequently the most effective.

▶ Air pollution poses risks to all humans, **but** it can be

deadly for asthma sufferers.

▶ Air pollution poses risks to all humans/; it can be deadly for asthma sufferers.

▶ Air pollution poses risks to all humans/. *It* it can be deadly for asthma sufferers.

▶ *Although air* ~~Air~~ pollution poses risks to all humans, it can be deadly for asthma sufferers.

15a Revision with a comma and a coordinating conjunction

When a coordinating conjunction (*and, but, or, nor, for, so, yet*) joins independent clauses, it is usually preceded by a comma.

▶ Most of his friends had made plans for their retirement, *but* Tom had not.

15b Revision with a semicolon (or a colon or a dash)

When the independent clauses are closely related and their relation is clear without a coordinating conjunction, a semicolon is an acceptable method of revision.

▶ Tragedy depicts the individual confronted with the fact of death/; comedy depicts the adaptability of human society.

A semicolon is required between independent clauses that have been linked with a conjunctive adverb such as *however* or *therefore* or a transitional phrase such as *in fact* or *of course*. (See p. 66 for a longer list.)

▶ The timber wolf looks like a large German shepherd/; however, the wolf has longer legs, larger feet, and a wider head.

If the first independent clause introduces a quoted sentence, use a colon.

▶ Carolyn Heilbrun says this about the future/:
                                                   ^

   "Today's shocks are tomorrow's conventions."

Either a colon or a dash may be appropriate when the second clause summarizes or explains the first. (See 18b and 21d.)

15c Revision by separating sentences

If both independent clauses are long— or if one is a question and the other is not— consider making them separate sentences.

▶ Why should we spend money on expensive space
                                    ? We
   exploration/ ~~we~~ have enough underfunded
                 ^

   programs here on Earth.

15d Revision by restructuring the sentence

For sentence variety, consider restructuring the run-on sentence, perhaps by turning one of the independent clauses into a subordinate clause or a phrase.

▶ Of the many geysers in Yellowstone National Park,
                                          which
   the most famous is Old Faithful, ~~it~~ sometimes
                                     ^

   reaches 150 feet in height.

▶ Mary McLeod Bethune, ~~was~~ the seventeenth
                        ^

   child of former slaves, ~~she~~ founded the National

   Council of Negro Women in 1935.

ON THE WEB > dianahacker.com/pocket > Language Debates >
Comma splices

ON THE WEB > dianahacker.com/pocket > Grammar exercises >
Grammar > E-ex 15–1 to 15–3

16 Edit for common ESL challenges.

16a Verbs

This section offers a brief review of English verb forms and tenses and the passive voice.

Verb forms. Every main verb in English has five forms (except *be*, which has eight). These forms are used to create all of the verb tenses in standard English. The following list shows these forms for the regular verb *help* and the irregular verb *give*.

	REGULAR	IRREGULAR
VERB FORM	*HELP*	*GIVE*
BASE FORM	help	give
PAST TENSE	helped	gave
PAST PARTICIPLE	helped	given
PRESENT PARTICIPLE	helping	giving
-S FORM	helps	gives

Verb tense. Here are descriptions of the tenses and progressive forms in standard English. Also see 11b.

The simple tenses show general facts, states of being, and habitual actions.

Simple present tense (base form or -s form) expresses general facts, constant states, habitual or repetitive actions, or scheduled future events: *The sun rises in the east. The plane leaves tomorrow at 6:30.*

NOTE: The verb *be* has three present-tense forms: *is*, *am*, and *are*. See page 29.

Simple past tense (base form + -ed or -d or irregular form) is used for actions that happened at a specific time or during a specific period in the past or for repetitive actions that have ended: *She drove to Montana three years ago. When I was young, I walked to school.*

NOTE: The verb *be* has two past-tense forms: *was* and *were*. See page 29.

Simple future tense (will + base form) expresses actions that will occur at some time in the future and promises or predictions of future events: *I will call you next week.*

The simple progressive forms show continuing action.

Present progressive (*am, is, are* + present participle) shows actions in progress that are not expected to remain constant: *We are building our house at the shore.*

Past progressive (*was, were* + present participle) shows actions in progress at a specific past time or a continuing action that was interrupted: *Roy was driving his new car yesterday. When she walked in, we were planning her party.*

Future progressive (*will* + *be* + present participle) expresses actions that will be in progress at a certain time in the future: *Nan will be flying home tomorrow.*

TIP: Certain verbs that express a state of being or mental activity are not used in the progressive sense in English. Common examples are *appear, believe, belong, contain, have, hear, know, like, need, see, seem, taste, think, understand,* and *want.* There are exceptions, however, that you must notice as you encounter them: W*e are thinking of buying a summer home.*

The perfect tenses show actions that happened or will happen before another time.

Present perfect tense (*have, has* + past participle) expresses actions that began in the past and continue to the present or actions that happened at an unspecific time in the past: *She has not spoken of her grandfather in a long time. They have traveled to Africa twice.*

Past perfect tense (*had* + past participle) expresses an action that began in the past and continued to a more recent past time or an action that happened at an unspecified time before another past event: *By the time Hakan was fifteen, he had learned to drive. I had just finished my walk when my brother drove up.*

Future perfect tense (*will* + *have* + past participle) expresses actions that will be completed before or at a specific future time: *By the time I graduate, I will have taken five composition classes.*

The perfect progressive forms show continuous past actions before another time.

Present perfect progressive (*have, has* + *been* + **present participle**) expresses continuous actions that began in the past and continue to the present: *My sister has been living in Oregon since 2001.*

Past perfect progressive (*had* + *been* + **present participle**) conveys actions that began and continued in the past until some other past action: *By the time I moved to Georgia, I had been supporting myself for five years.*

Future perfect progressive (*will* + *have* + *been* + **present participle**) expresses actions that are or will be in progress before another specified time in the future: *By the time we reach the register, we will have been waiting in line for two hours.*

Modal verbs. The nine modal verbs—*can, could, may, might, must, shall, should, will,* and *would*—are used with the base form of verbs to show certainty, necessity, or possibility. Modals do not change form to indicate tense.

► My cousin will sends us photographs from her

   wedding.

► We could ~~spoke~~ speak Portuguese when we were young.

Passive voice. When a sentence is written in the passive voice, the subject receives the action instead of doing it. To form the passive voice, use a form of *be—am, is, are, was, were, being, be,* or *been*—followed by the past participle of the main verb. (For appropriate uses of the passive voice, see 2b.)

   The control group *was given* a placebo.

   Senator Dixon *will be defeated.*

NOTE: Verbs that do not take direct objects—such as *occur, happen, sleep, die,* and *fall*—do not form the passive voice.

ON THE WEB > dianahacker.com/pocket > Grammar exercises > Grammar > E-ex 16–1 and 16–2

16b Articles (*a, an, the*)

Articles and other noun markers. Articles (*a, an, the*) are part of a category of words known as *noun markers* or *determiners*. Noun markers identify the nouns that follow them.

Besides articles, noun markers include possessive nouns (*Elena's*, *child's*); possessive pronoun/adjectives (*my*, *your*, *their*); demonstrative pronoun/adjectives (*this*, *that*); quantifiers (*all*, *few*, *neither*, *some*); and numbers (*one*, *twenty-six*).

      ART N
Felix is reading a book about mythology.

      ART ADJ   N
We took an exciting trip to Alaska last summer.

When to use a or an. Use *a* or *an* with singular count nouns that refer to one unspecific item (not a whole category). *Count nouns* refer to persons, places, things, or ideas that can be counted: *one girl, two girls; one city, three cities; one goose, four geese.*

▶ My English professor asked me to bring ^*a* dictionary to class.

▶ We want to rent ^*an* apartment close to the lake.

When to use the. Use *the* with most nouns that the reader can identify specifically. Usually the identity will be clear to the reader for one of the following reasons:

1. The noun has been previously mentioned.

▶ A truck cut in front of our van. When ^*the* truck skidded a few seconds later, we almost crashed into it.

2. A phrase or clause following the noun restricts its identity.

▶ Bryce warned me that ^*the* computer on his desk had just crashed.

3. A superlative adjective such as *best* or *most intelligent* makes the noun's identity specific. (See also 13c.)

▶ Our petite daughter dated ^*the* tallest boy in her class.

4. The noun describes a unique person, place, or thing.

▶ During an eclipse, one should not look directly at *the* sun.

5. The context or situation makes the noun's identity clear.

▶ Please don't slam *the* door when you leave.

6. The noun is singular and refers to a class or category of items (most often animals, musical instruments, and inventions).

▶ *The assembly* ~~Assembly~~ line transformed manufacturing in the United States.

When not to use articles. Do not use *a* or *an* with noncount nouns. *Noncount nouns* refer to things or abstract ideas that cannot be counted or made plural: *salt, silver, air, furniture, patience, knowledge.* (See the chart on p. 53.)

To express an approximate amount of a noncount noun, use a quantifier such as *some* or *more*: *some water, enough coffee, less violence.*

▶ Dr. Snyder gave us ~~an~~ information about the Peace Corps.

▶ Claudia said she had *some* ~~a~~ news that would surprise her parents.

Do not use articles with nouns that refer to all of something or something in general.

▶ *Kindness* ~~The kindness~~ is a virtue.

The noun represents *kindness* in general; it does not represent a specific type of kindness.

▶ In some parts of the world, ~~a~~ rice is preferred to all other grains.

The noun *rice* represents rice in general, not a specific type or serving of rice.

Commonly used noncount nouns

FOOD AND DRINK

beef, bread, butter, candy, cereal, cheese, cream, meat, milk, pasta, rice, salt, sugar, wine

NONFOOD SUBSTANCES

air, cement, coal, dirt, gasoline, gold, paper, petroleum, plastic, rain, silver, snow, soap, steel, wood, wool

ABSTRACT NOUNS

advice, anger, beauty, confidence, courage, employment, fun, happiness, health, honesty, information, intelligence, knowledge, love, poverty, satisfaction, wealth

OTHER

biology (and other areas of study), clothing, equipment, furniture, homework, jewelry, luggage, machinery, mail, money, news, poetry, pollution, research, scenery, traffic, transportation, violence, weather, work

NOTE: A few noncount nouns can also be used as count nouns: *The plants need water every day. The patrol boat strayed into international waters.*

When to use articles with proper nouns. Do not use articles with most singular proper nouns: *Prime Minister Brown, Jamaica, Lake Huron, Ivy Street, Mount Everest.* Use *the* with most plural proper nouns: *the McGregors, the Bahamas, the Finger Lakes, the United States.* Also use *the* with large regions, oceans, rivers, and mountain ranges: *the Sahara, the Indian Ocean, the Amazon River, the Rocky Mountains.*

There are, however, many exceptions, especially with geographic names. Note exceptions when you encounter them or consult a native speaker or an ESL dictionary.

ON THE WEB > dianahacker.com/pocket > Grammar exercises > Grammar > E-ex 16–3 and 16–4

16c Sentence structure

This section focuses on the major challenges that multilingual students face when constructing sentences in English.

Omitted verbs. Some languages do not use linking verbs (*am, is, are, was, were*) between subjects and complements (nouns or adjectives that rename or describe the subject). Every English sentence, however, must include a verb.

▶ **Jim ^ intelligent.** [inserted: *is*]

▶ **Many streets in San Francisco ^ very steep.** [inserted: *are*]

Omitted subjects. Some languages do not require a subject in every sentence. Every English sentence, however, needs a subject.

▶ **Your aunt is very energetic. ~~Seems~~ young for her age.** [inserted: *She seems*]

EXCEPTION: In commands, the subject *you* is understood but not present in the sentence: *Give to the poor.*

The word *it* is used as the subject of a sentence describing the weather or temperature, stating the time, indicating distance, or suggesting an environmental fact. Do not omit *it* in such sentences.

> *It* is raining in the valley and snowing in the mountains.
>
> In July, *it* is very hot in Arizona.
>
> *It* is 9:15 a.m.
>
> *It* is three hundred miles to Chicago.

In some English sentences, the subject comes after the verb, and a placeholder—*there* or *it*—comes before the verb.

> There [EXP] are [V] many people [S] here today. (Many people [S] are [V] here today.)
>
> It [EXP] is [V] important to study [S] daily. (To study [S] daily is [V] important.)

▶ **~~Is~~ an apple in the refrigerator.** [inserted: *There is*]

▶ **As you know, ^ many religious sects in India.** [inserted: *there are*]

Repeated subjects, objects, and adverbs. English does not allow a subject to be repeated in its own clause.

▶ The doctor ~~she~~ advised me to cut down on salt.

> The pronoun *she* cannot repeat the subject, *doctor*.

Do not add a pronoun even when a word group comes between the subject and the verb.

▶ The car that had been stolen ~~it~~ was found.

> The pronoun *it* cannot repeat the subject, *car*.

Do not repeat an object or an adverb in an adjective clause. Adjective clauses begin with relative pronouns (*who, whom, whose, which, that*) or relative adverbs (*when, where*). Relative pronouns usually serve as subjects or objects in the clauses they introduce; another word in the clause cannot serve the same function. Relative adverbs should not be repeated by other adverbs later in the clause.

▶ The cat ran under the car that ~~it~~ was parked on

the street.

> The relative pronoun *that* is the subject of the adjective clause, so the pronoun *it* cannot be added as the subject.

If the clause begins with a relative adverb, do not use another adverb with the same meaning later in the clause.

▶ The office where I work ~~there~~ is one hour from

the city.

> The adverb *there* cannot repeat the relative adverb *where*.

ON THE WEB > dianahacker.com/pocket > Grammar exercises > Grammar > E-ex 16–5 and 16–6

16d Prepositions showing time and place

The chart on page 56 is limited to three troublesome prepositions that show time and place: *at, on,* and *in.* Not every possible use is listed in the chart, so don't be surprised when you encounter exceptions and idiomatic uses that you must learn one at a time. For example, in English, we ride *in* a car but *on* a bus, plane, train, or subway.

At, *on*, and *in* to show time and place

SHOWING TIME

AT *at* a specific time: *at* 7:20, *at* dawn, *at* dinner

ON *on* a specific day or date: *on* Tuesday, *on* June 4

IN *in* a part of a day: *in* the afternoon, *in* the daytime [but *at* night]

   in a year or month: *in* 1999, *in* July

   in a period of time: finished *in* three hours

SHOWING PLACE

AT *at* a meeting place or location: *at* home, *at* the club

   at the edge of something: sitting *at* the desk

   at the corner of something: turning *at* the intersection

   at a target: throwing the snowball *at* Lucy

ON *on* a surface: placed *on* the table, hanging *on* the wall

   on a street: the house *on* Spring Street

   on an electronic medium: *on* television, *on* the Internet

IN *in* an enclosed space: *in* the garage, *in* an envelope

   in a geographic location: *in* San Diego, *in* Texas

   in a print medium: *in* a book, *in* a magazine

ON THE WEB > dianahacker.com/pocket > Grammar exercises > Grammar > E-ex 16–7

Punctuation

17 The comma

The comma was invented to help readers. Without it, sentence parts can collide into one another unexpectedly, causing misreadings.

CONFUSING   If you cook Elmer will do the dishes.

CONFUSING   While we were eating a rattlesnake
                  approached our campsite.

Add commas in the logical places (after *cook* and *eating*), and suddenly all is clear. No longer is Elmer being cooked, the rattlesnake being eaten.

Various rules have evolved to prevent such misreadings and to guide readers through complex grammatical structures. According to most experts, you should use a comma in the following situations.

17a Before a coordinating conjunction joining independent clauses

When a coordinating conjunction connects two or more independent clauses—word groups that could stand alone as separate sentences—a comma must precede it. There are seven coordinating conjunctions in English: *and, but, or, nor, for, so,* and *yet.*

A comma tells readers that one independent clause has come to a close and that another is about to begin.

▶ **Nearly everyone has heard of love at first sight,**

   but I fell in love at first dance.

EXCEPTION: If the two independent clauses are short and there is no danger of misreading, the comma may be omitted.

    The plane took off and we were on our way.

TIP: Do *not* use a comma to separate compound elements that are not independent clauses. See 17j.

17b After an introductory word group

Use a comma after an introductory clause or phrase. A comma tells readers that the introductory word group has come to a close and that the main part of the sentence is about to begin. The most common introductory word groups are adverb clauses, prepositional phrases, and participial phrases.

▶ **When Strom Thurmond ran for president in 1948,**

   he was a staunch segregationist.

▶ **Near a small stream at the bottom of the canyon,**

   we discovered an abandoned shelter.

▶ **Buried under layers of younger rocks, the earth's**

   oldest rocks contain no fossils.

EXCEPTION: The comma may be omitted after a short clause or phrase if there is no danger of misreading.

   In no time we were at 2,800 feet.

17c Between items in a series

Use a comma between all items in a series, including the last two.

▶ **Bubbles of air, leaves, ferns, bits of wood, and**

   insects are often found trapped in amber.

Although some writers view the comma between the last two items as optional, most experts advise using it because its omission can result in ambiguity or misreading.

ON THE WEB > dianahacker.com/pocket > Language Debates > Commas with items in a series

17d Between coordinate adjectives

Use a comma between coordinate adjectives, those that each modify a noun separately.

▶ **Patients with severe, irreversible brain damage**

   should not be put on life support systems.

Adjectives are coordinate if they can be connected with *and*: *severe and irreversible*.

NOTE: Do not use a comma between cumulative adjectives, those that do not each modify the noun separately.

Three large gray shapes moved slowly toward us.

Adjectives are cumulative if they cannot be connected with *and*. It would be very odd to say *three and large and gray shapes*.

17e To set off a nonrestrictive element

A *restrictive* element defines or limits the meaning of the word it modifies and is therefore essential to the meaning of the sentence. It is not set off with commas. A *nonrestrictive* element describes a word whose meaning already is clear. It is not essential to the meaning of the sentence and is set off with commas.

RESTRICTIVE

For camp the children needed clothes *that were washable.*

NONRESTRICTIVE

For camp the children needed sturdy shoes, *which were expensive.*

If you remove a restrictive element from a sentence, the meaning changes significantly, becoming more general than intended. The writer of the first sample sentence does not mean that the children needed clothes in general. The meaning is more restricted: The children needed *washable* clothes.

If you remove a nonrestrictive element from a sentence, the meaning does not change significantly. Some meaning is lost, to be sure, but the defining characteristics of the person or thing described remain the same. The children needed *sturdy shoes*, and these happened to be expensive.

Elements that may be restrictive or nonrestrictive include adjective clauses, adjective phrases, and appositives.

Adjective clauses   Adjective clauses, which usually follow the noun or pronoun they describe, begin with a relative pronoun (*who, whom, whose, which, that*) or a relative adverb (*when, where*). When an adjective clause is nonrestrictive, set it off with commas; when it is restrictive, omit the commas.

NONRESTRICTIVE CLAUSE

▶ A 1911 fire at the Triangle Shirtwaist Company,
which killed 146 sweatshop workers, led to reforms
in working conditions.

RESTRICTIVE CLAUSE

▶ A corporation / that has government contracts / must
maintain careful personnel records.

NOTE: Use *that* only with restrictive clauses. Many writers
use *which* only with nonrestrictive clauses, but usage varies.

> ON THE WEB > dianahacker.com/pocket > Language Debates >
> *that* versus *which*

Adjective phrases   Prepositional or verbal phrases functioning as adjectives may be restrictive or nonrestrictive.
Nonrestrictive phrases are set off with commas; restrictive
phrases are not.

NONRESTRICTIVE PHRASE

▶ The helicopter, with its million-candlepower
spotlight illuminating the area, circled above.

RESTRICTIVE PHRASE

▶ One corner of the attic was filled with newspapers /
dating from the 1920s.

Appositives   An appositive is a noun or pronoun that renames a nearby noun. Nonrestrictive appositives are set
off with commas; restrictive appositives are not.

NONRESTRICTIVE APPOSITIVE

▶ Darwin's most important book, *On the Origin of
Species*, was the result of many years of research.

RESTRICTIVE APPOSITIVE

▶ The song / "Vertigo /" was blasted out of amplifiers
ten feet tall.

17f To set off transitional and parenthetical expressions, absolute phrases, and contrasted elements

Transitional expressions   Transitional expressions serve as bridges between sentences or parts of sentences. They include conjunctive adverbs such as *however, therefore,* and *moreover* and transitional phrases such as *for example* and *as a matter of fact.* For a longer list, see page 66.

When a transitional expression appears between independent clauses in a compound sentence, it is preceded by a semicolon and usually followed by a comma.

▶   Minh did not understand our language; moreover, he was unfamiliar with our customs.

When a transitional expression appears at the beginning of a sentence or in the middle of an independent clause, it is usually set off with commas.

▶   As a matter of fact, American football was established by fans who wanted to play a more organized game of rugby.

▶   Natural foods are not always salt free; celery, for example, contains more sodium than most people would imagine.

Parenthetical expressions   Expressions that are distinctly parenthetical, interrupting the flow of a sentence, should be set off with commas.

▶   Evolution, so far as we know, does not work this way.

Absolute phrases   An absolute phrase consists of a noun followed by a participle or participial phrase. It modifies the whole sentence and should be set off with commas.

▶   Our grant having been approved, we were at last able to begin the archaeological dig.

Contrasted elements Sharp contrasts beginning with words such as *not* and *unlike* are set off with commas.

▶ The Epicurean philosophers sought mental, not

bodily, pleasures.

17g To set off nouns of direct address, the words *yes* and *no*, interrogative tags, and mild interjections

▶ Forgive us, Dr. Atkins, for eating rolls.

▶ Yes, the loan will probably be approved.

▶ The film was faithful to the book, wasn't it?

▶ Well, cases like this are difficult to decide.

17h To set off direct quotations introduced with expressions such as *he said*

▶ Naturalist Arthur Cleveland Bent remarked, "In

part the peregrine declined unnoticed because it is

not adorable."

17i With dates, addresses, and titles

Dates In dates, the year is set off from the rest of the sentence with commas.

▶ On December 12, 1890, orders were sent out for

the arrest of Sitting Bull.

EXCEPTIONS: Commas are not needed if the date is inverted or if only the month and year are given: *The 15 April 2007 deadline is approaching. May 2006 was a surprisingly cold month.*

Addresses The elements of an address or a place name are separated by commas. A zip code, however, is not preceded by a comma.

▶ Greg lived at 708 Spring Street, Washington,

Illinois 61571.

Titles If a title follows a name, separate it from the rest of the sentence with a pair of commas.

▶ Sandra Barnes, MD, was appointed to the board.

17j Misuses of the comma

Do not use commas unless you have a good reason for using them. In particular, avoid using the comma in the following situations.

BETWEEN COMPOUND ELEMENTS THAT ARE NOT INDEPENDENT CLAUSES

▶ Marie Curie discovered radium/and later applied her work on radioactivity to medicine.

TO SEPARATE A VERB FROM ITS SUBJECT

▶ Zoos large enough to give the animals freedom to roam/are becoming more popular.

BETWEEN CUMULATIVE ADJECTIVES (See p. 60.)

▶ Joyce was wearing a slinky/red silk gown.

TO SET OFF RESTRICTIVE ELEMENTS (See pp. 60–61.)

▶ Drivers/who think they own the road/make cycling a dangerous sport.

▶ Margaret Mead's book/*Coming of Age in Samoa/* caused controversy when it was published.

AFTER A COORDINATING CONJUNCTION

▶ Occasionally soap operas are live, but/more often they are taped.

AFTER *SUCH AS* OR *LIKE*

▶ Plants such as/begonias and impatiens add color to a shady garden.

BEFORE *THAN*

▶ Touring Crete was more thrilling for us/than visiting the Greek islands frequented by the rich.

BEFORE A PARENTHESIS

▶ At Nextel, Sylvia began at the bottom/(with only a
cubicle and a swivel chair), but within three years
she had been promoted to supervisor.

TO SET OFF AN INDIRECT (REPORTED) QUOTATION

▶ Samuel Goldwyn once said/that a verbal contract
isn't worth the paper it's written on.

WITH A QUESTION MARK OR AN EXCLAMATION POINT

▶ "Why don't you try it?/" she coaxed.

ON THE WEB > dianahacker.com/pocket > Grammar exercises >
Punctuation > E-ex 17–1 to 17–4

18 The semicolon and the colon

18a The semicolon

The semicolon is used between independent clauses not
joined with a coordinating conjunction. It can also be used
between items in a series containing internal punctuation.

The semicolon is never used between elements of un-
equal grammatical rank.

Between independent clauses   When related independent
clauses appear in one sentence, they are usually connected with a comma and a coordinating conjunction
(*and, but, or, nor, for, so, yet*). The coordinating conjunction expresses the relation between the clauses. If the relation is clear without a conjunction, a writer may choose
to connect the clauses with a semicolon instead.

> Injustice is relatively easy to bear; what stings is
> justice.   —H. L. Mencken

A writer may also connect the clauses with a semicolon
and a conjunctive adverb such as *however* or a transitional
phrase such as *for example*. (See p. 66.)

> He swallowed a lot of wisdom; however, it seemed as if
> all of it had gone down the wrong way.
>   —G. C. Lichtenberg

CONJUNCTIVE ADVERBS

accordingly, also, anyway, besides, certainly,
consequently, conversely, finally, furthermore, hence,
however, incidentally, indeed, instead, likewise,
meanwhile, moreover, nevertheless, next, nonetheless,
now, otherwise, similarly, specifically, still, subsequently,
then, therefore, thus

TRANSITIONAL PHRASES

after all, as a matter of fact, as a result, at any rate, at
the same time, even so, for example, for instance, in
addition, in conclusion, in fact, in other words, in the
first place, on the contrary

NOTE: A semicolon must be used whenever a coordinating
conjunction does not appear between independent clauses.
To use merely a comma — or to use a comma and a conjunctive adverb or transitional expression — creates an
error known as a *comma splice*. (See 15.)

Between items in a series containing internal punctuation
Items in a series are usually separated by commas. If one
or more of the items contain internal punctuation, however, a writer may use semicolons instead.

> Classic science fiction sagas are *Star Trek*, with Mr. Spock
> and his large pointed ears; *Battlestar Galactica*, with
> its Cylons; and *Star Wars*, with Han Solo, Luke
> Skywalker, and Darth Vader.

Misuses of the semicolon   Do not use a semicolon in the
following situations.

BETWEEN AN INDEPENDENT CLAUSE AND A SUBORDINATE CLAUSE

▶ The media like to portray my generation as lazy;,

although polls show that we work as hard as the

twentysomethings before us.

BETWEEN AN APPOSITIVE AND THE WORD IT REFERS TO

▶ We were fascinated by the species *Argyroneta*

aquatica;, a spider that lives underwater.

TO INTRODUCE A LIST

▶ Some of my favorite film stars have home pages

on the Web;: Jennifer Hudson, Jamie Foxx, and

Charlize Theron.

BETWEEN INDEPENDENT CLAUSES JOINED BY *AND, BUT, OR, NOR, FOR, SO,* OR *YET*

▶ Five of the applicants had worked with spread-

sheets/, but only one was familiar with database

management.

18b The colon

The colon is used after an independent clause to call attention to the words that follow it. The colon also has certain conventional uses.

Main uses of the colon   After an independent clause, a writer may use a colon to direct readers' attention to a list, an appositive, or a quotation.

A LIST

The routine includes the following: twenty knee bends, fifty leg lifts, and five minutes of running in place.

AN APPOSITIVE

My roommate is guilty of two of the seven deadly sins: gluttony and sloth.

A QUOTATION

Consider the words of Benjamin Franklin: "There never was a good war or a bad peace."

For other ways of introducing quotations, see pages 73–74.

A colon may also be used between independent clauses if the second summarizes or explains the first.

Faith is like love: It cannot be forced.

The second clause may begin with a capital or a lowercase letter: *Minds are like parachutes: They* [or *they*] *function only when open.*

Other uses   Use a colon after the salutation in a formal letter, to indicate hours and minutes, to show proportions, between a title and a subtitle, and to separate city and publisher in bibliographic entries.

Dear Sir or Madam:

5:30 p.m.

The ratio of women to men was 2:1.

Alvin Ailey: A Life in Dance

Boston: Bedford, 2007

NOTE: In biblical references, a colon is ordinarily used between chapter and verse (Luke 2:14). The Modern Language Association recommends a period (Luke 2.14).

Misuses of the colon   A colon must be preceded by an independent clause. Therefore, avoid using it in the following situations.

BETWEEN A VERB AND ITS OBJECT OR COMPLEMENT

▶ Some important vitamins found in vegetables are꞉ vitamin A, thiamine, niacin, and vitamin C.

BETWEEN A PREPOSITION AND ITS OBJECT

▶ The heart's two pumps each consist of꞉ an upper chamber, or atrium, and a lower chamber, or ventricle.

AFTER *SUCH AS, INCLUDING*, OR *FOR EXAMPLE*

▶ The trees on campus include fine Japanese specimens such as꞉ black pines, ginkgos, and cutleaf maples.

ON THE WEB > dianahacker.com/pocket > Grammar exercises > Punctuation > E-ex 18–1 to 18–3

---

19 The apostrophe

The apostrophe indicates possession and marks contractions. In addition, it has a few conventional uses.

19a To indicate possession

The apostrophe is used to indicate that a noun or an indefinite pronoun is possessive. Possessives usually indicate ownership, as in *Tim's hat, the editor's desk,* or *someone's gloves.* Frequently, however, ownership is only loosely implied: *the tree's roots, a day's work.* If you are not sure whether a noun or an indefinite pronoun is possessive, try turning it into an *of* phrase: *the roots of the tree, the work of a day.*

When to add -'s   Add -'s if the noun does not end in -s or if the noun is singular and ends in -s or an s sound.

> Luck often propels a rock musician's career.

> Thank you for refunding the children's money.

> Lois's sister spent last year in India.

> Her article presents an overview of Marx's teachings.

EXCEPTION: If pronunciation would be awkward with the added -'s, some writers use only the apostrophe: *Sophocles' plays*.

ON THE WEB > dianahacker.com/pocket **>** Language Debates >
-'s for singular nouns ending in -s or an s sound

When to add only an apostrophe   If the noun is plural and ends in -s, add only an apostrophe.

> Both diplomats' briefcases were stolen.

Joint possession   To show joint possession, use -'s (or -s') with the last noun only; to show individual possession, make all nouns possessive.

> Have you seen Joyce and Greg's new camper?

> Hernando's and Maria's expectations were quite different.

Compound nouns   If a noun is compound, use -'s (or -s') with the last element.

> Her father-in-law's sculpture won first place.

Indefinite pronouns such as someone   Use -'s to indicate that an indefinite pronoun is possessive. Indefinite pronouns refer to no specific person or thing: *everyone, someone, no one*, and so on.

> This diet will improve almost anyone's health.

NOTE: Possessive pronouns (*its, his*, and so on) do not use an apostrophe. (See 19d.)

19b To mark contractions

In a contraction, an apostrophe takes the place of missing letters.

> It's a shame that Frank can't go on the tour.

It's stands for *it is, can't* for *cannot*.

The apostrophe is also used to mark the omission of the first two digits of a year (*the class of '07*) or years (*the '60s generation*).

19c Conventional uses

An apostrophe typically is not used to pluralize numbers, letters, abbreviations, or words mentioned as words. Note the few exceptions and be consistent in your writing.

Plural numbers and abbreviations   Omit the apostrophe in the plural of all numbers (including decades) and of all abbreviations.

> Peggy skated nearly perfect figure 8s.

> We collected only four IOUs out of forty.

Plural letters   Italicize the letter and use roman font style for the *-s* ending. Use of an apostrophe is usually optional; the Modern Language Association recommends the apostrophe.

> Two large *J*s [or *J*'s] were painted on the door.

Plural of words mentioned as words   Italicize the word and use roman font style for the *-s* ending.

> We've heard enough *maybe*s.

Words mentioned as words may also appear in quotation marks. When you choose this option, use the apostrophe: *We've heard enough "maybe's."*

19d Misuses of the apostrophe

Do not use an apostrophe in the following situations.

WITH NOUNS THAT ARE PLURAL BUT NOT POSSESSIVE

▶ Some ~~outpatient's~~ *outpatients* are given special parking permits.

IN THE POSSESSIVE PRONOUNS *ITS, WHOSE, HIS, HERS, OURS, YOURS,* AND *THEIRS*

▶ Each area has ~~it's~~ *its* own conference room.

It's means "it is." The possessive pronoun *its* contains no apostrophe despite the fact that it is possessive.

ON THE WEB > dianahacker.com/pocket > Grammar exercises > Punctuation > E-ex 19–1

20 Quotation marks

Quotation marks are used to enclose direct quotations. They are also used around some titles and to set off words used as words.

20a To enclose direct quotations

Direct quotations of a person's words, whether spoken or written, must be in quotation marks.

> "A foolish consistency is the hobgoblin of little minds," wrote Ralph Waldo Emerson.

EXCEPTION: When a long quotation has been set off from the text by indenting, quotation marks are not needed. (See pp. 111–12, 162–63, and 203–4.)

Use single quotation marks to enclose a quotation within a quotation.

> According to Paul Eliott, Eskimo hunters "chant an ancient magic song to the seal they are after: 'Beast of the sea! Come and place yourself before me in the early morning!' "

NOTE: Do not use quotation marks around indirect quotations, which report what a person said without using the person's exact words: *Emerson believed that consistency for its own sake is the mark of a small mind.*

20b Around titles of short works

Use quotation marks around titles of newspaper and magazine articles, poems, short stories, songs, episodes of television and radio programs, and chapters or subdivisions of books.

> The poem "Mother to Son" is by Langston Hughes.

NOTE: Titles of books, plays, Web sites, television and radio programs, films, magazines, and newspapers are put in italics. (See pp. 85–86.)

20c To set off words used as words

Although words used as words are ordinarily italicized (see p. 86), quotation marks are also acceptable.

> The words "affect" and "effect" are frequently confused.

20d Other punctuation with quotation marks

This section describes the conventions to observe in placing various marks of punctuation inside or outside quotation marks. It also explains how to punctuate when introducing quoted material.

Periods and commas   Place periods and commas inside quotation marks.

> "This is a stick-up," said the well-dressed young couple. "We want all your money."

This rule applies to single and double quotation marks, and it applies to all uses of quotation marks.

EXCEPTION: In MLA and APA parenthetical in-text citations, the period follows the citation in parentheses. MLA: *According to Cole, "The instruments of science have vastly extended our senses" (53).* APA: *According to Cole (1999), "The instruments of science have vastly extended our senses" (p. 53).*

Colons and semicolons   Put colons and semicolons outside quotation marks.

> Harold wrote, "I regret that I cannot attend the fundraiser for AIDS research"; his letter, however, contained a contribution.

Question marks and exclamation points   Put question marks and exclamation points inside quotation marks unless they apply to the sentence as a whole.

> Contrary to tradition, bedtime at my house is marked by "Mommy, can I tell you a story now?"

> Have you heard the old proverb "Do not climb the hill until you reach it"?

In the first sentence, the question mark applies only to the quoted question. In the second sentence, the question mark applies to the whole sentence.

Introducing quoted material After a word group introducing a quotation, use a colon, a comma, or no punctuation at all, whichever is appropriate in context.

If a quotation has been formally introduced, a colon is appropriate. A formal introduction is a full independent clause, not just an expression such as *he said* or *she writes*.

> Morrow views personal ads as an art form: "The personal ad is like a haiku of self-celebration, a brief solo played on one's own horn."

If a quotation is introduced or followed by an expression such as *he said* or *she writes*, use a comma.

> Stephen Leacock once said, "I am a great believer in luck, and I find the harder I work the more I have of it."

> "You can be a little ungrammatical if you come from the right part of the country," writes Robert Frost.

When you blend a quotation into your own sentence, use either a comma or no punctuation, depending on the way the quotation fits into your sentence structure.

> The champion could, as he put it, "float like a butterfly and sting like a bee."

> Hudson notes that the prisoners escaped "by squeezing through a tiny window eighteen feet above the floor of their cell."

If a quotation appears at the beginning of a sentence, set it off with a comma unless the quotation ends with a question mark or an exclamation point.

> "I've always thought of myself as a reporter," claimed American poet Gwendolyn Brooks.

> "What is it?" I asked, bracing myself.

If a quoted sentence is interrupted by explanatory words, use commas to set off the explanatory words.

> "A great many people think they are thinking," observed William James, "when they are merely rearranging their prejudices."

If two successive quoted sentences from the same source are interrupted by explanatory words, use a comma before the explanatory words and a period after them.

> "I was a flop as a daily reporter," admitted E. B. White. "Every piece had to be a masterpiece—and before you knew it, Tuesday was Wednesday."

20e Misuses of quotation marks

Avoid using quotation marks in the following situations.

FAMILIAR SLANG, TRITE EXPRESSIONS, OR HUMOR

▶ Between Thanksgiving and Super Bowl Sunday, many American wives become /football widows./

INDIRECT QUOTATIONS

▶ After leaving the scene of the domestic quarrel, the officer said that /he was due for a coffee break./

NOTE: Do not use quotation marks around the title of your own essay.

ON THE WEB > dianahacker.com/pocket > Grammar exercises > Punctuation > E-ex 20–1

21 Other marks

21a The period

Use a period to end all sentences except direct questions or genuine exclamations.

> Celia asked whether the picnic would be canceled.

A period is conventionally used with personal titles, Latin abbreviations, and designations for time.

Mr.	i.e.	a.m. (or AM)
Ms.	e.g.	p.m. (or PM)
Dr.	etc.	

A period is not used in US postal service abbreviations for states, organization names, most capitalized abbreviations, academic degrees, and designations for eras.

CA	UNESCO	NATO	IRS	BS	BC
NY	USA	AFL-CIO	FCC	PhD	BCE

NOTE: If a sentence ends with a period marking an abbreviation, do not add a second period.

21b The question mark

Use a question mark after a direct question.

> What is the horsepower of a 747 engine?

NOTE: Use a period, not a question mark, after an indirect question, one that is reported rather than asked directly.

> He asked me who was teaching the mythology course.

21c The exclamation point

Use an exclamation point after a sentence that expresses exceptional feeling or deserves special emphasis.

> We yelled to the police officer, "He's not drunk! He's in diabetic shock!"

TIP: Do not overuse the exclamation point.

▶ **In the fisherman's memory, the fish lives on, increasing in length and weight with each passing year, until at last it is big enough to shade a fishing boat/.**

This sentence doesn't need to be pumped up with an exclamation point. It is emphatic enough without it.

21d The dash

The dash may be used to set off material that deserves special emphasis. When typing, use two hyphens to form a dash (- -), with no spaces before or after the dash. (If your word processing program has what is known as an "em-dash," you may use it instead, with no space before or after it.)

Use a dash to introduce a list, a restatement, an amplification, or a dramatic shift in tone or thought.

> Along the wall are the bulk liquids—sesame seed oil, honey, safflower oil, and half-liquid peanut butter.

> Consider the amount of sugar in the average person's diet—104 pounds per year.

> Kiere took a few steps back, came running full speed, kicked a mighty kick—and missed the ball.

In the first two examples, the writer could also use a colon. (See 18b.) The colon is more formal than the dash and not quite as dramatic.

Use a pair of dashes to set off parenthetical material that deserves special emphasis or to set off an appositive that contains commas.

> Everything that went wrong—from the peeping Tom at her window to my head-on collision—was blamed on our move.

> In my hometown, the basic needs of people—food, clothing, and shelter—are less costly than in Denver.

TIP: Unless you have a specific reason for using the dash, avoid it. Unnecessary dashes create a choppy effect.

21e Parentheses

Use parentheses to enclose supplemental material, minor digressions, and afterthoughts.

> After taking her vital signs (temperature, pulse, and blood pressure), the nurse made Becky comfortable.

Use parentheses to enclose letters or numbers labeling items in a series.

> There are three points of etiquette in poker: (1) allow someone to cut the cards, (2) don't forget to ante up, and (3) never stack your chips.

TIP: Do not overuse parentheses. Often a sentence reads more gracefully without them.

▶ Researchers have said that ~~thirteen million~~ *from thirteen to eighteen million*
^
~~(estimates run as high as eighteen million)~~

Americans have diabetes.

21f Brackets

Use brackets to enclose any words or phrases inserted into an otherwise word-for-word quotation.

> *Audubon* reports that "if there are not enough young to balance deaths, the end of the species [California condor] is inevitable."

The *Audubon* article did not contain the words *California condor* in the sentence quoted.

The Latin word "sic" in brackets indicates that an error in a quoted sentence appears in the original source.

> According to the review, Nelly Furtado's performance was brilliant, "exceding [sic] the expectations of even her most loyal fans."

21g The ellipsis mark

Use an ellipsis mark, three spaced periods, to indicate that you have deleted material from an otherwise word-for-word quotation.

> Reuben reports that "when the amount of cholesterol circulating in the blood rises over . . . 300 milligrams per 100, the chances of a heart attack increase dramatically."

If you delete a full sentence or more in the middle of a quoted passage, use a period before the three ellipsis dots.

TIP: Do not use the ellipsis mark at the beginning of a quotation; do not use it at the end of a quotation unless you have cut some words from the end of the final sentence quoted.

21h The slash

Use the slash to separate two or three lines of poetry that have been run into your text. Add a space both before and after the slash.

In the opening lines of "Jordan," George Herbert pokes fun at popular poems of his time: "Who says that fictions only and false hair / Become a verse? Is there in truth no beauty?"

Use the slash sparingly, if at all, to separate options: *pass/fail*, *producer/director*. Put no space around the slash. Avoid using a slash for *he/she*, *and/or*, and *his/her*.

ON THE WEB > dianahacker.com/pocket > Grammar exercises > Punctuation > E-ex 21–1

Mechanics

22 Capitalization

In addition to the following guidelines, a good dictionary can often tell you when to use capital letters.

22a Proper vs. common nouns

Proper nouns and words derived from them are capitalized; common nouns are not. Proper nouns name specific persons, places, and things. All other nouns are common nouns.

The following types of words are usually capitalized: names of deities, religions, religious followers, and sacred books; words of family relationships used as names; particular places; nationalities and their languages, races, and tribes; educational institutions, departments, degrees, particular courses; government departments, organizations, political parties; historical movements, periods, events, documents; specific electronic sources; and trade names.

PROPER NOUNS	COMMON NOUNS
God (used as a name)	a god
Book of Jeremiah	a sacred book
Grandmother Bishop	my grandmother
Father (used as a name)	my father
Lake Superior	a picturesque lake
the Capital Center	a center for the arts
the South	a southern state
Japan, a Japanese garden	an ornamental garden
University of Wisconsin	a good university
Geology 101	a geology course
Veterans Administration	a federal agency
Phi Kappa Psi	a fraternity
the Democratic Party	a political party
the Enlightenment	the eighteenth century
the Great Depression	a recession
the Declaration of Independence	a treaty
the World Wide Web, the Web	a home page
the Internet, the Net	a computer network
Advil	a painkiller

Months, holidays, and days of the week are capitalized: *May*, *Labor Day*, *Monday*. The seasons and numbers of the days of the month are not: *summer*, *the fifth of June*.

Names of school subjects are capitalized only if they are names of languages: *geology*, *history*, *English*, *French*. Names of particular courses are capitalized: *Geology 101*, *Principles of Economics*.

TIP: Do not capitalize common nouns to make them seem important: *Our company is currently hiring technical support staff* [not *Company*, *Technical Support Staff*].

22b Titles with proper names

Capitalize a title when used as part of a proper name but usually not when used alone.

> Prof. Margaret Burnes; Dr. Harold Stevens; John Scott Williams Jr.; Anne Tilton, LLD

> District Attorney Mill was ruled out of order.

> The district attorney was elected for a two-year term.

Usage varies when the title of an important public figure is used alone: *The president* [or *President*] *vetoed the bill.*

22c Titles of works

Major words should be capitalized in both titles and subtitles of works such as books, articles, and songs. Minor words—articles, prepositions, and coordinating conjunctions—are not capitalized unless they are the first or last word of a title or subtitle.

> *The Impossible Theater: A Manifesto*

> "Man in the Middle"

> "I Want to Hold Your Hand"

22d First word of a sentence or quoted sentence

The first word of a sentence should be capitalized. Capitalize the first word of a quoted sentence but not a quoted phrase.

> In *Time* magazine, Robert Hughes writes, "There are only about sixty Watteau paintings on whose authenticity all experts agree."

> Russell Baker has written that sports are "the opiate of the masses."

If a quoted sentence is interrupted by explanatory words, do not capitalize the first word after the interruption.

> "When we all think alike," he said, "no one is thinking."

22e First word following a colon

Capitalize the first word after a colon if it begins an independent clause.

> There is one glaring omission in the Bill of Rights: the right to vote.

> I came to a startling conclusion: The house must be haunted.

NOTE: MLA and *Chicago* styles use a lowercase letter to begin an independent clause following a colon. APA style uses a capital letter.

22f Abbreviations

Capitalize abbreviations for departments and agencies of government, other organizations, and corporations; capitalize trade names and the call letters of radio and television stations.

> EPA, FBI, OPEC, IBM, Xerox, WCRB, KNBC-TV

ON THE WEB > dianahacker.com/pocket > Grammar exercises > Mechanics > E-ex 22–1

23 Abbreviations, numbers, and italics

23a Abbreviations

Use abbreviations only when they are clearly appropriate.

Appropriate abbreviations Use standard abbreviations for titles immediately before and after proper names.

TITLES BEFORE PROPER NAMES	TITLES AFTER PROPER NAMES
Mr. Ralph Meyer	Thomas Hines Jr.
Ms. Nancy Linehan	Anita Lor, PhD
Dr. Margaret Simmons	Robert Simkowski, MD

TITLES BEFORE PROPER NAMES	TITLES AFTER PROPER NAMES
Rev. John Stone	William Lyons, MA
St. Joan of Arc	Margaret Chin, LLD
Prof. James Russo	Polly Stern, DDS

Do not abbreviate a title if it is not used with a proper name: *My history professor* [not *prof.*] *was an expert on naval warfare.*

Familiar abbreviations for the names of organizations, corporations, and countries are also acceptable: *CIA, FBI, AFL-CIO, NAACP, IBM, UPI, CBS, USA.*

> The CIA was established in 1947 by the National Security Act.

When using an unfamiliar abbreviation (such as NAB for National Association of Broadcasters) throughout a paper, write the full name followed by the abbreviation in parentheses at the first mention of the name. You may use the abbreviation in the rest of the paper.

Other commonly accepted abbreviations include *BC, AD, a.m., p.m., No.,* and *$.* The abbreviation *BC* ("before Christ") follows a date, and *AD* (*"anno Domini"*) precedes a date. Acceptable alternatives are *BCE* ("before the common era") and *CE* ("common era").

40 BC (or 40 BCE)	4:00 a.m. (or AM)	No. 12 (or no. 12)
AD 44 (or 44 CE)	6:00 p.m. (or PM)	$150

Avoid using *a.m., p.m., No.,* or *$* when not accompanied by a specific figure: *We set off for the lake early in the morning* [not *a.m.*].

Inappropriate abbreviations In formal writing, abbreviations for the following are not commonly accepted.

PERSONAL NAME   Charles (*not* Chas.)

UNITS OF MEASUREMENT   pound (*not* lb.)

DAYS OF THE WEEK   Monday (*not* Mon.)

HOLIDAYS   Christmas (*not* Xmas)

MONTHS   January, February (*not* Jan., Feb.)

COURSES OF STUDY   political science (*not* poli. sci.)

DIVISIONS OF WRITTEN WORKS   chapter, page (*not* ch., p.)

STATES AND COUNTRIES   Florida (*not* FL or Fla.)

PARTS OF A BUSINESS NAME   Adams Lighting Company (*not* Adams Lighting Co.); Kim and Brothers, Inc. (*not* Kim and Bros., Inc.)

Although Latin abbreviations are appropriate in footnotes and bibliographies and in informal writing, use the appropriate English phrases in formal writing.

cf. (Latin *confer*, "compare")

e.g. (Latin *exempli gratia*, "for example")

et al. (Latin *et alii*, "and others")

etc. (Latin *et cetera*, "and so forth")

i.e. (Latin *id est*, "that is")

N.B. (Latin *nota bene*, "note well")

ON THE WEB > dianahacker.com/pocket > Grammar exercises > Mechanics > E-ex 23–1

23b Numbers

Spell out numbers of one or two words. Use figures for numbers that require more than two words to spell out.

▶ The 1980 eruption of Mount St. Helens blasted
ash ~~16~~ *sixteen* miles into the sky and devastated ~~two hundred thirty~~ *230* square miles of land.

EXCEPTION: In technical and some business writing, figures are preferred even when spellings would be brief, but usage varies.

If a sentence begins with a number, spell out the number or rewrite the sentence.

▶ ~~150~~ *One hundred fifty* children in our program need expensive dental treatment.

Generally, figures are acceptable for the following.

DATES   July 4, 1776, 56 BC, AD 30

ADDRESSES   77 Latches Lane, 519 West 42nd Street

PERCENTAGES   55 percent (or 55%)

FRACTIONS, DECIMALS $^1/_2$, 0.047

SCORES   7 to 3, 21–18

STATISTICS   average age 37

SURVEYS   4 out of 5

EXACT AMOUNTS OF MONEY $105.37, $0.05

DIVISIONS OF BOOKS   volume 3, chapter 4, page 189

DIVISIONS OF PLAYS   act 3, scene 3 (or act III, scene iii)

IDENTIFICATION NUMBERS   serial no. 1098

TIME OF DAY   4:00 p.m., 1:30 a.m.

ON THE WEB > dianahacker.com/pocket > Grammar exercises > Mechanics > E-ex 23–2

23c Italics

This section describes conventional uses for italics: for titles of works; names of ships, aircraft, and spacecraft; foreign words; and words as words.

NOTE: In handwritten material, underlining is used in place of italics. If your instructor prefers underlining, simply substitute underlining for italics in the examples in this section.

Titles of works   Titles of the following works are italicized.

TITLES OF BOOKS   *The Color Purple, Middlesex, Encarta*

MAGAZINES   *Time, Scientific American, Salon.com*

NEWSPAPERS   the *Baltimore Sun*, the *New York Times on the Web*

PAMPHLETS   *Common Sense, Facts about Marijuana*

LONG POEMS   *The Waste Land, Paradise Lost*

PLAYS   *King Lear, Rent*

FILMS   *Casablanca, American Beauty*

TELEVISION PROGRAMS   *American Idol, Frontline*

RADIO PROGRAMS   *All Things Considered*

MUSICAL COMPOSITIONS   *Porgy and Bess*

CHOREOGRAPHIC WORKS   *Brief Fling*

WORKS OF VISUAL ART   *American Gothic*

COMIC STRIPS   *Dilbert*

ELECTRONIC DATABASES   *InfoTrac*

WEB SITES   *Salon.com, Google*

ELECTRONIC GAMES   *Everquest, The Sims*

The titles of other works, such as short stories, essays, songs, and short poems, are enclosed in quotation marks. (See 20b.)

NOTE: Do not use italics when referring to the Bible; titles of books in the Bible (Genesis, not *Genesis*); the titles of legal documents (the Constitution, not the *Constitution*); or the titles of your own papers.

Names of ships, aircraft, spacecraft Italicize names of specific ships, aircraft, and spacecraft.

> *Challenger, Spirit of St. Louis, Queen Elizabeth II*

Foreign words Italicize foreign words used in an English sentence.

> Caroline's *joie de vivre* should be a model for all of us.

EXCEPTION: Do not italicize foreign words that have become part of the English language—"laissez-faire," "fait accompli," "modus operandi," and "per diem," for example.

Words as words, etc. Italicize words used as words, letters mentioned as letters, and numbers mentioned as numbers.

> Tomás assured us that the chemicals could probably be safely mixed, but his *probably* stuck in our minds.

> Speakers of some dialects have trouble pronouncing the letter *r*.

> A big *3* was painted on the door to the lab.

NOTE: Quotation marks may be used instead of italics to set off words mentioned as words. (See 20c.)

Inappropriate italics Italicizing to emphasize words or ideas is distracting and should be used sparingly.

ON THE WEB > dianahacker.com/pocket > Grammar exercises > Mechanics > E-ex 23–3

24 Spelling and the hyphen

24a Spelling

A word processing program equipped with a spell checker is a useful tool, but be aware of its limitations. A spell checker will not tell you how to spell words not listed in its dictionary; nor will it help you catch words commonly confused, such as *accept* and *except*, or common typographical errors, such as *own* for *won*. You will still need to proofread, and for some words you may need to turn to the dictionary.

NOTE: To check for correct use of commonly confused words (*accept* and *except*, *its* and *it's*, and so on), consult section 44, the glossary of usage.

Major spelling rules If you need to improve your spelling, review the following rules and exceptions.

1. Use *i* before *e* except after *c* or when sounded like "ay," as in *neighbor* and *weigh*.

I BEFORE *E*	relieve, believe, sieve, niece, fierce, frieze
E BEFORE *I*	receive, deceive, sleigh, freight, eight
EXCEPTIONS	seize, either, weird, height, foreign, leisure

2. Generally, drop a final silent *-e* when adding a suffix that begins with a vowel. Keep the final *-e* if the suffix begins with a consonant.

desire, desiring   achieve, achievement
remove, removable   care, careful

Words such as *changeable*, *judgment*, *argument*, and *truly* are exceptions.

3. When adding *-s* or *-ed* to words ending in *-y*, ordinarily change *-y* to *-i* when the *-y* is preceded by a consonant but not when it is preceded by a vowel.

comedy, comedies   monkey, monkeys
dry, dried   play, played

With proper names ending in *-y*, however, do not change the *-y* to *-i* even if it is preceded by a consonant: *the Dougherty family, the Doughertys.*

4. If a final consonant is preceded by a single vowel *and* the consonant ends a one-syllable word or a stressed syllable, double the consonant when adding a suffix beginning with a vowel.

bet, betting   occur, occurrence
commit, committed

5. Add *-s* to form the plural of most nouns; add *-es* to singular nouns ending in *-s*, *-sh*, *-ch*, and *-x*.

table, tables   church, churches
paper, papers   dish, dishes

Ordinarily add *-s* to nouns ending in *-o* when the *-o* is preceded by a vowel. Add *-es* when it is preceded by a consonant.

radio, radios   hero, heroes
video, videos   tomato, tomatoes

To form the plural of a hyphenated compound word, add the *-s* to the chief word even if it does not appear at the end.

mother-in-law, mothers-in-law

NOTE: English words derived from other languages such as Latin, Greek, or French sometimes form the plural as they would in their original language.

medium, media   chateau, chateaux
criterion, criteria

Spelling variations   Following is a list of some common words spelled differently in American and British English. Consult a dictionary for others.

AMERICAN	BRITISH
canceled, traveled	cancelled, travelled
color, humor	colour, humour
judgment	judgement
check	cheque
realize, apologize	realise, apologise
defense	defence
anemia, anesthetic	anaemia, anaesthetic
theater, center	theatre, centre
fetus	foetus
mold, smolder	mould, smoulder
civilization	civilisation
connection, inflection	connexion, inflexion
licorice	liquorice

24b The hyphen

In addition to the following guidelines, a dictionary will help you make decisions about hyphenation.

Compound words   The dictionary will tell you whether to treat a compound word as a hyphenated compound (*water-repellent*), as one word (*waterproof*), or as two words (*water table*). If the compound word is not in the dictionary, treat it as two words.

▶ The prosecutor chose not to cross-examine any

 witnesses.

▶ Imogen kept her sketches in a small note book.

▶ Alice walked through the looking/glass into a

 backward world.

Words functioning together as an adjective   When two or more words function together as an adjective before a noun, connect them with a hyphen. Generally, do not use a hyphen when such compounds follow the noun.

▶ Pat Hobbs is not yet a well-known candidate.

▶ After our television campaign, Pat Hobbs will be

 well/known.

Do not use a hyphen to connect *-ly* adverbs to the words they modify.

▶ A slowly/moving truck tied up traffic.

NOTE: In a series, hyphens are suspended: *Do you prefer first-, second-, or third-class tickets?*

Conventional uses   Hyphenate the written form of fractions and of compound numbers from twenty-one to ninety-nine. Also use the hyphen with the prefixes *all-*, *ex-*, and *self-* and with the suffix *-elect*.

▶ One-fourth of my income goes for rent.

▶ The charity is funding more self-help projects.

Division of a word at the end of a line   If a word must be divided at the end of a line, use these guidelines.

1. Divide words between syllables.
2. Never divide one-syllable words.

3. Never divide a word so that a single letter stands alone at the end of a line or fewer than three letters begin a line.

4. When dividing a compound word at the end of a line, either make the break between the words that form the compound or put the whole word on the next line.

Division of an e-mail address or Internet address (URL)
Break an e-mail address after the @ symbol or before a period. Break a URL after a colon, a slash, or a double slash or before a period or another punctuation mark. Do not insert a hyphen at the break.

NOTE: For breaks in URLs in MLA, APA, and *Chicago* documentation styles, see pages 150, 187, and 226, respectively.

ON THE WEB > **dianahacker.com/pocket** > Grammar exercises > Mechanics > E-ex 24–1

Research

College research assignments ask you to pose a question worth exploring, to read widely in search of possible answers, to interpret what you read, to draw reasoned conclusions, and to support those conclusions with valid and well-documented evidence.

For help writing the actual paper—from forming a thesis to documenting your sources—consult one of the following color-coded sections, depending on the type of paper you have been assigned: MLA papers (orange), APA papers (green), or *Chicago* papers (brown).

25 Posing a research question

Working within the guidelines of your assignment, pose a few questions that seem worth researching. As you formulate possible questions, make sure that they are appropriate lines of inquiry for a research paper. Choose questions that are narrow (not too broad), challenging (not too bland), and grounded (not too speculative).

25a Choosing a narrow question

If your initial question is too broad, given the length of the paper you plan to write, look for ways to restrict your focus. Here, for example, is how two students narrowed their initial questions.

TOO BROAD

What are the hazards of fad diets?

Is the United States seriously addressing the problem of prisoner abuse?

NARROWER

What are the hazards of low-carbohydrate diets?

To what extent has the US military addressed the problem of prisoner abuse since the Abu Ghraib discoveries?

25b Choosing a challenging question

Your research paper will be more interesting to both you and your audience if you base it on an intellectually challenging line of inquiry. Avoid bland questions that fail to provoke thought or engage readers in a debate.

TOO BLAND

> What is obsessive-compulsive disorder?
>
> How does DNA testing work?

CHALLENGING

> What treatments for obsessive-compulsive disorder show the most promise?
>
> How reliable is DNA testing?

You may need to address a bland question in the course of answering a more challenging one, but it would be a mistake to use the bland question as the focus for the whole paper.

25c Choosing a grounded question

Finally, you will want to make sure that your research question is grounded, not too speculative. Although speculative questions—such as those that address philosophical, ethical, or religious issues—are worth asking and may receive some attention in a research paper, they are inappropriate central questions. The central argument of a research paper should be grounded in facts; it should not be based entirely on beliefs.

TOO SPECULATIVE

> Is it wrong to share music files on the Internet?
>
> Do medical students have the right to experiment on animals?

GROUNDED

> How has Internet file sharing affected the earning potential of musicians?
>
> How have breakthroughs in technology made medical experiments on animals increasingly unnecessary?

ON THE WEB > dianahacker.com/pocket > Research exercises > Researching > E-ex 25–1

26 Finding appropriate sources

Depending on your research question, some sources will prove more useful than others. For example, if your research question addresses a historical issue, you might look at reference works, books, scholarly articles, and primary sources such as speeches. If your research question addresses a current political issue, however, you might turn to magazine and newspaper articles, Web sites, and government documents.

> **ON THE WEB** > dianahacker.com/pocket > Research and Documentation Online > Humanities/Social Sciences/History/Sciences > Finding sources

26a Locating reference works

For some topics, you may want to begin your search by consulting general or specialized reference works. Check with a reference librarian to see which works are available in electronic format.

General reference works include encyclopedias, almanacs, atlases, and biographical references. Many specialized reference works are available: *Encyclopedia of Bioethics*, *Almanac of American Politics*, *The Historical and Cultural Atlas of African Americans*, and *The New Grove Dictionary of Music and Musicians*, to name a few.

26b Locating articles

Libraries subscribe to a variety of electronic databases (sometimes called *periodical databases*) that give students access to articles and other materials without charge. Because many databases are limited to relatively recent works, you may need to consult a print index as well.

What databases offer   Your library's databases can lead you to articles in newspapers, magazines, and scholarly or technical journals. Some databases cover several subjects; others cover one subject in depth. Your library might subscribe to some of the following resources.

GENERAL DATABASES

> *EBSCOhost.* A portal to databases that include periodical articles, government documents, pamphlets, and other documents.
>
> *InfoTrac.* A collection of databases, some of which index periodical articles.
>
> *LexisNexis.* A set of databases particularly strong in news, business, legal, and political topics.
>
> *ProQuest.* A database of periodical articles.

SUBJECT-SPECIFIC DATABASES

ERIC. An education database.

PubMed. A database with abstracts of medical studies.

MLA Bibliography. A database of literary criticism.

PsycINFO. A database of psychology research.

Many databases include the full text of at least some articles; others list only citations or citations with short summaries called *abstracts*. When full text is not available, the citation will give you enough information to track down an article.

How to search a database   To find articles on your topic in a database, start with a keyword search. If the first keyword you try results in no matches, experiment with synonyms. If your keyword search results in too many matches, narrow it by using one of the strategies in the following chart.

Refining keyword searches in databases and search engines

Although command terms and characters vary among electronic databases and Web search engines, some of the most commonly used functions are listed here.

- Use quotation marks around words that are part of a phrase: "Broadway musicals".

- Use AND to connect words that must appear in a document: Ireland AND peace. Some search engines require a plus sign instead: Ireland+peace.

- Use NOT in front of words that must not appear in a document: Titanic NOT movie. Some search engines require a minus sign (hyphen) instead: Titanic -movie.

- Use OR if only one of the terms must appear in a document: "mountain lion" OR cougar.

- Use an asterisk as a substitute for letters that might vary: "marine biolog*" (to find *marine biology* or *marine biologist*).

- Use parentheses to group a search expression and combine it with another: (cigarettes OR tobacco OR smok*) AND lawsuits.

NOTE: Many search engines and databases offer an advanced search option that makes it easy to refine your search.

26c Locating books

The books your library owns are listed in its computer catalog, along with other resources such as videos. You can search the catalog by author, title, or topic keywords.

Don't be surprised if your first search calls up too few or too many results. If you have too few results, try different keywords or search for books on broader topics. If a search gives you too many results, use the strategies in the chart on page 95.

When a book looks promising, you can usually print out its bibliographic information along with its call number. The call number is the book's address on the library shelf.

26d Locating Web resources

For some (but not all) topics, the Web is an excellent resource. For example, government agencies post information on the Web, and the sites of many organizations are filled with information about the issues they cover. Museums and libraries often post digital versions of primary sources, such as photographs, political speeches, and classic literary texts.

Although the Web can be a rich source of information, it lacks quality control. Anyone can publish on the Web, so you'll need to evaluate online sources with special care (see 27c).

This section describes the following Web resources: search engines, directories, digital archives, government and news sites, and discussion forums.

Search engines   Search engines take your search terms and seek matches among millions of Web pages. Often it is a good idea to try more than one search engine since each locates sources in its own way. For current information about search engines, visit *Search Engine Showdown* at <http://www.searchengineshowdown.com>. This site classifies search engines, evaluates them, and provides updates on new search features.

When using a search engine, focus your search as narrowly as possible. You can sharpen your search by using the tips listed in the chart on page 95 or by using a search engine's advanced search form.

Directories   Unlike search engines, which hunt for Web pages automatically, directories are put together by information specialists who arrange reputable sites by topic: education, health, politics, and so on.

Some directories are more selective and therefore more useful for scholarly research than search engines. The following directories are especially useful:

Internet Scout Project <http://scout.wisc.edu/Archives>

Librarian's Internet Index <http://lii.org>

Open Directory Project <http://dmoz.org>

WWW Virtual Library <http://vlib.org>

Digital archives   Archives may contain the texts of poems, books, speeches, political cartoons, and historically significant documents such as the Declaration of Independence and the Emancipation Proclamation. The following online archives are impressive collections:

American Memory <http://memory.loc.gov>

Archival Research Catalog <http://www.archives.gov/research/arc>

Avalon Project <http://yale.edu/lawweb/avalon/avalon.htm>

Electronic Text Center <http://etext.lib.virginia.edu>

Eurodocs <http://eudocs.lib.byu.edu>

Internet History Sourcebooks <http://www.fordham.edu/halsall>

Making of America <http://moa.umdl.umich.edu>

Online Books Page <http://onlinebooks.library.upenn.edu>

Government and news sites   For current topics, both government and news sites can prove useful. Many government agencies at every level provide online information. Government-maintained sites include resources such as facts and statistics, legal texts, government reports, and searchable reference databases. Here are just a few government sites:

Census Bureau <http://www.census.gov>

Fedstats <http://www.fedstats.gov>

FirstGov <http://www.usa.gov>

GPO Access <http://www.gpoaccess.gov>

United Nations <http://www.un.org>

Many news organizations offer up-to-date information on the Web. Some allow nonsubscribers to read current stories for free. Others allow users to search archives without cost but often charge users a fee to access full articles. Your library may subscribe to news archives that you can access at no charge. The following are some free news sites:

Google News <http://news.google.com>

Kidon Media-Link <http://www.kidon.com/media-link>

NewsLink <http://newslink.org>

Discussion forums   The Web offers various ways of communicating with experts and others who have an interest in your topic. You might join an online mailing list or search a newsgroup's postings. Newsgroups resemble bulletin boards on which messages are posted and connected through response "threads." In addition, you might log on to real-time discussion forums. To find mailing lists, newsgroups, and forums, try one of these sites:

CataList <http://www.lsoft.com/catalist.html>

Google Groups <http://groups.google.com>

Tile.Net <http://tile.net/lists>

27 Evaluating sources

With electronic search tools, you can often locate dozens or even hundreds of potential sources for your topic—far more than you will have time to read. Your challenge will be to determine what kinds of sources you need and to find a reasonable number of quality sources.

Later, once you have chosen worthwhile sources, your challenge will be to read them with an open mind and a critical eye.

27a Selecting sources

Determining how sources contribute to your writing   Before starting your research, think about how the sources you encounter could help you make your argument. How you plan to use a source affects how you evaluate it.

Sources can have various functions in a paper. They can

- provide background information or context for your topic
- explain terms or concepts that readers might not understand
- provide evidence for your argument
- lend authority to your argument
- offer counterevidence and alternative interpretations to your argument

For examples of how student writers use sources for a variety of purposes, see 30, 36, and 41.

Scanning search results   The chart on page 95 shows how to refine your searches in databases and search engines; these techniques can also be applied to library book catalog searches. This section explains how to scan through the results for the most useful and reliable sources.

Book catalogs   The library's book catalog usually gives you a short list of hits. A book's title and date of publication are often your first clues as to whether the book is worth consulting. If a title looks interesting, you can click on it for further information.

Determining if a source is scholarly

Many college assignments require you to use scholarly sources. Written by experts for a knowledgeable audience, these sources often go into more depth than books and articles written for a general audience. To determine if a source is scholarly, look for the following:

- Formal language and presentation
- Authors who are academics or scientists, not journalists
- Footnotes or a bibliography documenting the works cited by the author in the source
- Original research and interpretation (rather than a summary of other people's work)
- Quotations from and analysis of primary sources
- A description of research methods or a review of related research

Databases   Most databases, such as *ProQuest* and *Lexis-Nexis*, can help you decide if a source is relevant, current, scholarly enough, and a suitable length.

> Title and brief description (How relevant?)
>
> Date (How current?)
>
> Name of periodical (How scholarly?)
>
> Length (How extensive in coverage?)

Search engines   Unreliable Web sites often masquerade as legitimate sources of information. Look for the following clues about the probable relevance, currency, and reliability of a site—but be aware that the clues are by no means foolproof.

> Title, keywords, and lead-in text (How relevant?)
>
> A date (How current?)
>
> An indication of the site's sponsor or purpose (How reliable?)
>
> The URL, especially the domain name: .com, .edu, .gov, or .org (How relevant? How reliable?)

27b Reading with an open mind and a critical eye

As you begin reading the sources you have chosen, keep an open mind. Do not let your personal beliefs prevent you from listening to new ideas and opposing viewpoints. Your research question—not a snap judgment about the question—should guide your reading.

When you read critically, you are not necessarily judging an author's work harshly; you are simply examining its assumptions, assessing its evidence, and weighing its conclusions. Questions such as those in the following chart can help you weigh the strengths and weaknesses of the sources you read.

Evaluating all sources

CHECKING FOR SIGNS OF BIAS

■ Does the author or publisher have political leanings or religious views that could affect objectivity?

■ Is the author or publisher associated with a special-interest group, such as Greenpeace or the National Rifle Association, that might see only one side of an issue?   →

- How fairly does the author treat opposing views?
- Does the author's language show signs of bias?

ASSESSING AN ARGUMENT

- What is the author's central claim or thesis?
- How does the author support this claim—with relevant and sufficient evidence or with just a few anecdotes or emotional examples?
- Are statistics accurate and used fairly? Does the author explain where the statistics come from?
- Are any of the author's assumptions questionable?
- Does the author consider opposing arguments and refute them persuasively?

27c Assessing Web sources with special care

Web sources can be deceptive. Sophisticated-looking sites can be full of dubious information, and the identities of those who created a site are often hidden, along with their motives for having created it. Even hate sites may be cleverly disguised to look legitimate. In contrast, sites with reliable information can stand up to careful scrutiny. For a checklist on evaluating Web sources, see the following chart.

Evaluating Web sources

AUTHORSHIP

- Is there an author? You may need to do some clicking and scrolling to find the author's name. Check the home page or an "about this site" link.
- Can you tell whether an author is knowledgeable and credible? If the author's qualifications aren't listed on the site, look for links to the author's home page, which may provide evidence of his or her expertise.

SPONSORSHIP

- Who, if anyone, sponsors the site? The sponsor of a site is often named and described on the home page.
- What does the URL tell you? The URL ending often specifies the type of group hosting the site: commercial (.com), educational (.edu), nonprofit (.org), governmental →

Evaluating Web sources (continued)

SPONSORSHIP (continued)

(.gov), military (.mil), or network (.net). URLs may also indicate a country of origin: .uk (United Kingdom) or .jp (Japan), for instance.

PURPOSE AND AUDIENCE

- Why was the site created: To argue a position? To sell a product? To inform readers?
- Who is the site's intended audience?

CURRENCY

- How current is the site? Check for the date of publication or the latest update.
- How current are the site's links? If many of the links no longer work, the site may be too dated for your purposes.

TIP: If both the authorship and the sponsorship of a site are unclear, think twice about using the site for your research.

TIP: To discover a site's sponsor, you may have to truncate, or shorten, the URL. For example, to find the sponsor of a Web site featuring an article on environmentally friendly neighborhood development, you might need to shorten the full URL to its base URL.

FULL URL	\<http://www.bankof america.com/environment/dex.cfm?template=env_reports_speeches&context=smartgrowth\>
BASE URL	\<http://www.bankofamerica.com\>
SPONSOR	Bank of America

MLA Papers

Most assignments in English and other humanities classes are based to some extent on reading. At times, you will be asked to respond to one, two, or a few readings — such as essays or literary works. At other times, you may be asked to write a research paper that draws on a wide variety of sources.

Many English and humanities instructors will ask you to document your sources with the Modern Language Association (MLA) system of citations described in 32. When writing an MLA paper based on sources, you face three main challenges: (1) supporting a thesis, (2) citing your sources and avoiding plagiarism, and (3) integrating quotations and other source material.

28 Supporting a thesis

Most research assignments ask you to form a thesis, or main idea, and to support that thesis with well-organized evidence.

28a Forming a thesis

Once you have read a variety of sources and considered all sides of your issue, you are ready to form a tentative thesis—a one-sentence (or occasionally a two-sentence) statement of your central idea. The thesis expresses not just your opinion but also your informed, reasoned judgment. Usually your thesis will appear at the end of the first paragraph (see p. 151), but if you need to provide readers with more background information, you may place the thesis at the end of your second paragraph.

Because writing about a subject is a way of learning about it, your understanding of your subject will deepen as you write. After you have written a rough draft and done more reading and thinking, you may decide to revise your thesis.

In a research paper, your thesis will answer the central question that you pose, as in the following examples.

PUBLIC POLICY QUESTION

Should employers monitor their employees' online activities in the workplace?

POSSIBLE THESIS

Employers should not monitor their employees' online activities because electronic surveillance can compromise workers' privacy.

LITERATURE QUESTION

What does Stephen Crane's short story "The Open Boat" reveal about the relationship between humans and nature?

POSSIBLE THESIS

In Stephen Crane's gripping tale "The Open Boat," four men lost at sea discover not only that nature is indifferent to their fate but that their own particular talents make little difference as they struggle for survival.

MEDIA STUDIES QUESTION

What statement does the television show *ER* make about medical professionals in American society?

POSSIBLE THESIS

In dramatizing the experiences of doctors and nurses as they treat patients, navigate medical bureaucracy, and negotiate bioethical dilemmas, the TV show *ER* portrays health care professionals as unfailingly caring and noble.

Notice that each of these thesis statements takes a stand on a debatable issue—an issue about which intelligent, well-meaning people might disagree. Each writer's job will be to convince such people that his or her view is worth taking seriously.

ON THE WEB > dianahacker.com/pocket > Research exercises > MLA > E-ex 28–1 and 28–2

28b Organizing your evidence

The body of your paper will consist of evidence in support of your thesis. Instead of constructing a formal outline, list your key points, as Anna Orlov did in this simple plan.

- Employers monitor workers more efficiently with electronic surveillance.

- Companies may have financial and legal reasons to monitor employees' Internet usage.

- But monitoring employees' Internet usage may create distrust and lower worker productivity.

- Because laws do not protect employees' privacy rights, employees and employers must negotiate the risks and benefits of electronic surveillance.

After you have written a rough draft, a more formal outline can be a useful way to shape the complexities of your argument.

28c Using sources to inform and support your argument

Sources can play several different roles as you develop your points.

Providing background information or context   You can use facts and statistics to support generalizations or to establish the importance of your topic.

Explaining terms or concepts   Explain words, phrases, or ideas that might be unfamiliar to your readers. Quoting or paraphrasing a source can help you define terms and concepts in neutral, accessible language.

Supporting your claims   Back up your assertions with facts, examples, and other evidence from your research.

Lending authority to your argument   Expert opinion can give weight to your argument. But don't rely on experts to make your argument for you. Construct your argument in your own words and cite authorities in the field for support.

Anticipating and countering objections   Do not ignore sources that seem to contradict your position or that offer arguments different from your own. Instead, use them to give voice to opposing points of view before you counter them.

29 Avoiding plagiarism

Your research paper is a collaboration between you and your sources. To be fair and ethical, you must acknowledge your debt to the writers of those sources. If you don't, you commit plagiarism, a serious academic offense.

Three different acts are considered plagiarism: (1) failing to cite quotations and borrowed ideas, (2) failing to enclose borrowed language in quotation marks, and (3) failing to put summaries and paraphrases in your own words.

29a Citing quotations and borrowed ideas

You must cite all direct quotations and any ideas borrowed from a source: summaries and paraphrases; statistics and other specific facts; and visuals such as cartoons, graphs, and diagrams.

The only exception is common knowledge—information your readers could easily find in general sources. For example, it is well known that Martin Luther King Jr. won the Nobel Peace Prize in 1964 and that Emily Dickinson published only a handful of her many poems during her lifetime.

When you have seen information repeatedly in your reading, you don't need to cite it. However, when information has appeared in only one or two sources or when it is controversial, you should cite the source.

MLA recommends a system of in-text citations. Here, briefly, is how the MLA citation system usually works:

1. The source is introduced by a signal phrase that names its author.
2. The material being cited is followed by a page number in parentheses.
3. At the end of the paper, a list of works cited (arranged alphabetically by authors' last names) gives complete publication information about the source.

IN-TEXT CITATION

Legal scholar Jay Kesan points out that the law holds employers liable for employees' actions such as violations of copyright laws, the distribution of offensive or graphic sexual material, and illegal disclosure of confidential information (312).

ENTRY IN THE LIST OF WORKS CITED

Kesan, Jay P. "Cyber-Working or Cyber-Shirking? A First
    Principles Examination of Electronic Privacy in the
    Workplace." *Florida Law Review* 54.2 (2002): 289-332. Print.

Handling an MLA citation is not always this simple. For a detailed discussion of possible variations, see 32.

29b Enclosing borrowed language in quotation marks

To show that you are using a source's exact phrases or sentences, enclose them in quotation marks unless they have been set off from the text by indenting (see pp. 111–12). To omit the quotation marks is to claim—falsely—that the language is your own. Such an omission is plagiarism even if you have cited the source.

ORIGINAL SOURCE

> Without adequate discipline, the World Wide Web can be a tremendous time sink; no other medium comes close to matching the Internet's depth of materials, interactivity, and sheer distractive potential.
> —Frederick Lane, *The Naked Employee*, p. 142

PLAGIARISM

Frederick Lane points out that if people do not have adequate discipline, the World Wide Web can be a tremendous time sink; no other medium comes close to matching the Internet's depth of materials, interactivity, and sheer distractive potential (142).

BORROWED LANGUAGE IN QUOTATION MARKS

Frederick Lane points out that for those not exercising self-control, "the World Wide Web can be a tremendous time sink; no other medium comes close to matching the Internet's depth of materials, interactivity, and sheer distractive potential" (142).

29c Putting summaries and paraphrases in your own words

A summary condenses information from a source; a paraphrase repeats the information in about the same number of words as in the source. When you summarize or paraphrase, you must name the source and restate the source's meaning in your own language. You commit plagiarism if you half-copy the author's sentences—either by mixing the author's phrases with your own without quotation marks or by plugging your synonyms into the author's sentence structure.

The first paraphrase of the following source is plagiarized—even though the source is cited—because too much of its language is borrowed from the original. The underlined strings of words have been copied word-for-word (without quotation marks). In addition, the writer has closely echoed the sentence structure of the source, merely substituting some synonyms (*restricted* for *limited*, *modern era* for *computer age*, *monitoring* for *surveillance*, and *inexpensive* for *cheap*).

ORIGINAL SOURCE

> In earlier times, surveillance was limited to the information that a supervisor could observe and record firsthand and to primitive counting devices. In the computer age surveillance can be instantaneous, unblinking, cheap, and, maybe most importantly, easy.
>> —Carl Botan and Mihaela Vorvoreanu, "What Do Employees Think about Electronic Surveillance at Work?" p. 126

PLAGIARISM: UNACCEPTABLE BORROWING

Scholars Carl Botan and Mihaela Vorvoreanu argue that in earlier times monitoring of employees was restricted to the information that a supervisor could observe and record firsthand. In the modern era, monitoring can be instantaneous, inexpensive, and, most importantly, easy (126).

To avoid plagiarizing an author's language, don't look at the source while you are summarizing or paraphrasing. Write from memory, and then look at the source to check for accuracy.

ACCEPTABLE PARAPHRASE

Scholars Carl Botan and Mihaela Vorvoreanu claim that the nature of workplace surveillance has changed over time. Before the arrival of computers, managers could collect only small amounts of information about their employees based on what they saw or heard. However, because computers are now standard workplace technology, employers can monitor employees efficiently (126).

ON THE WEB > dianahacker.com/pocket > Research exercises >
MLA > E-ex 29–1 to 29–6

30 Integrating nonfiction sources

Quotations, summaries, paraphrases, and facts will help you make your argument, but they cannot speak for you. You can use several strategies to integrate information from research sources into your paper while maintaining your own voice.

30a Limiting your use of quotations

Using quotations appropriately   Because it is almost impossible to integrate numerous long quotations smoothly into your own text, do not quote excessively. Except for the following legitimate uses of quotations, use your own words to summarize and paraphrase your sources and to explain your own ideas.

WHEN TO USE QUOTATIONS

- When language is especially vivid or expressive
- When exact wording is needed for technical accuracy
- When it is important to let the debaters of an issue explain their positions in their own words
- When the words of an important authority lend weight to an argument
- When the language of a source is the topic of your discussion (as in an analysis or interpretation)

Often you can simply borrow a phrase or weave part of a source's sentence into your own sentence structure.

Kizza and Ssanyu observe that technology in the workplace has been accompanied by "an array of problems that needed quick answers," such as electronic monitoring to prevent security breaches (4).

Using the ellipsis mark   To condense a quoted passage, you can use the ellipsis mark (three periods, with spaces between) to indicate that you have omitted words. What remains must be grammatically complete.

Lane acknowledges the legitimate reasons that many companies have for monitoring their employees' online activities, particularly management's concern about preventing "the theft of information that can be downloaded to a . . . disk, e-mailed to oneself . . . , or even posted to a Web page for the entire world to see" (12).

The writer has omitted from the source the words *floppy or Zip* before *disk* and *or a confederate* after *oneself*.

If you want to omit a full sentence, use a period before the three ellipsis dots.

Charles Lewis, director of the Center for Public Integrity, points out that "by 1987, employers were administering nearly 2,000,000 polygraph tests a year to job applicants and employees. . . . Millions of workers were required to produce urine samples under observation for drug testing . . ." (22).

Ordinarily, do not use an ellipsis mark at the beginning or at the end of a quotation. Your readers will understand that the quoted material is taken from a longer passage. The only exception occurs when words have been dropped at the end of the final quoted sentence. In such cases, put three ellipsis dots before the closing quotation mark and parenthetical reference, as in the previous example.

Using brackets   Brackets allow you to insert your own words into quoted material—to explain a confusing reference or to keep a sentence grammatical in your context.

Legal scholar Jay Kesan notes that "a decade ago, losses [from employees' computer crimes] were already mounting to five billion dollars annually" (311).

To indicate an error such as a misspelling, insert [sic] right after the error.

Setting off long quotations   When you quote more than four typed lines of prose or more than three lines of poetry, set off the quotation by indenting it one inch (or ten spaces) from the left margin.

Long quotations should be introduced by an informative sentence, usually followed by a colon. Quotation marks are unnecessary because the indented format tells readers that the language is taken word-for-word from the source.

Botan and Vorvoreanu examine the role of gender in company practices of electronic surveillance:

> By the middle 1990s, estimates of the proportion of surveilled employees that were women ranged from 75% to 85%. . . . Ironically, this gender imbalance in workplace surveillance may be evening out today because advances in surveillance technology are making surveillance of traditionally male dominated fields, such as long-distance truck driving, cheap, easy, and frequently unobtrusive. (127)

At the end of an indented quotation, the parenthetical citation goes outside the final punctuation mark.

30b Using signal phrases to integrate sources

When you include a paraphrase, summary, or direct quotation in your paper, introduce it with a *signal phrase* naming the author of the source and providing some context for the source material.

Marking boundaries Readers need to move smoothly from your words to the words of a source. Avoid dropping quotations into the text without warning. Provide clear signal phrases, including at least the author's name, to indicate the boundary between your words and the source's words.

DROPPED QUOTATION

Some experts have argued that a range of legitimate concerns justifies employer monitoring of employee Internet usage. "Employees could accidentally (or deliberately) spill confidential corporate information . . . or allow worms to spread throughout a corporate network" (Tynan).

QUOTATION WITH SIGNAL PHRASE

Some experts have argued that a range of legitimate concerns justifies employer monitoring of employee Internet usage. As *PC World* columnist Daniel Tynan points out, companies that don't monitor network traffic can be penalized for their ignorance: "Employees could accidentally (or deliberately) spill confidential corporate information . . . or allow worms to spread throughout a corporate network."

Using signal phrases in MLA papers

To avoid monotony, try to vary both the language and the placement of your signal phrases.

MODEL SIGNAL PHRASES

In the words of researchers Greenfield and Davis, ". . ."

As legal scholar Jay Kesan has noted, ". . ."

The ePolicy Institute, an organization that advises companies about reducing risks from technology, reported that ". . ."

". . . ," writes Daniel Tynan, ". . ."

". . . ," claims attorney Schmitt.

Kizza and Ssanyu offer a persuasive counterargument: ". . ."

VERBS IN SIGNAL PHRASES

Are you providing background, explaining a concept, supporting a claim, lending authority, or refuting a belief? Choose a verb that is appropriate for the way you are using the source.

acknowledges	contends	notes
adds	declares	observes
admits	denies	points out
agrees	describes	reasons
argues	disputes	refutes
asserts	emphasizes	rejects
believes	endorses	reports
claims	grants	responds
comments	illustrates	suggests
compares	implies	thinks
confirms	insists	writes

NOTE: In MLA style, use present-tense verbs (*argues*) to introduce source material unless a date specifies the time of writing.

Establishing authority The first time you mention a source, briefly include the author's title, credentials, or experience to help your readers recognize the source's authority and your own credibility as a responsible researcher who has located reliable sources.

SOURCE WITH NO CREDENTIALS

Jay Kesan points out that the law holds employers liable for employees' actions such as violations of copyright laws, the distribution of offensive or graphic sexual material, and illegal disclosure of confidential information (312).

SOURCE WITH CREDENTIALS

Legal scholar Jay Kesan points out that the law holds employers liable for employees' actions such as violations of copyright laws, the distribution of offensive or graphic sexual material, and illegal disclosure of confidential information (312).

Introducing summaries and paraphrases   Introduce most summaries and paraphrases with a signal phrase that names the author and places the material in the context of your argument. Readers will then understand that everything between the signal phrase and the parenthetical citation summarizes or paraphrases the cited source.

Without the signal phrase (underlined) in the following example, readers might think that only the quotation at the end is being cited, when in fact the whole paragraph is based on the source.

Frederick Lane believes that the personal computer has posed new challenges for employers worried about workplace productivity. Whereas early desktop computers were primitive enough to prevent employees from using them to waste time, the machines have become so sophisticated that they now make non-work-related computer activities easy and inviting. Perhaps most problematic from the employer's point of view, Lane asserts, is giving employees access to the Internet, "roughly the equivalent of installing a gazillion-channel television set for each employee" (15-16).

Sometimes a summary or paraphrase does not require a signal phrase. When the context makes clear where the cited material begins, you may omit the signal phrase and include the author's last name in parentheses.

Putting direct quotations in context   A signal phrase can help you make the connection between a source and your own ideas by showing readers how a quotation supports or challenges a point you make.

Readers should not have to guess why a quotation appears in your paper. If you use another writer's words, you must explain how they contribute to your point. It's a good idea to embed a quotation—especially a long one—between interpretive comments that link the quotation to your paper's argument.

QUOTATION WITH EFFECTIVE CONTEXT

The difference, Lane argues, between these old methods of data gathering and electronic surveillance involves quantity:

> Technology makes it possible for employers to gather enormous amounts of data about employees, often far beyond what is necessary to satisfy safety or productivity concerns. And the trends that drive technology--faster, smaller, cheaper--make it possible for larger and larger numbers of employers to gather ever-greater amounts of personal data. (3-4)

In an age when employers can collect data whenever employees use their computers--when they send e-mail, surf the Web, or even arrive at or depart from their workstations--the challenge for both employers and employees is to determine how much is too much.

30c Integrating statistics and other facts

When you are citing a statistic or another specific fact, a signal phrase is often not necessary. In most cases, readers will understand that the citation refers to the statistic or fact (not the whole paragraph).

According to a 2002 survey, 60% of responding companies reported disciplining employees who had used the Internet in ways the companies deemed inappropriate; 30% had fired their employees for those transgressions (Greenfield and Davis 347).

There is nothing wrong, however, with using a signal phrase.

ON THE WEB > dianahacker.com/pocket > Research exercises > MLA > E-ex 30–1 to 30–4

31 Integrating literary quotations

Smoothly integrating quotations from a literary work into your own text can present a challenge. Do not be surprised to find yourself puzzling over the most graceful way to tuck in a short phrase or the clearest way to introduce a more extended passage from the work.

NOTE: The parenthetical citations at the ends of examples in this section tell readers where the quoted words can be found. They indicate the lines of a poem; the act, scene, and lines of a play; or the page number of a quotation from a short story or novel. (For guidelines on citing literary works, see pp. 126–27.)

31a Introducing literary quotations

When writing about nonfiction articles and books, you will introduce every quotation with a signal phrase naming the author (*John Smith points out . . .*; *Maura Jones presents a compelling argument . . .*). When writing about a single work of fiction, however, you do not need to include the author's name each time you quote from the work. Mention the author's name in the introduction to your paper; in your discussion of the work, refer, as appropriate, to the narrator of a story, the speaker of a poem, or the characters in a play. Make sure, however, that you do not confuse the author of the work with the narrator, speaker, or character.

INAPPROPRIATE

Poet Andrew Marvell describes his fear of death like this: "But at my back I always hear / Time's wingèd chariot hurrying near" (21-22).

APPROPRIATE

Addressing his beloved in an attempt to win her sexual favors, the speaker of the poem argues that death gives them no time to waste: "But at my back I always hear / Time's wingèd chariot hurrying near" (21-22).

APPROPRIATE

The poem "To His Coy Mistress" says as much about fleeting time and death as it does about sexual passion. Its most powerful lines may well be "But at my back I always hear / Time's wingèd chariot hurrying near" (21-22).

If you are quoting the words of a character in a story or a play, you should name the character who is speaking and provide a context for the quoted words. In the following example, the quoted dialogue is from Tennessee Williams's play *The Glass Menagerie*.

Laura is so completely under Amanda's spell that when urged to make a wish on the moon, she asks, "What shall I wish for, Mother?" (1.5.140).

For examples of quoted dialogue from a short story, see page 153.

31b Avoiding shifts in tense

Because it is conventional to write about literature in the present tense (see p. 30) and because literary works often use other tenses, you will need to exercise some care when weaving quotations into your own text. A first-draft attempt may result in an awkward shift, as it did for one student who was writing about Nadine Gordimer's short story "Friday's Footprint."

TENSE SHIFT

When Rita sees Johnny's relaxed attitude, "she blushed, like a wave of illness" (159).

To avoid the distracting shift from present to past tense, the writer decided to paraphrase the reference to Rita's blushing and reduce the length of the quotation.

REVISED

When Rita sees Johnny's relaxed attitude, she is overcome with embarrassment, "like a wave of illness" (159).

The writer could have changed the quotation to present tense, using brackets to indicate the change: *When Rita sees Johnny's relaxed attitude, "she blushe[s], like a wave of illness"* (159). (See also p. 111.)

31c Formatting literary quotations

MLA guidelines for formatting quotations and handling citations in the text of your paper differ somewhat for short stories or novels, poems, and plays.

Short stories or novels If a quotation from a short story or a novel takes up four or fewer typed lines in your paper, put it in quotation marks and run it into the text of your essay. Include a page number in parentheses after the quotation.

The narrator of Eudora Welty's "Why I Live at the P.O.," known to us only as "Sister," makes many catty remarks about her enemies. For example, she calls Mr. Whitaker "this photographer with the pop-eyes" (46).

If a quotation from a short story or a novel is five typed lines or longer in your paper, set it off from the text by indenting one inch (or ten spaces) from the left margin; do not use quotation marks. (See also pp. 111–12.) Put the page number in parentheses after the final mark of punctuation.

Sister's tale begins with "I," and she makes every event revolve around herself, even her sister's marriage:

> I was getting along fine with Mama, Papa-Daddy, and
> Uncle Rondo until my sister Stella-Rondo just
> separated from her husband and came back home
> again. Mr. Whitaker! Of course I went with Mr.
> Whitaker first, when he first appeared here in China
> Grove, taking "Pose Yourself" photos, and Stella-Rondo
> broke us up. (46)

Poems Enclose quotations of three or fewer lines of poetry in quotation marks within your text, and indicate line breaks with a slash with a space on each side. Include line numbers in parentheses at the end of the quotation. For the first reference, use the word "lines." Thereafter, use just numbers.

The opening of Frost's "Fire and Ice" strikes a conversational tone: "Some say the world will end in fire, / Some say in ice" (lines 1-2).

When you quote four or more lines of poetry, set the quotation off from the text by indenting one inch (or ten spaces) and omit the quotation marks. Put the line numbers in parentheses after the final mark of punctuation.

The opening stanza of Louise Bogan's "Women" startles readers by presenting a negative stereotype of women:

> Women have no wilderness in them,
>
> They are provident instead,
>
> Content in the tight hot cell of their hearts
>
> To eat dusty bread. (1-4)

Plays   If a quotation from a play takes up four or fewer typed lines in your paper and is spoken by only one character, put quotation marks around it and run it into the text of your essay. Whenever possible, include the act number, scene number, and line numbers in parentheses at the end of the quotation. Separate the numbers with periods, and use arabic numerals unless your instructor prefers roman numerals.

Two attendants silently watch as the sleepwalking Lady Macbeth subconsciously struggles with her guilt: "Here's the smell of blood still. All the perfumes of Arabia will not sweeten this little hand" (5.1.50-51).

32 MLA documentation style

To document sources, MLA recommends in-text citations that refer readers to a list of works cited.

DIRECTORY TO MLA IN-TEXT CITATION MODELS

BASIC RULES FOR PRINT AND ELECTRONIC SOURCES

VARIATIONS ON THE BASIC RULES

32a MLA in-text citations

MLA in-text citations are made with a combination of signal phrases and parenthetical references. A signal phrase introduces information taken from a source (a quotation, summary, paraphrase, or fact); usually the signal phrase includes the author's name. The parenthetical reference, which comes after the cited material, normally includes at least a page number. In the following models, the elements of the in-text citation are highlighted.

IN-TEXT CITATION

Kwon points out that the Fourth Amendment does not give employees any protections from employers' "unreasonable searches and seizures" (6).

Readers can look up the author's last name in the alphabetized list of works cited, where they will learn the work's title and other publication information. If readers decide to consult the source, the page number will direct them to the passage that has been cited.

Basic rules for print and electronic sources   The MLA system of in-text citations, which depends heavily on authors' names and page numbers, was created in the early 1980s with print sources in mind. Because some of today's electronic sources have unclear authorship and lack page numbers, they present a special challenge. Nevertheless, the basic rules are the same for print and electronic sources.

The models in this section (items 1–5) show how the MLA system usually works and explain what to do if your source has no author or page numbers.

■ **1. Author named in a signal phrase**   Ordinarily, introduce the material being cited with a signal phrase that includes the author's name. In addition to preparing readers for the source, the signal phrase allows you to keep the parenthetical citation brief.

Frederick Lane reports that employers can monitor their employees with "a hidden video camera pointed at an employee's monitor" and can even position a camera "so that a number of monitors [can] be viewed at the same time" (147).

The signal phrase — *Frederick Lane reports that* — names the author; the parenthetical citation gives the page number of the book in which the quoted words may be found.

Notice that the period follows the parenthetical citation. When a quotation ends with a question mark or an exclamation point, leave the end punctuation inside the quotation mark and add a period after the parentheses: "... ?" (8).

■ **2. Author named in parentheses**   If a signal phrase does not name the author, put the author's last name in parentheses along with the page number.

Companies can monitor employees' keystrokes without legal penalty, but they may have to combat low morale as a result (Lane 129).

Use no punctuation between the name and the page number.

■ **3. Author unknown**   Either use the complete title in a signal phrase or use a short form of the title in parentheses. Titles of books are italicized; titles of articles are put in quotation marks.

A popular keystroke logging program operates invisibly on workers' computers and provides supervisors with details of the workers' online activities ("Automatically").

NOTE: See the tip on page 130 about determining the author of a Web site; if the author is an organization or a government agency, see item 9 on page 123.

■ **4. Page number unknown** You may omit the page number if a work lacks page numbers, as is the case with many Web sources. Although printouts from Web sites usually show page numbers, printers don't always provide the same page breaks; for this reason, MLA recommends treating such sources as unpaginated.

As a 2005 study by *Salary.com* and *America Online* indicates, the Internet ranked as the top choice among employees for ways of wasting time on the job; it beat talking with co-workers--the second most popular method--by a margin of nearly two to one (Frauenheim).

When the pages of a Web source are stable (as in PDF files), however, supply a page number in your in-text citation.

NOTE: If a Web source numbers its paragraphs or screens, give the abbreviation "par." or "pars." or the word "screen" or "screens" in the parentheses: (Smith, par. 4).

■ **5. One-page source** For a one-page source, MLA allows (but does not require) you to omit the page number. Many instructors will want you to supply the page number because without it readers may not know where your citation ends or may not realize that you have provided a citation at all.

Anush Yegyazarian reports that in 2000 the National Labor Relations Board's Office of the General Counsel helped win restitution for two workers who had been dismissed because their employers were displeased by the employees' e-mails about work-related issues (62). This case points to the ongoing struggle to define what constitutes protected speech in the workplace.

Variations on the basic rules This section describes the MLA guidelines for handling a variety of situations not covered by the basic rules just given. These rules on in-text citations are the same for both print sources and electronic sources.

■ **6. Two or more titles by the same author** If your list of works cited includes two or more titles by the same author, mention the title of the work in the signal phrase or include a short version of the title in the parentheses.

The American Management Association and ePolicy Institute have tracked employers' practices in monitoring employees' e-mail use. The groups' 2003 survey found that one-third of companies had a policy of keeping and reviewing employees' e-mail messages ("2003 E-mail" 2); in 2005, more than 55% of companies engaged in e-mail monitoring ("2005 Electronic" 1).

Titles of articles and other short works are placed in quotation marks, as in the example just given. Titles of books are italicized.

When both the author's name and a short title must be given in parentheses, separate them with a comma.

A 2004 survey found that 20% of employers responding had employees' e-mail "subpoenaed in the course of a lawsuit or regulatory investigation," up 7% from the previous year (Amer. Management Assn. and ePolicy Inst., "2004 Workplace" 1).

■ **7. Two or three authors**   Name the authors in a signal phrase, as in the following example, or include their last names in the parenthetical reference: (Kizza and Ssanyu 2).

Kizza and Ssanyu note that "employee monitoring is a dependable, capable, and very affordable process of electronically or otherwise recording all employee activities at work . . ." (2).

When three authors are named in the parentheses, separate the names with commas: (Alton, Davies, and Rice 56).

■ **8. Four or more authors**   Name all of the authors or include only the first author's name followed by "et al." (Latin for "and others"). Make sure that your citation matches the entry in the list of works cited (see item 2 on pp. 129–30).

The study was extended for two years, and only after results were reviewed by an independent panel did the researchers publish their findings (Blaine et al. 35).

■ **9. Corporate author**   When the author is a corporation, an organization, or a government agency, name the corporate author either in the signal phrase or in the parentheses.

According to a 2001 survey of human resources managers by the American Management Association, more than three-quarters of the respondents reported disciplining employees for "misuse or personal use of office telecommunications equipment" (2).

In the list of works cited, the American Management Association is treated as the author and alphabetized under *A*.

When a government agency is treated as the author, it will be alphabetized in the list of works cited under the name of the government, such as "United States" (see item 3 on p. 130). For this reason, you must name the government in your in-text citation.

The United States Department of Transportation provides nationwide statistics on traffic fatalities.

■ **10. Authors with the same last name** If your list of works cited includes works by two or more authors with the same last name, include the author's first name in the signal phrase or first initial in the parentheses.

Estimates of the frequency with which employers monitor employees' use of the Internet vary widely (A. Jones 15).

■ **11. Indirect source (source quoted in another source)** When a writer's or a speaker's quoted words appear in a source written by someone else, begin the parenthetical citation with the abbreviation "qtd. in."

Researchers Botan and McCreadie point out that "workers are objects of information collection without participating in the process of exchanging the information . . ." (qtd. in Kizza and Ssanyu 14).

■ **12. Encyclopedia or dictionary** Unless an encyclopedia or a dictionary has an author, it will be alphabetized in the list of works cited under the word or entry that you consulted—not under the title of the reference work itself (see item 13 on p. 133). Either in your text or in the parenthetical citation, mention the word or the entry. No page number is required, since readers can easily look up the word or entry.

The word *crocodile* has a surprisingly complex etymology ("Crocodile").

13. Multivolume work If your paper cites more than one volume of a multivolume work, indicate in the parentheses the volume you are referring to, followed by a colon and the page number.

In his studies of gifted children, Terman describes a pattern of accelerated language acquisition (2: 279).

14. Two or more works To cite more than one source in the parentheses, give the citations in alphabetical order and separate them with a semicolon.

The effects of sleep deprivation have been well documented (Cahill 42; Leduc 114; Vasquez 73).

15. An entire work Use the author's name in a signal phrase or a parenthetical citation. There is no need to use a page number.

Lane explores the evolution of surveillance in the workplace.

16. Work in an anthology Put the name of the author of the work (not the editor of the anthology) in the signal phrase or the parentheses.

In "A Jury of Her Peers," Mrs. Hale describes both a style of quilting and a murder weapon when she utters the last words of the story: "We call it--knot it, Mr. Henderson" (Glaspell 210).

In the list of works cited, the work is alphabetized under the author of the work, not under the name of the editor of the anthology. (See item 10 on p. 131.)

17. Historical and legal documents For well-known historical documents, such as the United States Constitution, provide a parenthetical citation using common abbreviations: (US Const., art. 1, sec. 2). Cite other historical documents as you would any other work, by the first element in the works cited entry. (See item 55 on p. 145.)

For legislative acts (laws) and court cases, name the act or case either in a signal phrase or in parentheses. In the text of a paper, names of cases are italicized, but names of acts are not.

The Jones Act of 1917 granted US citizenship to Puerto Ricans.

In 1857, Chief Justice Roger B. Taney declared in the case of *Dred Scott v. Sandford* that blacks, whether enslaved or free, could not be citizens of the United States.

Literary works and sacred texts   Literary works and sacred texts are usually available in a variety of editions. Your list of works cited will specify which edition you are using. When possible, give enough information—such as book parts, play divisions, or line numbers—so that readers can locate the cited passage in any edition of the work.

■ **18. Literary works without parts or line numbers**   When a work has no parts or line numbers, cite the page number.

At the end of Kate Chopin's "The Story of an Hour," Mrs. Mallard drops dead upon learning that her husband is alive. In the final irony of the story, doctors report that she has died of a "joy that kills" (25).

■ **19. Verse plays and poems**   If possible, give act, scene, and line numbers for verse plays.

In Shakespeare's *King Lear*, Gloucester, blinded for suspected treason, learns a profound lesson from his tragic experience: "A man may see how this world goes / with no eyes" (4.2.148-49).

For a poem, cite the part, stanza, and line numbers, if it has them, separated by periods.

The Green Knight claims to approach King Arthur's court "because the praise of you, prince, is puffed so high, / And your manor and your men are considered so magnificent" (1.12.258-59).

For poems that are not divided into numbered parts or stanzas, use line numbers. For a first reference, use the word "lines": (lines 5-8). Thereafter use just the numbers: (12-13).

■ **20. Novels with numbered divisions**   Give the page number followed by a semicolon, and then indicate the book, part, or chapter in which the passage may be found. Use abbreviations such as "pt." and "ch."

One of Kingsolver's narrators, teenager Rachel, pushes her vocabulary beyond its limits. For example, Rachel complains that being forced to live in the Congo with her missionary family is "a sheer tapestry of justice" because her chances of finding a boyfriend are "dull and void" (117; bk. 2, ch. 10).

■ **21. Sacred texts**   When citing a sacred text such as the Bible or the Qur'an, name the edition in your works cited entry (see item 14, p. 133). In your parenthetical citation, give the book, chapter, and verse (or their equivalent), separated by periods. Common abbreviations for books of the Bible are acceptable.

Consider the words of Solomon: "If your enemy is hungry, give him bread to eat; and if he is thirsty, give him water to drink" (*Oxford Annotated Bible*, Prov. 25.21).

ON THE WEB > dianahacker.com/pocket > Research exercises > MLA > E-ex 32–1 and 32–2

32b MLA list of works cited

An alphabetized list of works cited, which appears at the end of your research paper, gives publication information for each of the sources you have cited in the paper. (For information about preparing this list, see pp. 149–50; for sample lists of works cited, see pp. 152 and 154.)

NOTE: Unless your instructor asks for them, omit sources not actually cited in the paper, even if you read them.

DIRECTORY TO MLA WORKS CITED MODELS

→

NOTE: MLA requires the medium of publication in all works cited entries, usually at the end of the entry (neither italicized nor in quotation marks). Typical designations for the medium are "Print," "Web," "Television," "Film," and "Lecture." (See specific items throughout this section.)

General guidelines for listing authors Alphabetize entries in the list of works cited by authors' last names (if a work has no author, alphabetize it by its title).

NAME CITED IN TEXT

According to Nancy Flynn, . . .

BEGINNING OF WORKS CITED ENTRY

Flynn, Nancy.

Items 1–5 show how to begin an entry for a work with a single author, multiple authors, a corporate author, an unknown author, and multiple works by the same author. What comes after this first element of your citation will depend on the kind of source you are citing (see items 6–63).

NOTE: For a book, an entry in the works cited list will sometimes begin with an editor (see item 9 on p. 131).

■ **1. Single author** Begin the entry with the author's last name, a comma, the author's first name, and a period.

Tannen, Deborah.

■ **2. Multiple authors** For works with two or more authors, reverse the name of only the first author.

Wilmut, Ian, Keith Campbell, and Colin Tudge.

When a work has four or more authors, either name all of the authors or name the first author followed by "et al." (Latin for "and others").

Sloan, Frank A., Emily M. Stout, Kathryn Whetten-Goldstein, and
     Lan Liang.

Sloan, Frank A., et al.

■ **3. Corporate author** When the author of a print document or a Web site is a corporation, a government agency, or some other organization, begin with the name of the group.

First Union.

United States. Bureau of the Census.

American Automobile Association.

NOTE: Make sure that your in-text citation also treats the organization as the author (see item 9 on p. 123).

■ **4. Unknown author** When the author is unknown, begin with the work's title. Titles of articles and other short works, such as brief documents from Web sites, are put in quotation marks. Titles of books and other long works, such as entire Web sites, are italicized.

Article or other short work
"Media Giants."

Book, entire Web site, or other long work
Atlas of the World.

TIP: Before concluding that a Web source has no author, check carefully. The name of the author may appear at the end of the source, in tiny print, or on another page of the site, such as the home page.

■ **5. Two or more works by the same author** First alphabetize the works by title (ignoring the article *A*, *An*, or *The* at the beginning of a title). Use the author's name for the first entry only; for subsequent entries, use three hyphens followed by a period. The three hyphens must stand for exactly the same name or names as in the first entry.

Knopp, Lisa. *Field of Vision*. Iowa City: U of Iowa P, 1996. Print.

---. *The Nature of Home: A Lexicon and Essays*. Lincoln: U of
    Nebraska P, 2002. Print.

Books

■ **6. Basic format for a book** For most books, arrange the information into four units, each followed by a period and one space: the author's name; the title and subtitle, italicized; the place of publication, the publisher, and the date; and the medium. (For an annotated example, see p. 132.)

Tan, Amy. *Saving Fish from Drowning*. New York: Putnam, 2005.
    Print.

■ **7. Author with an editor**

Plath, Sylvia. *The Unabridged Journals of Sylvia Plath*. Ed. Karen
    V. Kukil. New York: Anchor-Doubleday, 2000. Print.

■ **8. Author with a translator**

Allende, Isabel. *Zorro*. Trans. Margaret Sayers Peden. London:
    Fourth Estate, 2005. Print.

■ **9. Editor**

Craig, Patricia, ed. *The Oxford Book of Travel Stories*. Oxford:
    Oxford UP, 1996. Print.

■ **10. Work in an anthology** Begin with (1) the name of the author of the selection. Then give (2) the title of the selection; (3) the title of the anthology; (4) the name of the editor of the anthology (preceded by "Ed." for "Edited by"); (5) publication information; (6) the pages on which the selection appears; and (7) the medium.

Desai, Anita. "Scholar and Gypsy." *The Oxford Book of Travel*
    Stories. Ed. Patricia Craig. Oxford: Oxford UP, 1996. 251-73.
    Print.

Citation at a glance
Book (MLA)

To cite a print book in MLA style, include the following elements:

1 Author
2 Title and subtitle
3 City of publication
4 Publisher
5 Date of publication
6 Medium

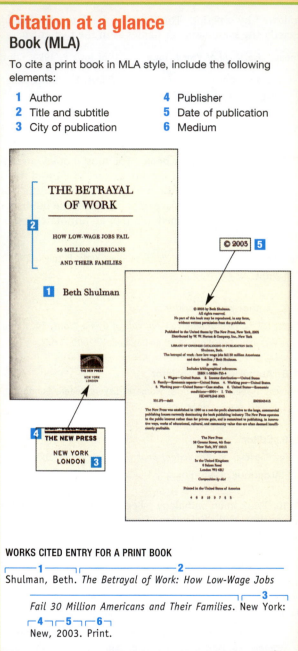

WORKS CITED ENTRY FOR A PRINT BOOK

Shulman, Beth. *The Betrayal of Work: How Low-Wage Jobs Fail 30 Million Americans and Their Families*. New York: New, 2003. Print.

For more on citing books in MLA style, see pages 131–34.

■ 11. Edition other than the first

Auletta, Ken. *The Underclass*. 2nd ed. Woodstock, NY: Overlook, 2000. Print.

■ 12. Multivolume work

Stark, Freya. *Letters*. Ed. Lucy Moorehead. Vol. 5. Salisbury: Compton, 1978. Print. 8 vols.

■ 13. Encyclopedia or dictionary entry

Posner, Rebecca. "Romance Languages." *The New Encyclopaedia Britannica: Macropaedia*. 15th ed. 1987. Print.

"Sonata." *The American Heritage Dictionary of the English Language*. 4th ed. 2000. Print.

■ 14. Sacred text

The Oxford Annotated Bible with the Apocrypha. Ed. Herbert G. May and Bruce M. Metzger. New York: Oxford UP, 1965. Print. Rev. Standard Vers.

The Qur'an: Translation. Trans. Abdullah Yusuf Ali. Elmhurst: Tahrike, 2000. Print.

■ 15. Foreword, introduction, preface, or afterword

Morris, Jan. Introduction. *Letters from the Field, 1925-1975*. By Margaret Mead. New York: Perennial-Harper, 2001. xix-xxiii. Print.

■ 16. Book with a title in its title

Hawkins, Hunt, and Brian W. Shaffer, eds. *Approaches to Teaching Conrad's* Heart of Darkness *and "The Secret Sharer."* New York: MLA, 2002. Print.

■ 17. Book in a series

Malena, Anne. *The Dynamics of Identity in Francophone Caribbean Narrative*. New York: Lang, 1998. Print. Francophone Cultures and Lits. Ser. 24.

■ 18. Republished book

Hughes, Langston. *Black Misery*. 1969. Afterword Robert O'Meally. New York: Oxford UP, 2000. Print.

■ **19. Publisher's imprint**

Truan, Barry. *Acoustic Communication*. Westport: Ablex-
Greenwood, 2000. Print.

Articles in periodicals   This section shows how to prepare
works cited entries for articles in magazines, scholarly
journals, and newspapers. In addition to consulting the
models in this section, you may need to turn to other
models as well:

More than one author: see item 2

Corporate author: see item 3

Unknown author: see item 4

Article from a database: see item 31

Online article: see items 32 and 33

Put titles of articles in quotation marks; italicize titles
of magazines, journals, and newspapers. For dates requiring a month, abbreviate all months except May, June, and
July. For articles appearing on consecutive pages, provide
the range of pages (see items 21 and 22). When an article
does not appear on consecutive pages, give the number of
the first page and a plus sign: 32+. Add the medium at the
end of the entry. (For an annotated example of an article
in a periodical, see p. 135.)

■ **20. Article in a magazine**   If the magazine is issued
monthly, give just the month and year.

Fay, J. Michael. "Land of the Surfing Hippos." *National
Geographic* Aug. 2004: 100+. Print.

If the magazine is issued weekly, give the exact date.

Lord, Lewis. "There's Something about Mary Todd." *US News and
World Report* 19 Feb. 2001: 53. Print.

■ **21. Article in a journal paginated by volume**   Give both
volume and issue numbers for all journals, even those with
pagination continuing through all issues of the volume.
Separate the volume and issue numbers with a period.

Ryan, Katy. "Revolutionary Suicide in Toni Morrison's Fiction."
African American Review 34.3 (2000): 389-412. Print.

Citation at a glance
Article in a periodical (MLA)

To cite an article in a print periodical in MLA style, include the following elements:

1 Author
2 Title and subtitle of article
3 Name of periodical
4 Volume and issue numbers (for scholarly journal)
5 Date or year of publication
6 Page numbers
7 Medium

WORKS CITED ENTRY FOR AN ARTICLE IN A PRINT PERIODICAL

<u>1</u> <u>2</u> <u>3</u>
McGrath, Anne. "A Loss of Foreign Talent." *US News and*

<u>5</u> <u>6</u> <u>7</u>
World Report 22 Nov. 2004: 76. Print.

For more on citing periodical articles in MLA style, see pages 134–36.

■ **22. Article in a journal paginated by issue** Give both volume and issue numbers, separated with a period.

Wood, Michael. "Broken Dates: Fiction and the Century." *Kenyon Review* 22.3 (2000): 50-64. Print.

■ **23. Article in a daily newspaper**

Brummitt, Chris. "Indonesia's Food Needs Expected to Soar." *Boston Globe* 1 Feb. 2005: A7. Print.

Wilford, John Noble. "In a Golden Age of Discovery, Faraway Worlds Beckon." *New York Times* 9 Feb. 1997, late ed., sec. 1: 1+. Print.

■ **24. Editorial in a newspaper**

"All Wet." Editorial. *Boston Globe* 12 Feb. 2001: A14. Print.

■ **25. Letter to the editor**

Shrewsbury, Toni. Letter. *Atlanta Journal-Constitution* 17 Feb. 2001: A13. Print.

■ **26. Book or film review**

Gleick, Elizabeth. "The Burdens of Genius." Rev. of *The Last Samurai,* by Helen DeWitt. *Time* 4 Dec. 2000: 171. Print.

Denby, David. "On the Battlefield." Rev. of *The Hurricane,* dir. Norman Jewison. *New Yorker* 10 Jan. 2000: 90-92. Print.

Online sources This section shows how to prepare works cited entries for a variety of online sources, including Web sites, online books and articles, blogs, and e-mail.

MLA guidelines assume that readers can locate most online sources by entering the author, title, or other identifying information in a search engine or a database. Consequently, MLA does not require a Web address (URL) in citations for online sources. Some instructors may require a URL; for an example, see the note at the end of item 27.

MLA style calls for a sponsor or publisher for most online sources. If a source has no sponsor or publisher, use the abbreviation "N.p." (for "No publisher") in the sponsor position. If there is no date of publication or update, use "n.d." (for "no date") after the sponsor. For an article in an online scholarly journal or an article from a database, give page numbers if they are available; if they are not, use the abbreviation "n. pag." (See item 32.)

How to cite a source without a model

Sometimes you may consult sources for which there is no direct citation model. When you encounter such a source, gather the same kinds of information as you do for other sources—author/creator, title, sponsor, date of creation or update, medium of publication or delivery. Then consult the models in this section to see which ones are similar to your source. You may need to combine elements from different models.

Your goal is always to provide readers with enough information to locate the source and to assess its reliability. The following points may help.

- Is the source originally video, audio, or both? (See items 44–49.)

- What kinds of sources are similar to this source? For instance, an audio file without a model may be similar to a podcast (item 49), a sound recording (item 44), or a radio or television program (item 47).

- Is the source an electronic or online version of a print source? Start with the model for the relevant print source. Then include information specific to the electronic or online version, such as the date of creation or update and the medium.

When citing any source for which you have to combine information from various models, check your work with your instructor.

■ **27. Entire Web site** Begin with the name of the author, editor, or the corporate author (if known) and the title of the site, italicized. Then give the sponsor and the date of publication or last update. End with the medium and your date of access. The following models show a Web site with an author, with an editor, with a corporate (group) author, and with no author.

Peterson, Susan Lynn. *The Life of Martin Luther*.
    Susan Lynn Peterson, 2005. Web. 24 Jan. 2009.

Halsall, Paul, ed. *Internet Modern History Sourcebook*. Fordham
    U, 22 Sept. 2001. Web. 19 Jan. 2009.

United States. Environmental Protection Agency. *Drinking Water
    Standards*. EPA, 28 Nov. 2006. Web. 24 Jan. 2007.

Margaret Sanger Papers Project. History Dept., New York U,
    18 Oct. 2000. Web. 6 Jan. 2009.

Citation at a glance
Short work from a Web site (MLA)

To cite a short work from a Web site in MLA style, include the following elements:

1 Author
2 Title of short work
3 Title of Web site
4 Sponsor of Web site
5 Update date ("n.d." if there is no date)
6 Medium
7 Date of access

BROWSER PRINTOUT OF SHORT WORK

conferences   http://web.mit.edu/comm-forum/papers/bearings.html

home
calendar
forums
conferences   **3**
papers   mit **communications**   mailing list
search   **forum**   about this site
                                                    4 **mit**

2 **Bearings**
    by Henry Jenkins **1**

How new is news?

Representative democracy emerged in the context of a relatively slow flow of information between the capital and the periphery. Elected representatives were delegated to make decisions for the public, in part because they had quicker access to reliable information. The earliest American newspapers were content to reproduce "intelligence" gathered from ships as they passed through their harbours, information about events that might have occurred months earlier at some other port of call. It is remarkable, given the geographic distance separating the thirteen original colonies, that they were able to think of themselves as having collective interests, as forming, in Benedict Anderson's terms, an "imaginary community" that could stand firm against distant European powers. The complex balance between federal and state authority established in the U.S. Constitution might be understood as a negotiation between the ideal of local control and the recognition of the slow flow of information across those huge geographic distances. The introduction of the telegraph dramatically accelerated the flow of news, and it has been followed throughout the twentieth century by a succession of faster technologies that allow minute by minute, real time reporting of distance events.

In turn, these technologies have established public expectations about timely delivery of the news. The result of this urgency to give us the news as quickly as possible has been a complex layering of the television newscast – sometimes splitting the screen to report on simultaneous events worldwide (such as the simultaneous impeachment vote and American attacks on Baghdad), sometimes introducing multiple windows and layers of textual information (as with the "crawls"

| http://web.mit.edu/comm-forum/papers.html

home
calendar
forums
conferences   mit **communications**   mailing list
papers   **forum**   about this site
search   **mit**

                                                                6/16/05 4:56 PM

papers

This page contains links to papers and articles generated by the MIT Communications Forum, Comparative Media Studies conferences and the Media in Transition project.

Andrew Jakubowicz, *Discourses of the Social: Making Multicultural Australia - A Multimedia Documentary*
[6,443 words, posted december 19, 1999]

Henry Jenkins, *Bearings*
[287 words, posted February 19, 2002] **5**

                                                                6/16/05 4:56 PM

WEB SITE LINKS PAGE FOR SHORT WORK

138

WORKS CITED ENTRY FOR A SHORT WORK FROM A WEB SITE

Jenkins, Henry. "Bearings." *MIT Communications Forum.*

MIT, 19 Feb. 2002. Web. 16 June 2005.

For more on citing sources from Web sites in MLA style, see pages 136–43.

If a site has no title, substitute a description, such as "Home page," for the title.

Yoon, Mina. Home page. Oak Ridge Natl. Laboratory, 28 Dec.
    2006. Web. 12 Jan. 2009.

NOTE: If your instructor requires a URL for Web sources, include the URL, enclosed in angle brackets, at the end of the entry. If you must divide a URL at the end of a line in a works cited entry, break it after a slash. Do not insert a hyphen.

Peterson, Susan Lynn. *The Life of Martin Luther.* Susan
    Lynn Peterson, 2005. Web. 24 Jan. 2009.
    <http://www.susanlynnpeterson.com/index_files/
    luther.htm>.

■ **28. Short work from a Web site** Short works include articles, poems, and other documents that are not book length or that appear as internal pages on a Web site. Include the following elements: author's name; title of the short work, in quotation marks; title of the site, italicized; sponsor of the site; date of publication or last update; medium; and your date of access.

Shiva, Vandana. "Bioethics: A Third World Issue." *NativeWeb.*
    NativeWeb, n.d. Web. 22 Jan. 2009.

"Living Old." *Frontline.* PBS Online, 21 Nov. 2006. Web.
    19 Jan. 2009.

■ **29. Online book**   Cite a book or a book-length work, such as a play or a long poem, as you would a short work from a Web site (see item 28), but italicize the title of the work.

Milton, John. *Paradise Lost: Book I. Poetryfoundation.org*. Poetry
    Foundation, 2008. Web. 14 Dec. 2008.

Give the print publication information for the work, if available (see items 6–19), followed by the title of the Web site, the medium, and your date of access.

Jacobs, Harriet A. *Incidents in the Life of a Slave Girl: Written
    by Herself*. Ed. L. Maria Child. Boston, 1861. *Documenting
    the American South*. Web. 3 Feb. 2009.

■ **30. Part of an online book**
Adams, Henry. "Diplomacy." *The Education of Henry Adams*. By
    Adams. Boston: Houghton, 1918. N. pag. *Bartleby.com:
    Great Books Online*. Web. 17 Feb. 2009.

■ **31. Work from a database**   For sources retrieved from a library's subscription database, first list the publication information for the source (see items 20–26). Then give the name of the database, italicized; the medium; and your date of access. (For an annotated example, see p. 141.)

The following models are for articles retrieved from library databases: a scholarly article, an article in a magazine, and an article in a weekly newspaper.

Johnson, Kirk. "The Mountain Lions of Michigan." *Endangered
    Species Update* 19.2 (2002): 27-31. *Expanded Academic
    Index*. Web. 26 Nov. 2008.

Barrera, Rebeca María. "A Case for Bilingual Education."
    Scholastic Parent and Child Nov.-Dec. 2004: 72-73.
    Academic Search Premier. Web. 1 Feb. 2009.

Williams, Jeffrey J. "Why Today's Publishing World Is Reprising
    the Past." *Chronicle of Higher Education* 13 June 2008: 8+.
    LexisNexis Academic. Web. 29 Sept. 2008.

When you access a work through a personal subscription service, such as *America Online,* give the same information as for a library subscription database.

Citation at a glance
Article from a database (MLA)

To cite an article from a database in MLA style, include the following elements:

1 Author
2 Title of article
3 Name of periodical, volume and issue numbers
4 Date of publication
5 Inclusive pages
6 Name of database
7 Medium
8 Date of access

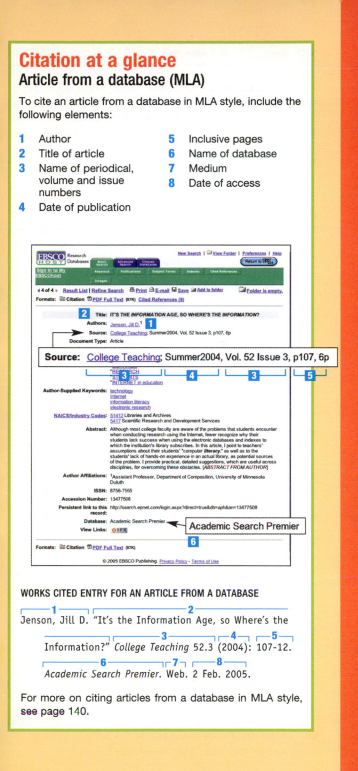

WORKS CITED ENTRY FOR AN ARTICLE FROM A DATABASE

```
      1                    2
Jenson, Jill D. "It's the Information Age, so Where's the

                    3            4       5
Information?" College Teaching 52.3 (2004): 107-12.

        6              7      8
Academic Search Premier. Web. 2 Feb. 2005.
```

For more on citing articles from a database in MLA style, see page 140.

■ **32. Article in an online journal** Give publication information as for a print journal (see items 21 and 22), using "n. pag." if the source does not have page numbers. Then give the medium and your date of access.

Belau, Linda. "Trauma and the Material Signifier." *Postmodern Culture* 11.2 (2001): n. pag. Web. 20 Feb. 2009.

■ **33. Article in an online magazine or newspaper** Give the author; the title of the article, in quotation marks; the title of the magazine or newspaper, italicized; the sponsor or publisher of the site (use "N.p." if there is none); the date of publication; the medium; and your date of access.

Paulson, Steve. "Buddha on the Brain." *Salon.com*. Salon Media Group, 27 Nov. 2006. Web. 18 Jan. 2009.

Rubin, Joel. "Report Faults Charter School." *Los Angeles Times*. Los Angeles Times, 22 Jan. 2005. Web. 24 Jan. 2009.

■ **34. Entire Weblog (blog)** Cite a blog as you would an entire Web site (see item 27). Give the author's name; the title of the blog, italicized; the sponsor or publisher of the blog (use "N.p." if there is none); the date of the most recent update; the medium; and your date of access.

Mayer, Caroline. *The Checkout*. Washington Post, 27 Apr. 2006. Web. 19 Jan. 2007.

■ **35. Entry in a Weblog (blog)** Begin with the author and the title of the entry or comment (a response to an entry). If the entry or comment has no title, use the label "Weblog entry" or "Weblog comment." Follow with the title of the blog, italicized, and the remaining information as for an entire blog in item 34.

Mayer, Caroline. "Some Surprising Findings about Identity Theft." *The Checkout*. Washington Post, 28 Feb. 2006. Web. 19 Jan. 2007.

Burdick, Dennis. Weblog comment. *The Checkout*. Washington Post, 28 Feb. 2006. Web. 19 Jan. 2007.

■ **36. CD-ROM**

"Pimpernel." *The American Heritage Dictionary of the English Language*. 4th ed. Boston: Houghton, 2000. CD-ROM.

■ **37. E-mail**

Lowe, Walter. "Review Questions." Message to the author. 15 Mar. 2007. E-mail.

■ **38. Posting to an online discussion list**

Fainton, Peter. "Re: Backlash against New Labour." *Media Lens Message Board*. Media Lens, 7 May 2008. Web. 2 June 2008.

Multimedia sources (including online versions)   Multimedia sources include visuals, audio works, audiovisuals, podcasts, and live events. Give the medium, usually at the end of the citation and not italicized or in quotation marks (for instance, "Print," "Web," "Radio," "Television," "CD," "Audiocassette," "Film," "Videocassette," "DVD," "Performance," "Lecture," "PDF file," "MP3 file," "*Microsoft Word* file," "JPEG file").

■ **39. Work of art**   Cite the artist's name; the title of the artwork, italicized; the date of composition; the medium of composition (for instance, "Photograph," "Charcoal on paper"); and the institution and city in which the artwork is located. For artworks found online, omit the medium of composition and include the title of the Web site, the medium ("Web"), and your date of access.

Constable, John. *Dedham Vale*. 1802. Oil on canvas. Victoria and Albert Museum, London.

van Gogh, Vincent. *The Starry Night*. 1889. Museum of Mod. Art, New York. *MoMA: The Museum of Modern Art*. Web. 14 Jan. 2009.

■ **40. Cartoon**

Sutton, Ward. "Why Wait 'til November?" Cartoon. *Village Voice* 7-13 July 2004: 6. Print.

■ **41. Advertisement**

Truth by Calvin Klein. Advertisement. *Vogue* Dec. 2000: 95-98. Print.

■ **42. Map or chart**

Serbia. Map. *Syrena Maps*. Syrena, 2 Feb. 2001. Web. 17 Mar. 2009.

Joseph, Lori, and Bob Laird. "Driving While Phoning Is Dangerous." Chart. *USA Today* 16 Feb. 2001: 1A. Print.

■ **43. Musical score**

Handel, G. F. *Messiah: An Oratorio*. N.d. *CCARH Publications: Scores and Parts*. Center for Computer Assisted Research in the Humanities, 2003. Web. 5 Jan. 2009.

■ **44. Sound recording**

Bizet, Georges. *Carmen*. Perf. Jennifer Laramore, Thomas Moser, Angela Gheorghiu, and Samuel Ramey. Bavarian State Orch. and Chorus. Cond. Giuseppe Sinopoli. Warner, 1996. CD.

Blige, Mary J. "Be without You." *The Breakthrough*. Geffen, 2005. CD.

■ **45. Film or video**

Finding Neverland. Dir. Marc Forster. Perf. Johnny Depp, Kate Winslet, Julie Christie, Radha Mitchell, and Dustin Hoffman. Miramax, 2004. DVD.

The Hours. Dir. Stephen Daldry. Perf. Meryl Streep, Julianne Moore, and Nicole Kidman. Paramount, 2002. Film.

■ **46. Special feature on a DVD**

"Sweeney's London." Prod. Eric Young. *Sweeney Todd: The Demon Barber of Fleet Street*. Dir. Tim Burton. DreamWorks, 2007. DVD. Disc 2.

■ **47. Radio or television program**

"New Orleans." *American Experience*. Narr. Jeffrey Wright. PBS. WGBH, Boston, 12 Feb. 2007. Television.

"Elif Shafak: Writing under a Watchful Eye." *Fresh Air*. Host Terry Gross. Natl. Public Radio, 6 Feb. 2007. *NPR.org*. Web. 22 Feb. 2009.

■ **48. Radio or television interview**

McGovern, George. Interview by Charlie Rose. *Charlie Rose*. PBS. WNET, New York, 1 Feb. 2001. Television.

■ 49. Podcast

Patterson, Chris. "Will School Consolidation Improve Education?"
  Host Michael Quinn Sullivan. *Texas PolicyCast*. Texas Public
  Policy Foundation, 13 Apr. 2006. MP3 file. 27 Apr. 2006.

■ 50. Online video clip

Murphy, Beth. "Tips for a Good Profile Piece." *Project: Report*.
  YouTube, 7 Sept. 2008. Web. 19 Sept. 2008.

■ 51. Live performance

Art. By Yasmina Reza. Dir. Matthew Warchus. Perf. Philip Franks,
  Leigh Lawson, and Simon Shephard. Whitehall Theatre,
  London. 3 Dec. 2001. Performance.

Cello Concerto no. 2. By Eric Tanguy. Cond. Seiji Ozawa. Perf.
  Mstislav Rostropovich. Boston Symphony Orch. Symphony
  Hall, Boston. 5 Apr. 2002. Performance.

■ 52. Lecture or public address

Wellbery, David E. "On a Sentence of Franz Kafka." Franke Inst.
  for the Humanities. Gleacher Center, Chicago. 1 Feb. 2006.
  Lecture.

■ 53. Personal interview

Akufo, Dautey. Personal interview. 11 Aug. 2008.

Other sources (including online versions) This section
includes a variety of sources not covered elsewhere. For
sources obtained on the Web, consult the appropriate
model in this section and give information required for
an online source (see items 27–38).

■ 54. Government publication

United States. Dept. of Labor. *America's Dynamic Workforce*.
  Washington: US Dept. of Labor, 2004. Print.

United States. Dept. of Transportation. Natl. Highway Traffic
  Safety Administration. *An Investigation of the Safety
  Implications of Wireless Communications in Vehicles*. Natl.
  Highway Traffic Safety Administration, Nov. 1999. Web.
  20 May 2008.

■ 55. Historical and legal sources For a well-known his-
torical document, such as the United States Constitution,

give the document title, neither italicized nor in quotation marks, the document date, and publication information. For less familiar documents, begin with the author, if the work has one, and give the title, date, and publication information.

Jefferson, Thomas. First Inaugural Address. 1801. *The American Reader*. Ed. Diane Ravitch. New York: Harper, 1990. 42-44. Print.

For a legislative act (law), give the name of the act, neither italicized nor in quotation marks, followed by the Public Law number, the Statutes at Large information, the date, and the medium.

Electronic Freedom of Information Act Amendments of 1996. Pub. L. 104-231. 110 Stat. 3048. 2 Oct. 1996. Print.

For a court case, name the first plaintiff and the first defendant. Then give the law report number, the court, the year, and publication information. In a works cited entry, do not italicize the name of the case. (For an in-text citation, see item 17 on p. 125.)

Utah v. Evans. 536 US 452. Supreme Court of the US. 2002. *Supreme Court Collection*. Legal Information Inst., Cornell U Law School, n.d. Web. 30 Apr. 2008.

■ 56. Pamphlet

Commonwealth of Massachusetts. Dept. of Jury Commissioner. *A Few Facts about Jury Duty*. Boston: Commonwealth of Massachusetts, 2004. Print.

■ 57. Dissertation

Jackson, Shelley. "Writing Whiteness: Contemporary Southern Literature in Black and White." Diss. U of Maryland, 2000. Print.

■ 58. Abstract of a dissertation

Chen, Shu-Ling. "Mothers and Daughters in Morrison, Tan, Marshall, and Kincaid." Diss. U of Washington, 2000. *DAI* 61.6 (2000): 2289. Print.

■ **59. Published proceedings of a conference**

Kartiganer, Donald M., and Ann J. Abadie, eds. *Faulkner at 100:*
    Retrospect and Prospect. Proc. of Faulkner and
    Yoknapatawpha Conf., 27 July-1 Aug. 1997, U of
    Mississippi. Jackson: UP of Mississippi, 2000. Print.

■ **60. Published interview**

Armstrong, Lance. "Lance in France." *Sports Illustrated* 28 June
    2004: 46+. Print.

■ **61. Personal letter**   At the end of the entry, add the
medium ("MS" for "manuscript," or a handwritten letter;
"TS" for "typescript," or a typed letter).

Primak, Shoshana. Letter to the author. 6 May 2006. TS.

■ **62. Published letter**

Wharton, Edith. Letter to Henry James. 28 Feb. 1915. *Henry*
    James and Edith Wharton: Letters, 1900-1915. Ed. Lyall H.
    Powers. New York: Scribner's, 1990. 323-26. Print.

■ **63. Entry in a wiki**   A wiki is an online reference that is
openly edited by its users. Because wiki content is collec-
tively edited and can be updated frequently, do not include an author. Treat an entry in a wiki as you would a
short work from a Web site.

"Hip Hop Music." *Wikipedia*. Wikimedia Foundation, 26 Sept.
    2008. Web. 18 Mar. 2009.

"Negation in Languages." *UniLang.org*. UniLang, 25 Oct. 2004.
    Web. 9 June 2009.

ON THE WEB > dianahacker.com/pocket > Research exercises >
MLA > E-ex 32–3 to 32–6

32c MLA information notes (optional)

Researchers who use the MLA system of in-text citations
(see 32a) may also use information notes for one of two
purposes:

1. to provide additional material that might interrupt
    the flow of the paper yet is important enough to
    include

2. to refer readers to several sources or to provide comments on sources

Information notes may be footnotes or endnotes. Footnotes appear at the foot of the page; endnotes appear on a separate page at the end of the paper, just before the list of works cited. For either style, the notes are numbered consecutively throughout the paper. The text of the paper contains a raised arabic numeral that corresponds to the number of the note.

TEXT

In the past several years, employees have filed a number of lawsuits against employers because of online monitoring practices.[1]

NOTE

[1] For a discussion of federal law applicable to electronic surveillance in the workplace, see Kesan 293.

33 MLA manuscript format; sample pages

33a MLA manuscript format

The following guidelines on formatting a paper and preparing a list of works cited are consistent with advice given in the *MLA Handbook for Writers of Research Papers,* 7th ed. (New York: MLA, 2009) and with typical requirements for student papers. For sample pages from two MLA papers, see 33b.

Formatting the paper MLA papers should be formatted as follows.

Title and identification MLA does not require a title page. On the first page of your paper, place your name, your instructor's name, the course title, and the date on separate lines against the left margin. Then center your title. (See pp. 151 and 153 for sample first pages.)

If your instructor requires a title page, ask for guidelines on formatting it. A format similar to the one on page 188 will most likely be acceptable.

Pagination   Put the page number preceded by your last name in the upper right corner of each page, one-half inch below the top edge. Use arabic numerals (1, 2, 3, and so on).

Margins, line spacing, and paragraph indents   Leave margins of one inch on all sides of the page. Left-align the text.

Double-space throughout the paper. Do not add extra lines of space above or below the title of the paper or between paragraphs.

Indent the first line of each paragraph one-half inch (or five spaces) from the left margin.

Long quotations   For MLA guidelines on setting off nonfiction quotations, see pages 111–12. For MLA guidelines on setting off literary quotations, see pages 118–19.

Web addresses   When a Web address (URL) mentioned in the text of your paper must be divided at the end of a line, do not insert a hyphen. Break the URL only after a slash. (See also p. 150.)

Headings   MLA neither encourages nor discourages the use of headings and currently provides no guidelines for their use.

Visuals   MLA classifies visuals as tables and figures (figures include graphs, charts, maps, photographs, and drawings). Label each table with an arabic numeral (Table 1, Table 2, and so on) and provide a clear caption that identifies the subject. The label and the caption should appear on separate lines above the table, flush left. Below the table, give its source in a note like this one:

Source: David N. Greenfield and Richard A. Davis; "Lost in Cyberspace: The Web @ Work"; *CyberPsychology and Behavior* 5.4 (2002): 349; print.

For each figure, place the figure number (using the abbreviation "Fig.") and a caption below the figure, flush left. Include source information following the caption.

Preparing the list of works cited   Begin the list of works cited on a new page at the end of the paper. Center the title Works Cited about one inch from the top of the page. Double-space throughout. See pages 152 and 154 for sample lists of works cited.

Alphabetizing the list   Alphabetize the list by the last names of the authors (or editors); if a work has no author or editor, alphabetize it by the first word of the title other than *A, An,* or *The.*

If your list includes two or more works by the same author, see item 5 on page 130.

Indenting   Do not indent the first line of each works cited entry, but indent any additional lines one-half inch (or five spaces).

Web addresses   If you need to include a Web addresss (URL) in a works cited entry, do not insert a hyphen when dividing it at the end of a line. Break the URL only after a slash. Insert angle brackets around the URL. (See the note following item 27 on p. 139.)

If your word processing program automatically turns Web addresses into links (by underlining them and highlighting them in color), turn off this feature.

33b Pages from two MLA papers

Following are excerpts from two MLA papers: a research paper written for a composition course and an analysis of a short story written for a literature class.

ON THE WEB > dianahacker.com/pocket > Model papers
> MLA papers: Orlov; Daly; Levi
> MLA literature papers: Peel; Larson
> MLA annotated bibliography: Orlov

Sample MLA page: Research paper

Orlov 1

Anna Orlov

Professor Willis

English 101

17 March 2006

Online Monitoring:

A Threat to Employee Privacy in the Wired Workplace

Company policies on Internet usage have become as common as policies regarding vacation days or sexual harassment. A 2005 study by the American Management Association and ePolicy **1** Institute found that 76% of companies monitor employees' use of the Web, and the number of companies that block employees' access to certain Web sites has increased 27% since 2001 (1). Unlike other company rules, however, Internet usage policies raise questions about rights in the workplace. Although companies often have legitimate concerns that lead them to monitor employees' Internet **2** usage, the benefits of electronic surveillance are outweighed by its costs to employees' privacy and autonomy.

While surveillance of employees is not new, electronic surveillance allows employers to monitor workers with unprecedented efficiency. In *The Naked Employee*, Frederick Lane **3** describes offline ways in which employers have been permitted to intrude on employees' privacy for decades. The difference, Lane argues, between the old methods and electronic surveillance involves quantity:

> **4**   Technology makes it possible for employers to gather
> enormous amounts of data about employees. . . . And the
> trends that drive technology—faster, smaller, cheaper—
> make it possible for larger and larger numbers of
> employers to gather ever-greater amounts of personal
> data. (3-4) **5**

1 Source provides background information. **2** Debatable thesis. **3** Signal phrase introduces quotation. **4** Long quotation indented 1″ (10 spaces); quotation marks omitted. **5** Page number in parentheses after final period.

(Annotations indicate MLA-style formatting and effective writing.)

Sample MLA list of works cited

Orlov 5

[1]   Works Cited

[2] Adams, Scott. *Dilbert and the Way of the Weasel*. New York:
          Harper, 2002. Print.

American Management Association and ePolicy Institute. "2005
          Electronic Monitoring and Surveillance Survey." *American
          Management Association*. Amer. Management Assn., 2005.
          Web. 15 Feb. 2006.

[3] "Automatically Record Everything They Do Online! Spector Pro
          5.0 FAQ's." *Netbus.org*. Netbus.Org, n.d. Web. 17 Feb.   [4]
          2006.

[5] Flynn, Nancy. "Internet Policies." *ePolicy Institute*. ePolicy
          Inst., n.d. Web. 15 Feb. 2006.

Frauenheim, Ed. "Stop Reading This Headline and Get Back to
     [6] Work." *CNET News.com*. CNET Networks, 11 July 2005. Web.
          17 Feb. 2006.

Gonsalves, Chris. "Wasting Away on the Web." *eWeek.com*. Ziff
     [7] Davis Enterprise Holdings, 8 Aug. 2005. Web. 16 Feb.
          2006.

Kesan, Jay P. "Cyber-Working or Cyber-Shirking? A First
[8]   Principles Examination of Electronic Privacy in the
          Workplace." *Florida Law Review* 54.2 (2002): 289-332.
          Print.

Lane, Frederick S., III. *The Naked Employee: How Technology Is
          Compromising Workplace Privacy*. New York: Amer.
          Management Assn., 2003. Print.

[9] Tam, Pui-Wing, et al. "Snooping E-Mail by Software Is Now a
          Workplace Norm." *Wall Street Journal* 9 Mar. 2005: B1+.
          Print.

[1] **Heading, centered.** [2] **Authors' names inverted; works alphabetized by last names.** [3] **Work without author listed by title.** [4] **Abbreviation "n.d." for online source with no update date.** [5] **Short work from Web site.** [6] **First line of entry at left margin; extra lines indented ½" (5 spaces).** [7] **Article from online periodical.** [8] **Double-spacing throughout.** [9] **Four authors listed by first author's name and the abbreviation "et al."**

Larson 1

Dan Larson

Professor Duncan

English 102

18 April 2005

The Transformation of Mrs. Peters: **1**

An Analysis of "A Jury of Her Peers"

In Susan Glaspell's 1917 short story "A Jury of Her Peers," two women accompany their husbands and a county attorney to an isolated house where a farmer named John Wright has been choked to death. The chief suspect is Wright's wife, Minnie, who is in jail awaiting trial. The sheriff's wife, Mrs. Peters, has come along to gather some items for Minnie, and Mrs. Hale has joined her. Initially, Mrs. Hale sympathizes with Minnie and objects to the male investigators "snoopin' round and criticizin' " her kitchen (200). **2** But Mrs. Peters shows respect for the law, saying that the men are doing "no more than their duty" (201). By the end of the story, however, Mrs. Peters has joined Mrs. Hale in lying to the men and committing a crime—hiding key evidence. What causes this dramatic change? **3**

One critic, Leonard Mustazza, argues that Mrs. Hale recruits Mrs. Peters "as a fellow 'juror' in the case, moving the sheriff's wife . . . towards identification with the accused woman" (494). However, Mrs. Peters also reaches insights on her own. Her **4** observations in the kitchen lead her to understand Minnie's plight:

> The sheriff's wife had looked from the stove to the
> sink—to the pail of water which had been carried in
> **5** from outside. . . . That look of seeing into things, of
> seeing through a thing to something else, was in the
> eyes of the sheriff's wife now. (203)

---

1 Title, centered. **2** Quotation from literary work followed by page number. **3** Writer's research question. **4** Debatable thesis. **5** Long quotation indented 1" (10 spaces); page number in parentheses after final period.

Sample MLA list of works cited

Larson 7

Works Cited

1 Ben-Zvi, Linda. " 'Murder, She Wrote': The Genesis of Susan
Glaspell's *Trifles*." *Theatre Journal* 44.2 (1992): 141-62.
Rpt. in *Susan Glaspell: Essays on Her Theater and Fiction*.
Ed. Linda Ben-Zvi. Ann Arbor: U of Michigan P, 1995.
19-48. Print.

Glaspell, Susan. "A Jury of Her Peers." *Literature and Its Writers:
A Compact Introduction to Fiction, Poetry, and Drama*. Ed.
Ann Charters and Samuel Charters. 3rd ed. Boston:
Bedford, 2004. 194-210. Print.

Hedges, Elaine. "Small Things Reconsidered: 'A Jury of Her
2 Peers.' " *Women's Studies* 12.1 (1986): 89-110. Rpt. in
Susan Glaspell: Essays on Her Theater and Fiction. Ed. Linda
Ben-Zvi. Ann Arbor: U of Michigan P, 1995. 49-69. Print.

Mustazza, Leonard. "Generic Translation and Thematic Shift in
3 Susan Glaspell's *Trifles* and 'A Jury of Her Peers.' " *Studies
in Short Fiction* 26.4 (1989): 489-96. Print.

1 List alphabetized by last names. **2** Article reprinted in
anthology. **3** Article in a journal paginated by volume.

APA Papers

Most writing assignments in the social sciences are either reports of original research or reviews of the literature written about a research topic. Often an original research report contains a "review of the literature" section that places the writer's project in the context of previous research.

Most social science instructors will ask you to document your sources with the American Psychological Association (APA) system of in-text citations and references described in 37. You face three main challenges when writing a social science paper that draws on written sources: (1) supporting a thesis, (2) citing your sources and avoiding plagiarism, and (3) integrating quotations and other source material.

34 Supporting a thesis

Most assignments ask you to form a thesis and to support it with well-organized evidence. A thesis, which usually appears at the end of the introduction, is a one-sentence (or occasionally a two-sentence) statement of your central idea. In a paper reviewing the literature on a topic, the thesis analyzes the often competing conclusions drawn by a variety of researchers.

34a Forming a thesis

You will be reading articles and other sources that address a central research question. Your thesis will express a reasonable answer to that question, given the current state of research in the field. Here are some examples.

RESEARCH QUESTION

Is medication the right treatment for the escalating problem of childhood obesity?

POSSIBLE THESIS

Understanding the limitations of medical treatments for children highlights the complexity of the childhood obesity problem in the United States and underscores the need for physicians, advocacy groups, and policymakers to search for other solutions.

RESEARCH QUESTION

How has the popularity of the Internet shaped presidential campaign strategies?

POSSIBLE THESIS

Because the Internet provides the public with more information about candidates' personal lives than ever before, campaigns now focus more on damage control than on developing substantive programs.

RESEARCH QUESTION

How has the managed care system affected the role of nurses on health care teams?

POSSIBLE THESIS

As HMOs seek to increase their profitability with new cost-control methods, nurses have taken on more job responsibilities, but not always with adequate compensation.

ON THE WEB > dianahacker.com/pocket > Research exercises > APA > E-ex 34–1

34b Organizing your evidence

APA encourages the use of headings to help readers follow the organization of a paper. For an original research report, the major headings often follow a standard model: Method, Results, Discussion. For a paper that reviews the literature on a research topic, headings will vary, depending on the topic. For an example of a heading in an APA paper, see page 189.

34c Using sources to inform and support your argument

Sources can play several different roles as you develop your points.

Providing background information or context You can use facts and statistics to support generalizations or to establish the importance of your topic.

Explaining terms or concepts Explain words, phrases, or ideas that might be unfamiliar to your readers. Quoting or paraphrasing a source can help you define terms and concepts in neutral, accessible language.

Supporting your claims Back up your assertions with facts, examples, and other evidence from your research.

Lending authority to your argument Expert opinion can give weight to your argument. But don't rely on experts to make your argument for you. Construct your argument in your own words and cite authorities in the field for support.

Anticipating and countering alternative interpretations Do not ignore sources that seem to contradict your position or that offer interpretations different from your own. Instead, use them to give voice to opposing points of view before you counter them.

35 Avoiding plagiarism

Your research paper is a collaboration between you and your sources. To be fair and ethical, you must acknowledge your debt to the writers of those sources. If you don't, you commit plagiarism, a serious academic offense.

Three different acts are considered plagiarism: (1) failing to cite quotations and borrowed ideas, (2) failing to enclose borrowed language in quotation marks, and (3) failing to put summaries and paraphrases in your own words.

35a Citing quotations and borrowed ideas

You must cite all direct quotations and any ideas borrowed from a source: summaries and paraphrases; statistics and other specific facts; and visuals such as cartoons, graphs, and diagrams.

The only exception is common knowledge—information that your readers may know or could easily locate in general sources. For example, the current population of the United States is common knowledge among sociologists and economists, and psychologists are familiar with Freud's theory of the unconscious. When you have seen certain information repeatedly in your reading, you don't need to cite it. However, when information has appeared in only a few sources, when it is highly specific (as with statistics), or when it is controversial, you should cite the source.

APA recommends an author-date style of citations. Here, briefly, is how the author-date system usually works. See 37 for a detailed discussion of variations.

1. The source is introduced by a signal phrase that includes the last names of the authors followed by the date of publication in parentheses.
2. The material being cited is followed by a page number in parentheses.
3. At the end of the paper, an alphabetized list of references gives publication information about the sources.

IN-TEXT CITATION

As researchers Yanovski and Yanovski (2002) have explained, obesity was once considered "either a moral failing or evidence of underlying psychopathology" (p. 592).

ENTRY IN THE LIST OF REFERENCES

Yanovski, S. Z., & Yanovski, J. A. (2002). Drug therapy: Obesity. *The New England Journal of Medicine, 346*(8), 591-602.

35b Enclosing borrowed language in quotation marks

To show that you are using a source's exact phrases or sentences, you must enclose them in quotation marks. To omit the quotation marks is to claim—falsely—that the language is your own. Such an omission is plagiarism even if you have cited the source.

ORIGINAL SOURCE

> In an effort to seek the causes of this disturbing trend,
> experts have pointed to a range of important potential
> contributors to the rise in childhood obesity that are
> unrelated to media.
> —Henry J. Kaiser Family Foundation, "The Role
> of Media in Childhood Obesity" (2004), p. 1

PLAGIARISM

According to the Henry J. Kaiser Family Foundation (2004),
experts have pointed to a range of important potential
contributors to the rise in childhood obesity that are
unrelated to media (p. 1).

BORROWED LANGUAGE IN QUOTATION MARKS

According to the Henry J. Kaiser Family Foundation (2004),
"experts have pointed to a range of important potential
contributors to the rise in childhood obesity that are
unrelated to media" (p. 1).

NOTE: When quoted sentences are set off from the text by
indenting, quotation marks are not needed (see p. 162).

35c Putting summaries and paraphrases in your own words

A summary condenses information; a paraphrase reports
information in about the same number of words as in the
source. When you summarize or paraphrase, you must
restate the source's meaning using your own language.
You commit plagiarism if you half-copy the author's sentences—either by mixing the author's phrases with your
own without using quotation marks or by plugging your
own synonyms into the author's sentence structure. The
following paraphrases are plagiarized—even though the
source is cited—because their language is too close to
that of the source.

ORIGINAL SOURCE

> In an effort to seek the causes of this disturbing trend,
> experts have pointed to a range of important potential
> contributors to the rise in childhood obesity that are
> unrelated to media.
> —Henry J. Kaiser Family Foundation, "The Role
> of Media in Childhood Obesity" (2004), p. 1

PLAGIARISM: UNACCEPTABLE BORROWING OF PHRASES
According to the Henry J. Kaiser Family Foundation (2004),
experts have indicated a range of significant potential
contributors to the rise in childhood obesity that are not
linked to media (p. 1).

PLAGIARISM: UNACCEPTABLE BORROWING OF STRUCTURE
According to the Henry J. Kaiser Family Foundation (2004),
experts have identified a variety of significant factors causing a
rise in childhood obesity, factors that are not linked to media
(p. 1).

To avoid plagiarizing an author's language, set the
source aside, write from memory, and consult the source
later to check for accuracy.

ACCEPTABLE PARAPHRASE
A report by the Henry J. Kaiser Family Foundation (2004)
described sources other than media for the childhood obesity
crisis.

ON THE WEB > dianahacker.com/pocket > Research exercises >
APA > E-ex 35–1 to 35–5

36 Integrating sources

Quotations, summaries, paraphrases, and facts will support your argument, but they cannot speak for you. You
can use several strategies to integrate information from
research sources into your paper while maintaining your
own voice.

36a Limiting your use of quotations

Using quotations appropriately   Because it is almost impossible to integrate numerous long quotations smoothly
into your own text, do not quote excessively. Often you
can simply borrow a phrase or weave part of a source's
sentence into your own sentence structure.

As researchers continue to face a number of unknowns about
obesity, it may be helpful to envision treating the disorder, as

Yanovski and Yanovski (2002) suggested, "in the same manner as any other chronic disease" (p. 592).

Using the ellipsis mark To condense a quoted passage, you can use the ellipsis mark (three periods, with spaces between) to indicate that you have omitted words. What remains must be grammatically complete.

Roman (2003) reported that "social factors are nearly as significant as individual metabolism in the formation of . . . dietary habits of adolescents" (p. 345).

The writer has omitted the words *both healthy and unhealthy* from the source.

When you want to omit a full sentence or more, use a period before the three ellipsis dots.

According to Sothern and Gordon (2003), "Environmental factors may contribute as much as 80% to the causes of childhood obesity. . . . Research suggests that obese children demonstrate decreased levels of physical activity and increased psychosocial problems" (p. 104).

Ordinarily, do not use an ellipsis mark at the beginning or at the end of a quotation. Readers will understand that the quoted material is taken from a longer passage. The only exception occurs when you think that the author's meaning might be misinterpreted without the ellipsis mark.

Using brackets Brackets allow you to insert your own words into quoted material to explain a confusing reference or to keep a sentence grammatical in your context.

The cost of treating obesity currently totals $117 billion per year—a price, according to the surgeon general, "second only to the cost of [treating] tobacco use" (Carmona, 2004).

To indicate an error in a quotation, insert [*sic*] right after the error. Notice that the term *sic* is italicized and appears in brackets.

Setting off long quotations When you quote forty or more words, set off the quotation by indenting it one-half inch (or five spaces) from the left margin. Use the normal right margin and do not single-space.

Long quotations should be introduced by an informative sentence, usually followed by a colon. Quotation marks are unnecessary because the indented format tells readers that the words are taken from the source.

Yanovski and Yanovski (2002) have traced the history of treatments for obesity:

> For many years, obesity was approached as if it were either a moral failing or evidence of underlying psychopathology. With the advent of behavioral treatments for obesity in the 1960s, hope arose that modification of maladaptive eating and exercise habits would lead to sustained weight loss, and that time-limited programs would produce permanent changes in weight. (p. 592)

36b Using signal phrases to integrate sources

Whenever you include a paraphrase, summary, or direct quotation in your paper, introduce it with a *signal phrase*. A signal phrase usually names the author of the source and gives the publication date in parentheses.

NOTE: It is generally acceptable in the social sciences to call authors by their last name only, even on first mention. If your paper refers to two authors with the same last name, use their initials as well.

Putting source material in context   Readers need to understand how your source is relevant to your paper's thesis. It's a good idea, therefore, to embed your quotation — especially a long one — between sentences of your own, introducing it with a signal phrase and following it up with interpretive comments that link the source material to your paper's thesis.

QUOTATION WITH EFFECTIVE CONTEXT

A report by the Henry J. Kaiser Family Foundation (2004) outlined trends that may have contributed to the childhood obesity crisis, including food advertising for children as well as

> a reduction in physical education classes . . . , an increase in the availability of sodas and snacks in public schools, the growth in the number of fast-food outlets . . . , and the increasing number of highly processed high-calorie and high-fat grocery products. (p. 1)

Using signal phrases in APA papers

To avoid monotony, try to vary the language and placement of your signal phrases.

MODEL SIGNAL PHRASES

In the words of Carmona (2004), ". . ."

As Yanovski and Yanovski (2002) have noted, ". . ."

Hoppin and Taveras (2004), medical researchers, pointed out that ". . ."

". . . ," claimed Critser (2003).

". . . ," wrote Duenwald (2004), ". . ."

Researchers McDuffie et al. (2003) have offered a compelling argument for this view: ". . ."

Hilts (2002) answered these objections with the following analysis: ". . ."

VERBS IN SIGNAL PHRASES

Are you providing background, explaining a concept, supporting a claim, lending authority, or refuting a belief? Choose a verb that is appropriate for the way you are using the source.

admitted	contended	reasoned
agreed	declared	refuted
argued	denied	rejected
asserted	emphasized	reported
believed	insisted	responded
claimed	noted	suggested
compared	observed	thought
confirmed	pointed out	wrote

NOTE: In APA style, use the past tense or present perfect tense to introduce quotations and other source material: *Davis (2005) noted that* or *Davis (2005) has noted that,* not *Davis (2005) notes that.* Use the present tense only to discuss the results of an experiment (*the results show*) or knowledge that has clearly been established (*researchers agree*).

Addressing each of these areas requires more than a doctor armed with a prescription pad; it requires a broad mobilization not just of doctors and concerned parents but of educators, food industry executives, advertisers, and media representatives.

Marking boundaries Avoid dropping direct quotations into your text without warning. Provide clear signal phrases, including at least the author's name and the date of publication. A signal phrase indicates the boundary between your words and the source's words.

DROPPED QUOTATION

Obesity was once considered in a very different light. "For many years, obesity was approached as if it were either a moral failing or evidence of underlying psychopathology" (Yanovski & Yanovski, 2002, p. 592).

QUOTATION WITH SIGNAL PHRASE

As researchers Yanovski and Yanovski (2002) have explained, obesity was once considered "either a moral failing or evidence of underlying psychopathology" (p. 592).

36c Integrating statistics and other facts

When you are citing a statistic or another specific fact, a signal phrase is often not necessary. In most cases, readers will understand that the citation refers to the statistic or fact (not the whole paragraph).

In purely financial terms, the drugs cost more than $3 a day on average (Duenwald, 2004).

There is nothing wrong, however, with using a signal phrase.

ON THE WEB > dianahacker.com/pocket > Research exercises > APA > E-ex 36–1 to 36–4

37 APA documentation style

To document sources, APA recommends in-text citations that refer readers to a list of references.

37a APA in-text citations

APA's in-text citations provide at least the author's last name and the year of publication. For direct quotations and some summaries and paraphrases, a page number is given as well. In the following models, the elements of the in-text citation are highlighted.

NOTE: APA style requires the use of the past tense or the present perfect tense in signal phrases introducing cited material: *Smith (2005) reported, Smith (2005) has argued.*

■ **1. A quotation** Ordinarily, introduce the quotation with a signal phrase that includes the author's last name followed by the year of publication in parentheses. Put the page number (preceded by "p.") in parentheses after the quotation.

Critser (2003) noted that despite growing numbers of overweight Americans, many health care providers still "remain either in ignorance or outright denial about the health danger to the poor and the young" (p. 5).

If the author is not named in the signal phrase, place the author's name, the year, and the page number in parentheses after the quotation: (Critser, 2003, p. 5).

NOTE: Do not include a month, even if the entry in the reference list includes the month and year.

■ **2. A summary or a paraphrase** Include the author's last name and the year in a signal phrase introducing the material or in parentheses following it. A page number or another locator is not required, but include one if it would help readers find the passage in a long work.

Yanovski and Yanovski (2002) explained that sibutramine suppresses appetite by blocking the reuptake of the neurotransmitters serotonin and norepinephrine in the brain (p. 594).

Sibutramine suppresses appetite by blocking the reuptake of the neurotransmitters serotonin and norepinephrine in the brain (Yanovski & Yanovski, p. 594).

■ **3. Two authors**   Name both authors in the signal phrase or parentheses each time you cite the work. In the parentheses, use "&" between the authors' names; in the signal phrase, use "and."

According to Sothern and Gordon (2003), "Environmental factors may contribute as much as 80% to the causes of childhood obesity" (p. 104).

Obese children often engage in limited physical activity (Sothern & Gordon, 2003, p. 104).

■ **4. Three to five authors**   Identify all authors in the signal phrase or parentheses the first time you cite the source.

In 2003, Berkowitz, Wadden, Tershakovec, and Cronquist concluded, "Sibutramine . . . must be carefully monitored in adolescents, as in adults, to control increases in [blood pressure] and pulse rate" (p. 1811).

In subsequent citations, use the first author's name followed by "et al." in either the signal phrase or the parentheses.

As Berkowitz et al. (2003) advised, "Until more extensive safety and efficacy data are available, . . . weight-loss medications should be used only on an experimental basis for adolescents" (p. 1811).

■ **5. Six or more authors**   Use the first author's name followed by "et al." in the signal phrase or the parentheses.

McDuffie et al. (2002) tested 20 adolescents, aged 12-16, over a three-month period and found that orlistat, combined with behavioral therapy, produced an average weight loss of 4.4 kg, or 9.7 pounds (p. 646).

■ **6. Unknown author**   If the author is unknown, mention the work's title in the signal phrase or give the first word or two of the title in the parenthetical citation. Titles of articles and chapters are put in quotation marks; titles of books and reports are italicized.

Children struggling to control their weight must also struggle with the pressures of television advertising that, on the one hand, encourages the consumption of junk food and, on the other, celebrates thin celebrities ("Television," 2002).

NOTE: In the rare case when "Anonymous" is specified as the author, treat it as if it were a real name: (Anonymous, 2001). In the list of references, also use the name Anonymous as author.

■ **7. Organization as author**   If the author is a government agency or another organization, name the organization in the signal phrase or in the parenthetical citation the first time you cite the source.

Obesity puts children at risk for a number of medical complications, including type 2 diabetes, hypertension, sleep apnea, and orthopedic problems (Henry J. Kaiser Family Foundation, 2004, p. 1).

If the organization has a familiar abbreviation, you may include it in brackets the first time you cite the source and use the abbreviation alone in later citations.

FIRST CITATION   (National Institute of Mental Health [NIMH], 2001)

LATER CITATIONS   (NIMH, 2001)

■ **8. Two or more works in the same parentheses**   When your parenthetical citation names two or more works, put them in the same order that they appear in the reference list, separated by semicolons.

Researchers have indicated that studies of pharmacological treatments for childhood obesity are inconclusive (Berkowitz et al., 2003; McDuffie et al., 2002).

■ **9. Authors with the same last name** To avoid confusion, use initials with the last names if your reference list includes two or more authors with the same last name.

Research by E. Smith (1989) revealed that . . .

■ **10. Personal communication** Cite interviews, memos, letters, e-mail, and similar unpublished person-to-person communications as follows:

One of Atkinson's colleagues, who has studied the effect of the media on children's eating habits, has contended that advertisers for snack foods will need to design ads responsibly for their younger viewers (F. Johnson, personal communication, October 20, 2004).

Do not include personal communications in your reference list.

■ **11. An electronic document** Cite an electronic document as you would any other document.

Atkinson (2001) found that children who spent at least four hours a day watching TV were less likely to engage in adequate physical activity during the week.

Electronic sources may lack page numbers, authors' names, or dates. Here are APA's guidelines for handling sources without these details.

Unknown author
If no author is named, mention the title of the document in a signal phrase or give the first word or two of the title in parentheses (see also item 6). (If an organization serves as the author, see item 7.)

The body's basal metabolic rate, or BMR, is a measure of its at-rest energy requirement ("Exercise," 2003).

Unknown date
When the date is unknown, APA recommends using the abbreviation "n.d." (for "no date").

Attempts to establish a definitive link between television programming and children's eating habits have been problematic (Magnus, n.d.).

No page numbers
APA ordinarily requires page numbers for quotations, and it recommends them for summaries or paraphrases from

long sources. When an electronic source lacks stable numbered pages, your citation should include information that will help readers locate the particular passage being cited.

When an electronic document has numbered paragraphs, use the paragraph number preceded by the abbreviation "para.": (Hall, 2001, para. 5). If neither a page nor a paragraph number is given and the document contains headings, cite the appropriate heading and indicate which paragraph under that heading you are referring to.

Hoppin and Taveras (2004) pointed out that several other medications were classified by the Drug Enforcement Administration as having the "potential for abuse" (Weight-Loss Drugs section, para. 6).

NOTE: Electronic files in portable document format (PDF) often have stable page numbers. For such sources, give the page number in the parenthetical citation.

■ **12. Indirect source**   If you use a source that was cited in another source (a secondary source), name the original source in your signal phrase. List the secondary source in your reference list and include it in your parenthetical citation, preceded by the words "as cited in." In the following example, Critser is the secondary source.

Former surgeon general Dr. David Satcher described "a nation of young people seriously at risk of starting out obese and dooming themselves to the difficult task of overcoming a tough illness" (as cited in Critser, 2003, p. 4).

■ **13. Two or more works by the same author in the same year**   When your list of references includes more than one work by the same author in the same year, use lowercase letters ("a," "b," and so on) with the year to order the entries in the reference list. (See item 6 on p. 173.) Use those same letters with the year in the in-text citation.

Research by Durgin (2003b) has yielded new findings about the role of counseling in treating childhood obesity.

ON THE WEB > dianahacker.com/pocket > Research exercises > APA > E-ex 37–1 to 37–3

37b APA references

In APA style, the alphabetical list of works cited, which appears at the end of the paper, is titled References. Following are models illustrating the form that APA recommends for entries in the list of references. Observe all details: capitalization, punctuation, use of italics, and so on. For advice on preparing the reference list, see pages 186–87. For sample reference lists, see pages 190, 193, and 195.

→

ON THE WEB > dianahacker.com/pocket > Research exercises > APA > E-ex 37–4

General guidelines for listing authors   Alphabetize entries in the list of references by authors' last names; if a work has no author, alphabetize it by its title. The first element of each entry is important because citations in the text of the paper refer to it and readers will be looking for it in the alphabetized list. The date of publication appears after the first element of the entry.

NAME AND YEAR CITED IN TEXT

Duncan (2006) has reported that . . .

BEGINNING OF ENTRY IN THE LIST OF REFERENCES

Duncan, B. (2006).

Items 1–4 show how to begin an entry for a work with a single author, multiple authors, an organization as author, and an unknown author. Items 5 and 6 show how to begin an entry when your list includes two or more works by the same author or two or more works by the same author in the same year.

What comes after the first element of your citation will depend on the kind of source you are citing (see items 7–34).

■ **1. Single author**   Begin the entry with the author's last name, followed by a comma and the author's initial(s). Then give the date in parentheses.

Perez, E. (2006).

■ **2. Multiple authors**   List up to seven authors by last names followed by initials. Use an ampersand (&) before the name of the last author. If there are more than seven authors, list the first six followed by three ellipsis dots and the last author's name.

Sloan, F. A., Stout, E. M., Whetten-Goldstein, K., & Liang, L.
     (2000).

Mulvaney, S. A., Mudasiru, E., Schlundt, D. G., Baughman, C. L.,
     Fleming, M., VanderWoude, A., . . . Rothman, R. (2008).

■ **3. Organization as author**   When the author is an organization, begin with the name of the organization.

American Psychiatric Association. (2005).

■ **4. Unknown author**   Begin with the work's title. Titles of books are italicized. Titles of articles are neither italicized nor put in quotation marks.

Oxford essential world atlas. (2001).

Omega-3 fatty acids. (2004, November 23).

■ **5. Two or more works by the same author**   Use the author's name for all entries. List the entries by year, the earliest first.

Schlechty, P. C. (1997).

Schlechty, P. C. (2001).

■ **6. Two or more works by the same author in the same year**   List the works alphabetically by title. In the parentheses, following the year add "a," "b," and so on. Use these same letters when giving the year in the in-text citation.

Durgin, P. A. (2003a). At-risk behaviors in children.

Durgin, P. A. (2003b). Treating obesity with psychotherapy.

Articles in periodicals   This section shows how to prepare an entry for an article in a scholarly journal, a magazine,

Citation at a glance
Article in a periodical (APA)

To cite an article in a periodical in APA style, include the following elements:

1 Author
2 Year of publication
3 Title of article
4 Name of periodical
5 Volume number; issue number if required (see item 8)
6 Page numbers

5 VOLUME 2, NUMBER 2

3

The POWER of PEERS

How does the makeup of a classroom influence achievement?

by CAROLINE M. HOXBY

1 by CAROLINE M. HOXBY

2 **4** **6**
SUMMER 2002/ EDUCATION NEXT 57

REFERENCE LIST ENTRY FOR AN ARTICLE IN A PERIODICAL

┌─**1**─┐ ┌─**2**─┐ ┌────**3**────┐ ┌────**4**────┐
Hoxby, C. M. (2002). The power of peers. *Education Next*,

┌─**5**─┐┌─**6**─┐
2(2), 57-63.

For more on citing articles in periodicals in APA style, see pages 173–75.

or a newspaper. You may also need to refer to items 1–6. (For an annotated example, see p. 174.)

NOTE: For articles on consecutive pages, provide the range of pages (see item 7). When an article does not appear on consecutive pages, give all page numbers: A1, A17.

■ 7. Article in a journal paginated by volume

Morawski, J. (2000). Social psychology a century ago. *American Psychologist, 55,* 427-431.

■ 8. Article in a journal paginated by issue

Smith, S. (2003). Government and nonprofits in the modern age. *Society, 40*(4), 36-45.

■ 9. Article in a magazine

Raloff, J. (2001, May 12). Lead therapy won't help most kids. *Science News, 159,* 292.

■ 10. Article in a newspaper

Lohr, S. (2004, December 3). Health care technology is a promise unfinanced. *The New York Times,* p. C5.

■ 11. Letter to the editor

Wright, M. J. (2006, December). Diminutive danger [Letter to the editor]. *Scientific American, 295*(6), 18.

■ 12. Review

Gleick, E. (2000, December 4). The burdens of genius [Review of the book *The Last Samurai,* by Helen DeWitt]. *Time, 156*(23), 171.

Books   In addition to consulting the items in this section, you may need to refer to items 1–6 on page 173. (For an annotated example, see p. 176.)

■ 13. Basic format for a book

Highmore, B. (2001). *Everyday life and cultural theory*. New York, NY: Routledge.

■ 14. Book with an editor   The first model is for a book with editors but no author; the second is for a book with an author and an editor. (For a work in an edited book, see item 17.)

Citation at a glance
Book (APA)

To cite a book in APA style, include the following elements:

1 Author
2 Year of publication
3 Title and subtitle
4 Place of publication
5 Publisher

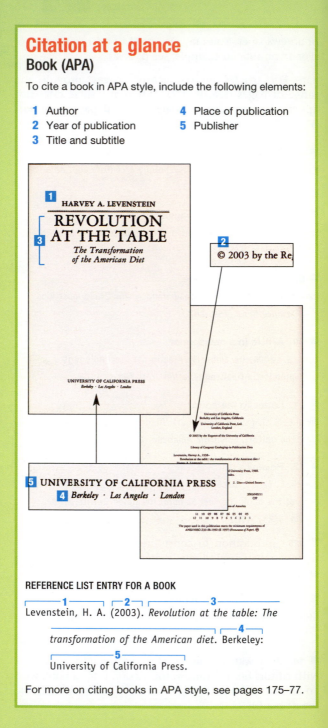

REFERENCE LIST ENTRY FOR A BOOK

———1——— ——2—— —————3—————
Levenstein, H. A. (2003). *Revolution at the table: The*

——————4——
transformation of the American diet. Berkeley:

———5———
University of California Press.

For more on citing books in APA style, see pages 175–77.

Bronfen, E., & Kavka, M. (Eds.). (2001). *Feminist consequences: Theory for a new century*. New York, NY: Columbia University Press.

Plath, S. (2000). *The unabridged journals* (K. V. Kukil, Ed.). New York, NY: Anchor.

■ **15. Translation**

Steinberg, M. D. (2003). *Voices of revolution, 1917* (M. Schwartz, Trans.). New Haven, CT: Yale University Press. (Original work published 2001)

■ **16. Edition other than the first**

Helfer, M. E., Keme, R. S., & Drugman, R. D. (1997). *The battered child* (5th ed.). Chicago, IL: University of Chicago Press.

■ **17. Article or chapter in an edited book**

Meskell, L. (2001). Archaeologies of identity. In I. Hodder (Ed.), *Archaeological theory today* (pp. 187-213). Cambridge, England: Polity Press.

■ **18. Multivolume work**

Luo, J. (Ed.). (2005). *China today: An encyclopedia of life in the People's Republic* (Vols. 1-2). Westport, CT: Greenwood Press.

Electronic sources

NOTE: The publication information for some online sources includes a DOI (digital object identifier). APA uses the DOI, when available, in reference list entries.

■ **19. Article from an online periodical** When citing online articles, include publication information as in items 7–12. If the article has a DOI, include that number.

Whitmeyer, J. M. (2000). Power through appointment. *Social Science Research, 29*, 535-555. doi:10.1006/ssre.2000.0680

If there is no DOI, include the URL for the journal's home page.

Ashe, D. D., & McCutcheon, L. E. (2001). Shyness, loneliness, and attitude toward celebrities. *Current Research in Social Psychology, 6*, 124-133. Retrieved from http://www.uiowa.edu/~grpproc/crisp/crisp.html

How to cite a source without a model

Sometimes you may consult sources for which APA does not yet provide citation models. When you encounter such a source, gather the same kinds of information as you do for other sources—author/creator, title, sponsor, date of creation or update. Then consult the available models in this section to see which models have similar features to your source. You may need to combine elements from different models.

Your goal is always to provide readers with enough information to locate the source and to assess its reliability. The following questions may help.

- Is the source originally video, audio, or both? (See items 33 and 34.)
- Is the source an electronic or audio/video version of a print source? (See the model for the relevant print source.)
- What kinds of sources are similar to this source?
- Does the source list a date on which it was created or updated?

When citing any source without a model, check your work with your instructor.

NOTE: When you have retrieved an article from a newspaper's searchable Web site, give the URL for the site, not for the exact source.

■ **20. Article from a database** To cite an article from a library's subscription database, include the publication information for the source (see items 7–12). If the article has a DOI, give that number at the end and do not include the database name. If there is no DOI, include the URL for the home page of the journal. (For an annotated example, see p. 180.)

Holliday, R. E., & Hayes, B. K. (2000). Dissociating automatic and intentional processes in children's eyewitness memory. *Journal of Experimental Child Psychology, 75,* 1-42. doi:10.1006/jecp.1999.2521

Howard, K. R. (2007). Childhood overweight: Parental perceptions and readiness for change. *The Journal of School Nursing, 23,* 73-79. Retrieved from http://jsn.sagepub.com/

■ **21. Document from a Web site**   APA refers to non-peer-reviewed work, such as reports, brochures, fact sheets, press releases, and newsletter articles, as "gray literature." List as many of the following elements as are available: author's name, publication date (or "n.d." for "no date"), title, and URL. Give your retrieval date only if the content of the source is likely to change.

Cain, A., & Burris, M. (1999, April). *Investigation of the use of mobile phones while driving*. Retrieved from http://www .cutr.eng.usf.edu/its/mobile_phone_text.htm

Archer, D. (n.d.). *Exploring nonverbal communication*. Retrieved from http://nonverbal.ucsc.edu

■ **22. Chapter or section in a Web document**   Begin with the author, the date, and the title of the chapter or section, not italicized. After the word "In," put the name of the editor of the Web site, if there is one; the title of the Web site, italicized; and the URL for the chapter or section. (For an annotated example, see p. 182.)

National Institute on Media and the Family. (2009). Mobile networking. In *Guide to social networking: Risks*. Retrieved from http://www.mediafamily.org/network_pdf /MediaWise_Guide_to_Social_Networking_Risks_09.pdf

■ **23. Weblog (blog) post**   Give the writer's name, the date of the post, the title or subject of the post, the label "Web log post," and the URL.

Kellermann, M. (2007, May 23). Disclosing clinical trials [Web log post]. Retrieved from http://www.iq.harvard.edu/blog /sss/archives/2007/05

■ **24. Podcast**   Include as much of the following information as is available: writer or producer of the podcast; the date it was produced or posted; the title; the number in parentheses (if any); and a label in brackets. Then give the series title (if there is one), in italics; a retrieval statement; and the URL.

National Academies (Producer). (2007, June 6). Progress in preventing childhood obesity: How do we measure up? [Audio podcast]. *The sounds of science podcast*. Retrieved from http://media.nap.edu/podcasts/

Citation at a glance
Article from a database (APA)

To cite an article from a database in APA style, include the following elements:

1 Author
2 Date of publication
3 Title of article
4 Name of periodical
5 Volume number; issue number, if required (see item 8)
6 Page numbers
7 DOI (digital object identifier)
8 URL for journal's home page (if there is no DOI)

ON-SCREEN VIEW OF DATABASE RECORD

REFERENCE LIST ENTRY FOR AN ARTICLE FROM A DATABASE

Poupart, L. M. (2002). Crime and justice in American

Indian communities. *Social Justice, 29,* 144-159.

Retrieved from http:www.socialjusticejournal.org/

For more on citing articles from a database in APA style, see item 20.

■ **25. Entry in a wiki** Begin with the title of the entry and the date of posting, if there is one (use "n.d." for "no date" if there is not). Then add your retrieval date, the name of the wiki, and the URL for the wiki entry. Unlike most other entries for electronic sources, the entry for a wiki includes the date of retrieval because the content of a wiki is often not stable. If an author or an editor is identified, include that name at the beginning of the entry.

Ethnomethodology. (n.d.). Retrieved August 22, 2008,

   from http://en.stswiki.org/index.php/Ethnomethodology

■ **26. E-mail** E-mail messages, letters, and other personal communications are not included in the list of references.

■ **27. Online posting** If an online posting is not archived, cite it as a personal communication in the text of your paper and do not include it in the list of references. If the posting is archived, give the URL and the name of the discussion list if it is not part of the URL.

McKinney, J. (2006, December 19). Adult education-healthcare

   partnerships [Electronic mailing list messge]. Retrieved

   from http://www.nifl.gov/pipermail/healthliteracy/2006

   /000524.html

Citation at a glance
Section in a Web document (APA)

To cite a section in a Web document in APA style, include the following elements:

1 Author
2 Date of publication or most recent update
3 Title of document on Web site
4 Title of Web site or section of site
5 URL of document

BROWSER PRINTOUT OF WEB SITE

2003 Minnesota Health Statistics Annual Summary - Min...   http://health.state.mn.us/divs/chs/03annsum/

1 *Minnesota Department of Health*
Protecting, maintaining and improving the health of all Minnesotans

MDH

4 2003 Minnesota Health Statistics Annual Summary

The Minnesota "Annual Summary" or "Minnesota Health Statistics" is a report published yearly. The most recent version of this report is **2003 Minnesota Health Statistics**, published February 2005. This report provides statistical data on the following seven subjects for the state of Minnesota.

2 February 2005.

To view the PDF files, you will need Adobe Acrobat Reader (

- **Overview of 2003 Annual Summary (PDF: 251KB/11 pages)**
- **Live Births (PDF: 608KB/21 pages)**
- **3 • Fertility (PDF: 80KB/2 pages)**
- **Infant Mortality and Fetal Deaths (PDF: 414KB/15 pages)**
- **General Mortality (PDF: 581KB/40 pages)**
- **Marriage (PDF: 83KB/4 pages)**
- **Divorce (PDF: 62KB/3 pages)**
- **Population (PDF: 29KB/12 pages)**

Note: Induced abortion statistics previously reported in this publication are now published separately.
See > Report to the Legislature: Induced Abortions in Minnesota

See also> Minnesota Health Statistics Annual Summary Main Page

For further information about the Annual Summary, please contact:

Center for Health Statistics
Minnesota Department of Health
Golden Rule Building, 3rd Floor
85 East Seventh Place
PO Box 64882
St. Paul, Minnesota, U.S.A. 55164-0882
E-mail: healthstats@health.state.mn.us

If you have questions or comments about this page, please contact the Minnesota Center for Health Statistics: healthstats@health.state.mn.us.

1 of 2   6/20/07 10:35 AM

ON-SCREEN VIEW OF DOCUMENT

Fertility Table 1
Total Reported Pregnancies by Outcome and Rate
Minnesota Residents, 1980 - 2003

Year	Total Reported Pregnancies*	Live Births	Induced Abortions	Fetal Deaths	Female Population Ages 15-44	Pregnancy Rate**
1980	84,782	67,843	16,490	449	958,773	88.4
1981	84,934	68,652	15,821	461	967,087	87.8
1982	84,500	68,512	15,559	429	977,905	86.4
1983	80,530	65,559	14,514	457	981,287	82.1
1984	82,736	66,715	15,556	465	985,608	83.9
1985	83,853	67,412	16,002	439	994,249	84.3
1986	81,882	65,766	15,716	400	997,501	82.1
1987	81,318	65,168	15,746	404	1,004,801	80.9
1988	83,335	66,745	16,124	466	1,020,209	81.7
1989	83,426	67,490	15,506	430	1,024,576	81.4
1990	83,714	67,985	15,280	449	1,025,919	81.6

REFERENCE LIST ENTRY FOR A SECTION FROM A WEB DOCUMENT

—1— —2—
Minnesota Department of Health. (2005, February).

—3— —4—
Fertility. In *2003 Minnesota health statistics annual*

—5—
summary. Retrieved from http://www.health.state.mn

.us/divs/chs/03annsum/fertility.pdf

For more on citing documents from Web sites in APA style,
see page 179.

■ **28. Computer program**

Kaufmann, W. J., III, & Comins, N. F. (2003). Discovering the
universe (Version 6.0) [Computer software]. New York, NY:
Freeman.

Other sources

■ **29. Dissertation from a database**

Hymel, K. M. (2009). Essays in urban economics (Doctoral
dissertation). Available from ProQuest Dissertations and
Theses database. (AAT 3355930)

■ **30. Government document**

U.S. Census Bureau. (2006). *Statistical abstract of the United
States*. Washington, DC: Government Printing Office.

■ **31. Report from a private organization**   If the publisher
and the author are the same, begin with the publisher. For
a print source, use "Author" as the publisher at the end;
for an online source, give the URL.

American Psychiatric Association. (2000). *Practice guidelines for
the treatment of patients with eating disorders* (2nd ed.).
Washington, DC: Author.

■ **32. Conference proceedings**

Stahl, G. (Ed.). (2002). *Proceedings of CSCL '02: Computer support
for collaborative learning*. Hillsdale, NJ: Erlbaum.

■ **33. Film or video (motion picture)**

Gaghan, S. (Director). (2005). *Syriana* [Motion picture]. United
States: Warner Brothers Pictures.

■ **34. Television broadcast or series episode**

Pratt, C. (Executive producer). (2006, February 19). *Face
the nation* [Television broadcast]. Washington, DC:
CBS News.

Loeterman, B. (Writer), & Gale, B. (Director). (2000). Real
justice [Television series episode]. In M. Sullivan (Executive
producer), *Frontline*. Boston, MA: WGBH.

ON THE WEB > dianahacker.com/pocket > Research exercises > APA > E-ex 37–5 and 37–6

38   APA manuscript format; sample pages

38a   APA manuscript format

Many instructors in the social sciences require students to follow the guidelines in the *Publication Manual of the American Psychological Association*, 6th ed. (Washington: APA, 2010), for formatting a paper and a list of references.

Formatting the paper   The guidelines and examples in 38a and 38b are consistent with APA's formatting for papers prepared for publication in a scholarly journal. The formatting on pages 194–95 is typical for a business report.

Title page   Most instructors will want you to include a title page. See pages 188 and 191.

Page numbers and running head   Number all pages with arabic numerals (1, 2, 3, and so on) in the upper right corner about one-half inch from the top of the page. Flush with the left margin and on the same line as the page number, type a running head consisting of the title of the paper (shortened to no more than fifty characters) in all capital letters. (See pp. 189–90 and 192–93.) On the title page only, include the words "Running head" followed by a colon before the title. (See pp. 188 and 191.)

Margins and line spacing   Use margins of one inch on all sides of the page. Left-align the text. Double-space throughout the paper.

Long quotations and footnotes   See pages 162–63 for APA's guidelines for formatting long quotations. Place footnotes at the bottom of the page on which the text reference occurs. Begin each note with the superscript arabic numeral that corresponds to the number in the text. Indent the first line one-half inch. See page 189.

Abstract   If your instructor requires one, include an abstract on its own page after the title page. Center the word Abstract one inch from the top of the page.

An abstract is a 100-to-150-word overview of your essay. It should express your main idea and key points; it might also suggest any implications or applications of the research you discuss in the paper.

Headings   Although headings are not always necessary, their use is encouraged in the social sciences. For college papers, one level of heading is usually sufficient.

In APA style, major headings are centered and bold-face. Capitalize the first word of the heading, along with all other words except articles, short prepositions, and coordinating conjunctions.

Visuals   APA classifies visuals as tables and figures (figures include graphs, charts, drawings, and photographs). Label each table with an arabic numeral (Table 1, Table 2) and provide a clear title. The label and title should appear on separate lines above the table, flush left and double-spaced. Below the table, give its source in a note.

Note. From "Innovation Roles: From Souls of Fire to Devil's Advocates," by M. Meyer, 2000, *The Journal of Business Communication, 37,* p. 338.

For each figure, place a label and a caption below the figure, flush left and double-spaced. They need not appear on separate lines.

Preparing the list of references   Begin your list of references on a new page at the end of the paper. Center the title References one inch from the top of the page. Double-space throughout. For sample reference lists, see pages 190, 193, and 195.

Indenting entries   Type the first line of each entry flush left and indent any additional lines one-half inch, as shown on pages 190, 193, and 195.

Alphabetizing the list   Alphabetize the reference list by the last names of the authors (or editors); when a work has no author or editor, alphabetize by the first word of the title other than *A, An,* or *The.*

If you list two or more works by the same author, arrange the entries by year, the earliest first. If you include two or more works by the same author in the same year, arrange them alphabetically by title. Add the letters "a," "b," and so on in the parentheses after the year. Use only the year and the letter for journal articles: (2003a). Use the full date and the letter for articles in magazines and newspapers in the reference list: (2005a, July 17). Use only the year and the letter in in-text citations.

Authors' names   Invert all authors' names and use initials instead of first names. With two or more authors, use an ampersand (&) before the last author's name. Separate the names with commas. Include names for the first seven authors; if there are eight or more authors, give the first six authors, three ellipsis dots, and the last author (see p. 173).

Titles of books and articles   Italicize the titles and subtitles of books; capitalize only the first word of the title and subtitle (and all proper nouns). Capitalize names of periodicals as you would capitalize them normally (see 22c).

Abbreviations for page numbers   Abbreviations for "page" and "pages" ("p." and "pp.") are used before page numbers of newspaper articles and articles in edited books (see item 10 on p. 175 and item 17 on p. 177) but not before page numbers of articles in magazines and scholarly journals (see items 7–9 on p. 175).

Breaking a URL   When a URL or a DOI (digital object identifier) must be divided, break it after a double slash or before any other mark of punctuation. Do not insert a hyphen, and do not add a period at the end.

38b Sample APA pages

Following are excerpts from a review of the literature paper written for a psychology class, a nursing practice paper, and a paper written for a business class.

**ON THE WEB > dianahacker.com/pocket > Model papers
> APA papers: Mirano
> APA annotated bibliography: Haddad
> APA nursing practice paper: Riss
> APA business proposal: Ratajczak**

Sample APA title page

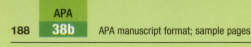

Running head: CAN MEDICATION CURE OBESITY IN CHILDREN?   1

Can Medication Cure Obesity in Children?

A Review of the Literature

Luisa Mirano

Northwest-Shoals Community College

Author Note

This paper was prepared for Psychology 108, Section B, taught by Professor Kang.

---

1 Short title in all capital letters on all pages; words "Running head" on title page only. **2** Arabic page number on all pages. **3** Full title and writer's name and affiliation, centered. **4** Author's note (optional) for extra information.

(Annotations indicate APA-style formatting and effective writing.)

Sample APA page

CAN MEDICATION CURE OBESITY IN CHILDREN?   3

Can Medication Cure Obesity in Children? **1**

A Review of the Literature

In March 2004, U.S. Surgeon General Richard Carmona called attention to a health problem in the United States that, until recently, has been overlooked: childhood obesity. Carmona said that the **2** "astounding" 15% child obesity rate constitutes an "epidemic." Since the early 1980s, that rate has "doubled in children and tripled in adolescents." Now more than 9 million children are classified as obese.[1] This literature review considers whether the use of medication is a promising approach for solving the childhood obesity problem by responding to the following questions:

1. What are the implications of childhood obesity? **3**
2. Is medication effective at treating childhood obesity?
3. Is medication safe for children?
4. Is medication the best solution?

Understanding the limitations of medical treatments for children **4** highlights the complexity of the childhood obesity problem in the United States and underscores the need for physicians, advocacy groups, and policymakers to search for other solutions.

What Are the Implications of Childhood Obesity? **5**

Obesity can be a devastating problem from both an individual and a societal perspective. Obesity puts children at risk for a number of medical complications, including type 2 diabetes, hypertension,

[1]Obesity is measured in terms of body-mass index (BMI): weight in **6** kilograms divided by square of height in meters. An adolescent with a BMI in the 95th percentile for his or her age and gender is considered obese.

---

1 Full title, centered. **2** Signal phrase introduces source. **3** Questions provide organization. **4** Paper's thesis. **5** Headings guide readers. **6** Footnote defines essential term without interrupting text.

Sample APA list of references

1   References

2 Berkowitz, R. I., Wadden, T. A., Tershakovec, A. M., & Cronquist, J. L.
    (2003). Behavior therapy and sibutramine for the treatment
    of adolescent obesity. *Journal of the American Medical
    Association, 289*, 1805-1812.

Carmona, R. H. (2004, March 2). *The growing epidemic of childhood*
    3 *obesity.* Testimony before the Subcommittee on Competition,
    Foreign Commerce, and Infrastructure of the U.S. Senate
    Committee on Commerce, Science, and Transportation.
    Retrieved from http://www.hhs.gov/asl/testify/t040302.html

Critser, G. (2003). *Fat land.* Boston, MA: Houghton Mifflin.

Duenwald, M. (2004, January 6). Slim pickings: Looking beyond ephedra.
    The New York Times, p. F1. Retrieved from http://nytimes.com/

4 Henry J. Kaiser Family Foundation. (2004, February). *The role of
    media in childhood obesity.* Retrieved from http://www
    .kff.org/entmedia/7030.cfm

Hilts, P. J. (2002, March 20). Petition asks for removal of diet drug from
    market. *The New York Times,* p. A26. Retrieved from http://
    nytimes.com/

Hoppin, A. G., & Taveras, E. M. (2004, June 25). Assessment and
    management of childhood and adolescent obesity. *Clinical
    Update.* Retrieved from http://www.medscape.com
    /viewarticle/481633

McDuffie, J. R., Calis, K. A., Uwaifo, G. I., Sebring, N. G., Fallon,
    E. M., Hubbard, V. S., & Yanovski, J. A. (2002). Three-month
    tolerability of orlistat in adolescents with obesity-related
    comorbid conditions. *Obesity Research, 10,* 642–650.

1 Reference list on new page, heading centered. **2** Authors' names inverted and alphabetized. **3** First line of entry flush left, subsequent lines indented ½". **4** Double-spaced throughout.

Sample APA title page

1 Running head: ALL AND HTN IN ONE CLIENT **2** 1

Acute Lymphoblastic Leukemia and Hypertension in One Client:

A Nursing Practice Paper

Julie Riss **3**

George Mason University

Author Note

This paper was prepared for Nursing 451, taught by
4 Professor Durham. The author wishes to thank the nursing
staff of Milltown General Hospital for help in understanding
client care and diagnosis.

1 Short title in all capital letters on all pages; words
"Running head" on title page only. **2** Arabic page number
on all pages. **3** Full title and writer's name and affiliation,
centered. **4** Author's note (optional) for extra information.

(Annotations indicate APA-style formatting and effective
writing.)

Sample APA page

1 Acute Lymphoblastic Leukemia and Hypertension in One Client:
A Nursing Practice Paper

2 Historical and Physical Assessment

3 Physical History

    E.B. is a 16-year-old white male 5'10" tall weighing 190 lb. He was admitted to the hospital on April 14, 2006, due to decreased platelets and a need for a PRBC transfusion. He was diagnosed in October 2005 with T-cell acute lymphoblastic leukemia (ALL), after a 2-week **4** period of decreased energy, decreased oral intake, easy bruising, and petechia. The client had experienced a 20-lb weight loss in the previous 6 months. At the time of diagnosis, his CBC showed a WBC count of 32, an H & H of 13/38, and a platelet count of 34,000. He began induction chemotherapy on October 12, 2005, receiving vincristine, 6-mercaptopurine, doxorubicin, intrathecal methotrexate, and then high-dose methotrexate per protocol. During his hospital stay he required packed red cells and platelets on two different occasions. He was diagnosed with hypertension (HTN) due to systolic blood pressure readings consistently ranging between 130s and 150s and was started on nifedipine. E.B. has a history of mild ADHD, migraines, and deep vein thrombosis (DVT). He has tolerated the induction and consolidation phases of chemotherapy well and is now in the maintenance phase.

Psychosocial History

    There is a possibility of a depressive episode a year previously when he would not attend school. He got into serious trouble and was sent to a shelter for 1 month. He currently lives with his mother, father, and 14-year-old sister.

Family History

    Paternal: prostate cancer and hypertension in grandfather
    Maternal: breast cancer and heart disease

1 Full title, centered. **2** First-level heading, boldface and centered. **3** Second-level heading, boldface and flush left. **4** Writer's summary of client's medical history.

Sample APA list of references

References

Hockenberry, M. (2003). *Wong's nursing care of infants and children*.
    St. Louis, MO: Mosby.

Lemone, P., & Burke, K. (2004). *Medical surgical nursing: Critical* **1**
    thinking in client care. Upper Saddle River, NJ: Pearson
    Education.

1 Ampersand used with multiple authors.

Sample proposal, APA style

MEMORANDUM

To: Jay Crosson, Senior Vice President, Human Resources
From: Kelly Ratajczak, Intern, Purchasing Department
Subject: Proposal to Add a Wellness Program
Date: April 24, 2006

Health care costs are rising. In the long run, implementing a wellness program in our corporate culture will decrease the company's health care costs.

Research indicates that nearly 70% of health care costs are from common illnesses related to high blood pressure, overweight, lack of exercise, high cholesterol, stress, poor nutrition, and other preventable health issues (Hall, 2006). Health care costs are a major expense for most businesses, and they do not reflect costs due to the loss of productivity or absenteeism. A wellness program would address most, if not all, of these health care issues and related costs.

Benefits of Healthier Employees

Not only would a wellness program substantially reduce costs associated with employee health care, but our company would prosper through many other benefits. Businesses that have wellness programs show a lower cost in production, fewer sick days, and healthier employees ("Workplace Health," 2006). Our healthier employees will help to cut not only our production and absenteeism costs but also potential costs such as higher turnover because of low employee morale.

Implementing the Program

Implementing a good wellness program means making small changes to the work environment, starting with a series of information sessions.

---

1 First page in memo format. **2** Clear point in first paragraph. **3** Introduction provides background information. **4** Headings define sections.

(Annotations indicate typical business-style formatting and effective writing.)

Wellness Program Proposal 3

References

Hall, B. (2006). Good health pays off! Fundamentals of health promotion
    incentives. *Journal of Deferred Compensation 11*(2), 16-26. Retrieved
    from http://www.aspenpublishers.com/

Springer, D. (2005, October 28). Key to business success? *La Crosse
    Tribune*. Retrieved from http://lacrossetribune.com/

White, M. (2005). The cost-benefit of well employees. *Harvard Business
    Review, 83*(12), 22.

Workplace health and productivity programs lower absenteeism, costs. [1]
    (2006). *Managing benefit plans 6*(2), 1-4. Retrieved from
    http:/www.ioma.com/

[1] Work with no author listed by title.

Chicago
Papers

Most assignments in history and other humanities classes are based to some extent on reading. At times you will be asked to respond to one or two readings, such as essays or historical documents. At other times you may be asked to write a research paper that draws on a wide variety of sources.

Most history instructors and some humanities instructors require the *Chicago*-style footnotes or endnotes explained in section 42. When you write a paper using sources, you face three main challenges in addition to documenting those sources: (1) supporting a thesis, (2) avoiding plagiarism, and (3) integrating quotations and other source material.

39 Supporting a thesis

Most assignments ask you to form a thesis, or main idea, and to support that thesis with well-organized evidence.

39a Forming a thesis

A thesis is a one-sentence (or occasionally a two-sentence) statement of your central idea. Usually your thesis will appear at the end of the first paragraph (as in the example on p. 228), but if you need to provide readers with considerable background information, you may place it in the second paragraph.

The thesis of your paper will be a reasoned answer to the central research question you pose, as in the following examples.

RESEARCH QUESTION

To what extent was Confederate Major General Nathan Bedford Forrest responsible for the massacre of Union troops at Fort Pillow?

POSSIBLE THESIS

Although we will never know whether Nathan Bedford Forrest directly ordered the massacre of Union troops at Fort Pillow, evidence suggests that he was responsible for it.

RESEARCH QUESTION

How did the 365-day combat tour affect soldiers' experiences of the Vietnam War?

POSSIBLE THESIS

Letters and diaries written by combat soldiers in Vietnam reveal that when soldiers' tours of duty were shortened, their investment in the war shifted from fighting for victory to fighting for survival.

Notice that each of these thesis statements expresses a view on a debatable issue — an issue about which intelligent, well-meaning people might disagree. The writer's job is to convince such readers that this view is worth taking seriously.

ON THE WEB > **dianahacker.com/pocket** > Research exercises > *Chicago* > E-ex 39–1

39b Organizing your evidence

The body of your paper will consist of evidence in support of your thesis. Instead of getting tangled up in a complex, formal outline, sketch an informal plan that organizes your evidence in bold strokes. The student who wrote about Fort Pillow used a simple list of questions as the blueprint for his paper. In the paper itself, these became headings that helped readers follow the writer's line of argument.

What happened at Fort Pillow?

Did Forrest order the massacre?

Can Forrest be held responsible for the massacre?

39c Using sources to inform and support your argument

Sources can play several different roles as you develop your points.

Providing background information or context You can use facts and statistics to support generalizations or to establish the importance of your topic.

Explaining terms or concepts Explain words, phrases, or ideas important to your topic that may be unfamiliar to readers. Quoting or paraphrasing a source can help you define terms and concepts in neutral, accessible language.

Supporting your claims Back up your assertions with facts, examples, and other evidence from your research.

Lending authority to your argument Expert opinion can give weight to your argument. But don't rely on experts to make your argument for you. Construct your argument in your own words and cite authorities in the field for support.

Anticipating and countering objections Do not ignore sources that seem contrary to your position or that offer arguments different from your own. Instead, use them to raise opposing points of view before you counter them.

40 Avoiding plagiarism

Your research paper is a collaboration between you and your sources. To be fair and ethical, you must acknowledge your debt to the writers of those sources. If you don't, you commit plagiarism, a serious academic offense.

Three different acts are considered plagiarism: (1) failing to cite quotations and borrowed ideas, (2) failing to enclose borrowed language in quotation marks, and (3) failing to put summaries and paraphrases in your own words.

40a Citing quotations and borrowed ideas

You must cite all direct quotations or ideas borrowed from a source: summaries and paraphrases; statistics and other specific facts; and visuals such as cartoons, graphs, and diagrams.

The only exception is common knowledge—information your readers could easily locate. For example, the population of the United States is common knowledge among sociologists and economists, and historians are familiar with facts such as the date of the Emancipation Proclamation. When you have seen certain general information repeatedly in your reading, you don't need to cite it. However, when information has appeared in only a few sources, when it is highly specific (as with statistics), or when it is controversial, you should cite it.

Chicago citations consist of superscript numbers in the text of the paper that refer readers to notes with corresponding numbers either at the foot of the page (footnotes) or at the end of the paper (endnotes).

TEXT

Governor John Andrew was not allowed to recruit black soldiers from out of state. "Ostensibly," writes Peter Burchard, "no recruiting was done outside Massachusetts, but it was an open secret that Andrew's agents were working far and wide."[1]

NOTE

1. Peter Burchard, *One Gallant Rush: Robert Gould Shaw and His Brave Black Regiment* (New York: St. Martin's, 1965), 85.

For detailed advice on using *Chicago* notes, see 42a. When you use footnotes or endnotes, you will usually need to provide a bibliography as well (see 42b).

40b Enclosing borrowed language in quotation marks

To show that you are using a source's exact phrases or sentences, you must enclose them in quotation marks. To omit the quotation marks is to claim—falsely—that the language is your own. Such an omission is plagiarism even if you have cited the source.

ORIGINAL SOURCE

> For many Southerners it was psychologically impossible to see a black man bearing arms as anything but an incipient slave uprising complete with arson, murder, pillage, and rapine.
> —Dudley Taylor Cornish, *The Sable Arm: Negro Troops in the Union Army, 1861–1865*, p. 158

PLAGIARISM

According to Civil War historian Dudley Taylor Cornish, for many Southerners it was psychologically impossible to see a black man bearing arms as anything but an incipient slave uprising complete with arson, murder, pillage, and rapine.[2]

BORROWED LANGUAGE IN QUOTATION MARKS

According to Civil War historian Dudley Taylor Cornish, "For many Southerners it was psychologically impossible to see a black man bearing arms as anything but an incipient slave uprising complete with arson, murder, pillage, and rapine."[2]

NOTE: When quoted sentences are set off from the text by indenting, quotation marks are not needed (see p. 203).

40c Putting summaries and paraphrases in your own words

A summary condenses information; a paraphrase reports information in about the same number of words as in the source. When you summarize or paraphrase, you must restate the source's meaning using your own language.

In the following example, the paraphrase is plagiarized — even though the source is cited — because too much of its language is borrowed from the source without quotation marks. The underlined phrases have been copied word-for-word. In addition, the writer has closely followed the sentence structure of the original source, merely plugging in some synonyms (such as *fifty percent* for *half* and *savage hatred* for *fierce, bitter animosity*).

ORIGINAL SOURCE

> Half of the force holding Fort Pillow were Negroes, former slaves now enrolled in the Union Army. Toward them Forrest's troops had the fierce, bitter animosity of men who had been educated to regard the colored race as inferior and who for the first time had encountered that race armed and fighting against white men. The sight enraged and perhaps terrified many of the Confederates and aroused in them the ugly spirit of a lynching mob.
>   — Albert Castel, "The Fort Pillow Massacre," pp. 46–47

PLAGIARISM: UNACCEPTABLE BORROWING

Albert Castel suggests that much of the brutality at Fort Pillow can be traced to racial attitudes. Fifty percent of the troops holding Fort Pillow were Negroes, former slaves who had joined the Union Army. Toward them Forrest's soldiers displayed the savage hatred of men who had been taught the inferiority of blacks and who for the first time had confronted them armed and fighting against white men. The vision angered and perhaps frightened the Confederates and aroused in them the ugly spirit of a lynching mob.[3]

To avoid plagiarizing an author's language, set the source aside, write from memory, and consult the source later to check for accuracy.

ACCEPTABLE PARAPHRASE

Albert Castel suggests that much of the brutality at Fort Pillow can be traced to racial attitudes. Nearly half of the Union troops were blacks, men whom the Confederates had been raised to consider their inferiors. The shock and perhaps fear of facing armed ex-slaves in battle for the first time may well have unleashed the fury that led to the massacre.[3]

ON THE WEB > dianahacker.com/pocket > Research exercises > *Chicago* > E-ex 40–1 to 40–5

---

41 Integrating sources

Quotations, summaries, paraphrases, and facts will support your argument, but they cannot speak for you. You can use several strategies to integrate information from research sources into your paper while maintaining your own voice.

41a Limiting your use of quotations

Using quotations appropriately   Because it is almost impossible to integrate numerous long quotations smoothly into your own text, do not quote excessively. Often you can simply borrow a phrase or weave part of a source's sentence into your own sentence structure.

As Hurst has pointed out, until "an outcry erupted in the Northern press," even the Confederates did not deny that there had been a massacre at Fort Pillow.[4]

Union surgeon Dr. Charles Fitch testified that after he was in custody he "saw" Confederate soldiers "kill every negro that made his appearance dressed in Federal uniform."[20]

Using the ellipsis mark You can use the ellipsis mark (three periods, with spaces between) to condense a quoted passage and indicate that you have omitted words. What remains must be grammatically complete.

Union surgeon Fitch's testimony that all women and children had been evacuated from Fort Pillow before the attack conflicts with Forrest's report: "We captured . . . about 40 negro women and children."[6]

The writer has omitted several words not relevant to the issue at hand: *164 Federals, 75 negro troops, and.*

When you want to omit a full sentence or more, use a period before the three ellipsis dots. For an example, see the long quotation on page 204.

You do not need an ellipsis mark at the beginning or at the end of a quotation. Readers will understand that the quoted material is taken from a longer passage.

Using brackets Brackets allow you to insert your own words into quoted material to explain a confusing reference or to keep a sentence grammatical in your context.

According to Albert Castel, "It can be reasonably argued that he [Forrest] was justified in believing that the approaching steamships intended to aid the garrison [at Fort Pillow]."[7]

NOTE: Use [*sic*] to indicate that an error in a quoted sentence appears in the original source. (An example appears on p. 204.) However, if a source is filled with errors, this use of [*sic*] can become distracting and should be avoided.

Setting off long quotations *Chicago* style allows you to set off a long quotation or run it into your text. For emphasis, you may want to set off a quotation of more than five lines; you should always set off quotations of ten lines or more. To set off a quotation, indent it one-half inch (or five spaces) from the left margin and keep the standard right margin. Double-space the quotation.

Introduce long quotations with an informative sentence, usually ending in a colon. Because the indented format tells readers that the words are taken directly from the source, you don't need quotation marks.

In a letter home, Confederate officer Achilles V. Clark recounted what happened at Fort Pillow:

> Words cannot describe the scene. The poor deluded negroes would run up to our men fall upon their knees and with uplifted hands scream for mercy but they were ordered to their feet and then shot down. The whitte [*sic*] men fared but little better. . . . I with several others tried to stop the butchery and at one time had partially succeeded[,] but Gen. Forrest ordered them shot down like dogs[,] and the carnage continued.[8]

41b Using signal phrases to integrate sources

Introduce any paraphrase, summary, or direct quotation of another writer in your paper with a *signal phrase*. A signal phrase usually names the author of the source and often provides some context for the source material.

NOTE: The first time you mention an author, use the full name: *Shelby Foote argues.* . . . When you refer to the author again, you may use the last name only: *Foote raises an important question.*

Marking boundaries   Avoid dropping direct quotations into your text without warning. Provide clear signal phrases, including at least the author's name. A signal phrase indicates the boundary between your words and the source's words.

DROPPED QUOTATION

Unionists claimed that their troops had abandoned their arms and were in full retreat. "The Confederates, however, all agreed that the Union troops retreated to the river with arms in their hands."[9]

QUOTATION WITH SIGNAL PHRASE

Unionists claimed that their troops had abandoned their arms and were in full retreat. "The Confederates, however," writes historian Albert Castel, "all agreed that the Union troops retreated to the river with arms in their hands."[9]

Introducing summaries and paraphrases   Introduce most summaries and paraphrases with a signal phrase that

Using signal phrases in *Chicago* papers

To avoid monotony, try to vary the language and placement of your signal phrases.

MODEL SIGNAL PHRASES

In the words of historian James M. McPherson, ". . ."[1]

As Dudley Taylor Cornish has argued, ". . ."[2]

In a letter to his wife, a Confederate soldier who witnessed the massacre wrote that ". . ."[3]

". . . ," claims Benjamin Quarles.[4]

". . . ," writes Albert Castel, ". . ."[5]

Shelby Foote offers an intriguing interpretation: ". . ."[6]

VERBS IN SIGNAL PHRASES

Are you providing background, explaining a concept, supporting a claim, lending authority, or refuting a belief? Choose a verb that is appropriate for the way you are using the source.

admits	contends	reasons
agrees	declares	refutes
argues	denies	rejects
asserts	emphasizes	reports
believes	insists	responds
claims	notes	suggests
compares	observes	thinks
confirms	points out	writes

NOTE: In *Chicago* style, use the present tense or present perfect tense to introduce quotations or other material from nonfiction sources: *Foote points out that* or *Foote has pointed out that*. Use the past tense only to emphasize that the author's language or opinion was articulated in the past.

mentions the author and places the material in context. Readers will then understand where the summary or paraphrase begins.

The signal phrase (underlined) in the following example shows that the whole paragraph, not just the last sentence, is based on the source.

According to Jack Hurst, official Confederate policy was that black soldiers were to be treated as runaway slaves; in addition, the Confederate Congress decreed that white Union officers commanding black troops be killed. Confederate Lieutenant General Kirby Smith went one step further, declaring that he would kill all captured black troops. Smith's policy never met with strong opposition from the Richmond government.[10]

Putting source material in context   Readers need to understand how your source is relevant to your paper's argument. It's a good idea to embed your quotation—especially a long one—between sentences of your own, introducing it with a signal phrase and following it up with interpretive comments.

QUOTATION WITH EFFECTIVE CONTEXT

In a respected biography of Nathan Bedford Forrest, Hurst suggests that the temperamental Forrest "may have ragingly ordered a massacre and even intended to carry it out--until he rode inside the fort and viewed the horrifying result" and ordered it stopped.[11] While this is an intriguing intepretation of events, even Hurst would probably admit that it is merely speculation.

41c Integrating statistics and other facts

When you cite a statistic or another specific fact, a signal phrase is often not necessary. In most cases, readers will understand that the citation refers to the statistic or fact (not the whole paragraph).

Of 295 white troops garrisoned at Fort Pillow, 168 were taken prisoner. Black troops fared worse, with only 58 of 262 captured and most of the rest presumably killed or wounded.[12]

There is nothing wrong, however, with using a signal phrase.

Shelby Foote notes that of 295 white troops garrisoned at Fort Pillow, 168 were taken prisoner but that black troops fared worse, with only 58 of 262 captured and most of the rest presumably killed or wounded.[12]

ON THE WEB > dianahacker.com/pocket > Research exercises > *Chicago* > E-ex 41–1 to 41–4

42 *Chicago* documentation style (notes and bibliography)

Professors in history and some humanities courses often require footnotes or endnotes based on *The Chicago Manual of Style* (see 42a). When you use *Chicago*-style notes, you will usually be asked to include a bibliography at the end of your paper (see 42b).

42a First and subsequent references to a source

The first time you cite a source, the note should include publication information for that work as well as the page number on which the passage you cite may be found.

   1. Peter Burchard, *One Gallant Rush: Robert Gould Shaw and His Brave Black Regiment* (New York: St. Martin's, 1965), 85.

   For subsequent references to a source you have already cited, you may simply give the author's last name, a short form of the title, and the page or pages cited. A short form of the title of a book is italicized; a short form of the title of an article is put in quotation marks.

   4. Burchard, *One Gallant Rush,* 31.

When you have two consecutive notes from the same source, you may use "Ibid." (meaning "in the same place") and the page number for the second note. Use "Ibid." alone if the page number is the same.

   5. Jack Hurst, *Nathan Bedford Forrest: A Biography* (New York: Knopf, 1993), 8.

   6. Ibid., 174.

42b *Chicago*-style bibliography

A bibliography, which appears at the end of your paper, lists every work you have cited in your notes; in addition, it may include works that you consulted but did not cite. For advice on constructing the list, see page 226. A sample bibliography appears on page 230.

NOTE: If you include a bibliography, *The Chicago Manual of Style* suggests that you shorten all notes, including the first reference to a source, as described in 42a. Check with your instructor, however, to see whether using an abbreviated note for a first reference to a source is acceptable.

42c Model notes and bibliography entries

The following models are consistent with guidelines in *The Chicago Manual of Style,* 16th edition. For each type of source, a note appears first, followed by a bibliography entry. The note shows the format you should use when citing a source for the first time. For subsequent citations of a source, use shortened notes (see 42a).

Some online sources use a permanent locator called a digital object identifier (DOI). Use the DOI, when available, in place of a URL in citations of online sources.

ON THE WEB > dianahacker.com/pocket > Research exercises > *Chicago* > E-ex 42–1

DIRECTORY TO *CHICAGO*-STYLE NOTES AND BIBLIOGRAPHY ENTRIES

Books (print and online)

■ 1. Basic format for a print book

1. William H. Rehnquist, *The Supreme Court: A History* (New York: Knopf, 2001), 204.

Rehnquist, William H. *The Supreme Court: A History*. New York: Knopf, 2001.

(For an annotated example, see p. 210.)

■ 2. Basic format for an online book

2. John Dewey, *Democracy and Education* (1916; ILT Digital Classics, 1994), chap. 4, http://www.ilt.columbia.edu /publications/dewey.html.

Dewey, John. *Democracy and Education*. 1916. ILT Digital Classics, 1994. http://www.ilt.columbia.edu/publications /dewey.html.

■ 3. Basic format for an e-book (electronic book)

3. Leo Tolstoy, *War and Peace*, trans. Richard Pevear and Larissa Volokhonsky (New York: Knopf, 2007), Kindle edition, vol. 1, pt. 1, chap. 3.

Tolstoy, Leo. *War and Peace*. Translated by Richard Pevear and Larissa Volokhonsky. New York: Knopf, 2007. Kindle edition.

■ 4. Two or more authors

Two or three authors

4. Michael D. Coe and Mark Van Stone, *Reading the Maya Glyphs* (London: Thames and Hudson, 2002), 129-30.

Coe, Michael D., and Mark Van Stone. *Reading the Maya Glyphs*. London: Thames and Hudson, 2002.

Citation at a glance
Book (*Chicago*)

To cite a print book in *Chicago* style, include the following elements:

1 Author
2 Title and subtitle
3 City of publication
4 Publisher

5 Year of publication
6 Page number(s) cited (for notes)

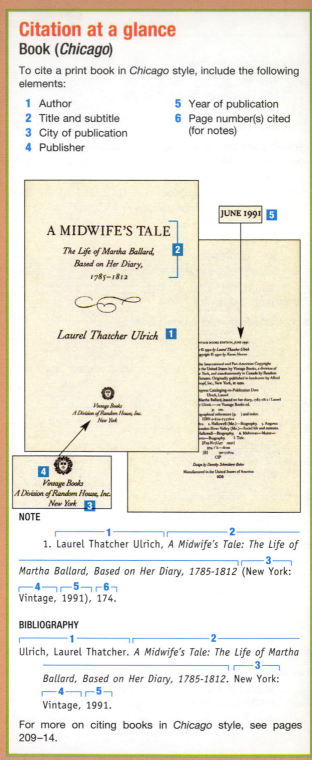

NOTE

1. Laurel Thatcher Ulrich, *A Midwife's Tale: The Life of Martha Ballard, Based on Her Diary, 1785-1812* (New York: Vintage, 1991), 174.

BIBLIOGRAPHY

Ulrich, Laurel Thatcher. *A Midwife's Tale: The Life of Martha Ballard, Based on Her Diary, 1785-1812*. New York: Vintage, 1991.

For more on citing books in *Chicago* style, see pages 209–14.

Four or more authors

4. Lynn Hunt et al., *The Making of the West: Peoples and Cultures,* 3rd ed. (Boston: Bedford/St. Martin's, 2009), 541.

Hunt, Lynn, Thomas R. Martin, Barbara H. Rosenwein, R. Po-chia Hsia, and Bonnie G. Smith. *The Making of the West: Peoples and Cultures.* 3rd ed. Boston: Bedford/St. Martin's, 2009.

■ 5. Unknown author

5. *The Men's League Handbook on Women's Suffrage* (London, 1912), 23.

The Men's League Handbook on Women's Suffrage. London, 1912.

■ 6. Edited work without an author

6. Jack Beatty, ed., *Colossus: How the Corporation Changed America* (New York: Broadway Books, 2001), 127.

Beatty, Jack, ed. *Colossus: How the Corporation Changed America.* New York: Broadway Books, 2001.

■ 7. Edited work with an author

7. Ted Poston, *A First Draft of History,* ed. Kathleen A. Hauke (Athens: University of Georgia Press, 2000), 46.

Poston, Ted. *A First Draft of History.* Edited by Kathleen A. Hauke. Athens: University of Georgia Press, 2000.

■ 8. Translated work

8. Tonino Guerra, *Abandoned Places,* trans. Adria Bernardi (Barcelona: Guernica, 1999), 71.

Guerra, Tonino. *Abandoned Places.* Translated by Adria Bernardi. Barcelona: Guernica, 1999.

■ 9. Edition other than the first

9. Andrew F. Rolle, *California: A History,* 5th ed. (Wheeling, IL: Harlan Davidson, 1998), 243.

Rolle, Andrew F. *California: A History.* 5th ed. Wheeling, IL: Harlan Davidson, 1998.

■ 10. Volume in a multivolume work

10. James M. McPherson, *Ordeal by Fire,* vol. 2, *The Civil War* (New York: McGraw-Hill, 1993), 205.

McPherson, James M. *Ordeal by Fire.* Vol. 2, *The Civil War.* New York: McGraw-Hill, 1993.

■ 11. Work in an anthology

11. Zora Neale Hurston, "From *Dust Tracks on a Road,*" in *The Norton Book of American Autobiography,* ed. Jay Parini (New York: Norton, 1999), 336.

Citation at a glance
Letter in a published collection (*Chicago*)

To cite a letter in a published collection in *Chicago* style, include the following elements:

1 Author of letter
2 Recipient of letter
3 Date of letter
4 Title of collection
5 Editor of collection
6 City of publication
7 Publisher
8 Year of publication
9 Page number(s) cited (for notes); page range of letter (for bibliography)

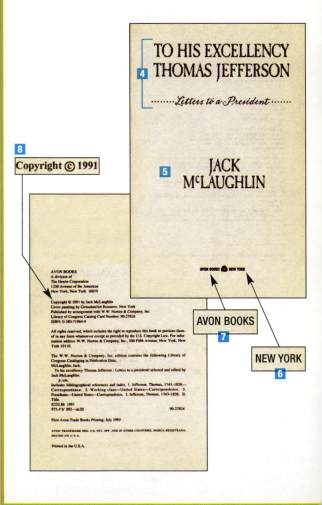

TO HIS EXCELLENCY
THOMAS JEFFERSON
········· *Letters to a President* ·······

JACK
McLAUGHLIN

Copyright © 1991

AVON BOOKS
A division of
The Hearst Corporation
1350 Avenue of the Americas
New York, New York 10019

Copyright © 1991 by Jack McLaughlin
Cover painting by Giraudon/Art Resource, New York
Published by arrangement with W.W. Norton & Company, Inc.
Library of Congress Catalog Card Number: 90-27824
ISBN: 0-380-71964-9

All rights reserved, which includes the right to reproduce this book or portions thereof in any form whatsoever except as provided by the U.S. Copyright Law. For information address W.W. Norton & Company, Inc., 500 Fifth Avenue, New York, New York 10110.

The W.W. Norton & Company, Inc. edition contains the following Library of Congress Cataloging in Publication Data:
McLaughlin, Jack.
   To his excellency Thomas Jefferson : Letters to a president/ selected and edited by Jack McLaughlin.
      p. cm.
   Includes bibliographical references and index. 1. Jefferson, Thomas, 1743–1826—Correspondence. 2. Working class—United States—Correspondence. 3. Presidents—United States—Correspondence. I. Jefferson, Thomas, 1743–1826. II. Title.
E332.86 1991
973.4'6' 092—dc20   90-27824

First Avon Trade Books Printing: July 1993

AVON TRADEMARK REG. U.S. PAT. OFF. AND IN OTHER COUNTRIES, MARCA REGISTRADA, HECHO EN U.S.A.

Printed in the U.S.A.

AVON BOOKS 🖙 NEW YORK

AVON BOOKS
7

NEW YORK
6

Washington 30th. Oct 1805 **3**

His Excellency Ths. Jefferson **2**

Sir,

I have not the honor to be personally known to your Excellency therefore you will no doubt think it strange to receive this letter from a person of whom you have not the smallest knowledge. But in order to state to your Excellency in as few words as possible the purport of this address, I am a young man, a Roman Catholic who had been born and partly educated in Ireland but finding like many others who

Patronage   6 1 **9**

your Excellency this very prolix letter which should it please your Excellency to give me some little Office or appointment in that extensive Country of Louisiana It should be my constant endeavour to merit the same by fidelity and an indefatigable attention to whatever business I should be assigned. May I have the satisfaction in whatsoever Country or situation [I] may be in to hear of your Excellencies long continuence of your Natural powers unempaired to conduct the Helm of this Extensive Country which are the sincere wishes of your Excellencies Mo. Obt. Hum. Servt.

1 JOHN O'NEILL

NOTE

1. John O'Neill to Thomas Jefferson, 30 October 1805, in To *His Excellency Thomas Jefferson: Letters to a President,* ed. Jack McLaughlin (New York: Avon Books, 1991), 61.

BIBLIOGRAPHY

O'Neill, John. John O'Neill to Thomas Jefferson, 30 October 1805. In *To His Excellency Thomas Jefferson: Letters to a President*, edited by Jack McLaughlin, 59–61. New York: Avon Books, 1991.

For another citation of a letter in *Chicago* style, see item 12.

Hurston, Zora Neale. "From *Dust Tracks on a Road.*" In *The Norton Book of American Autobiography,* edited by Jay Parini, 333-43. New York: Norton, 1999.

■ **12. Letter in a published collection** If the letter writer's name is part of the book title, begin the note with the writer's last name but begin the bibliography entry with the full name. (For an annotated example, see pp. 212–13.)

12. Mitford to Esmond Romilly, 29 July 1940, in *Decca: The Letters of Jessica Mitford*, ed. Peter Y. Sussman (New York: Knopf, 2006), 55-56.

Mitford, Jessica. *Decca: The Letters of Jessica Mitford.* Edited by Peter Y. Sussman. New York: Knopf, 2006.

■ **13. Work in a series**

13. R. Keith Schoppa, *The Columbia Guide to Modern Chinese History,* Columbia Guides to Asian History (New York: Columbia University Press, 2000), 256-58.

Schoppa, R. Keith. *The Columbia Guide to Modern Chinese History.* Columbia Guides to Asian History. New York: Columbia University Press, 2000.

■ **14. Encyclopedia or dictionary entry**

14. *Encyclopaedia Britannica,* 15th ed., s.v. "Monroe Doctrine."

The abbreviation "s.v." is for the Latin *sub verbo* ("under the word").

Reference works are usually not included in the bibliography.

■ **15. Sacred text**

15. Matt. 20:4-9 (Revised Standard Version).

15. Qur'an 18:1-3.

Sacred texts are usually not included in the bibliography.

Articles in periodicals (print and online)

■ **16. Article in a journal** For an article in a print journal, include the volume and issue numbers and the date; end the bibliography entry with the page range of the article. (For an annotated example, see p. 215.)

16. T. H. Breen, "Will American Consumers Buy a Second American Revolution?," *Journal of American History* 93, no. 2 (2006): 405.

Breen, T. H. "Will American Consumers Buy a Second American Revolution?" *Journal of American History* 93, no. 2 (2006): 404-8.

Citation at a glance
Article in a scholarly journal (*Chicago*)

To cite a print article in a scholarly journal in *Chicago* style, include the following elements:

1 Author
2 Title of article
3 Title of journal
4 Volume and issue numbers
5 Date of publication
6 Page number(s)

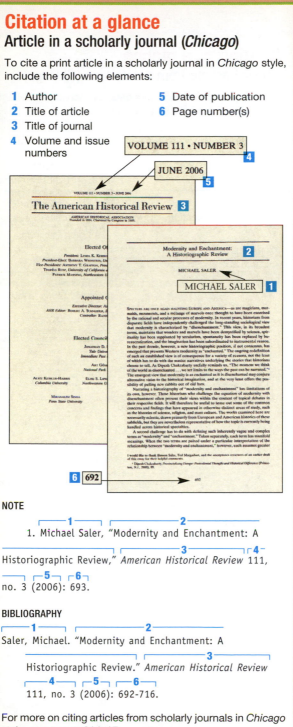

VOLUME 111 · NUMBER 3 4

JUNE 2006 5

The American Historical Review 3

Modernity and Enchantment: A Historiographic Review 2

MICHAEL SALER

MICHAEL SALER 1

6 692

NOTE

1 2
1. Michael Saler, "Modernity and Enchantment: A

3 4
Historiographic Review," *American Historical Review* 111,

5 6
no. 3 (2006): 693.

BIBLIOGRAPHY

1 2
Saler, Michael. "Modernity and Enchantment: A

3
Historiographic Review." *American Historical Review*

4 5 6
111, no. 3 (2006): 692-716.

For more on citing articles from scholarly journals in *Chicago* style, see pages 214–17.

Citation at a glance
Journal article from a database (*Chicago*)

To cite a journal article from a database service in *Chicago* style, include the following elements:

1 Author
2 Title of article
3 Title of journal
4 Volume and issue numbers
5 Year of publication

6 Page number(s) (for notes); page range (for bibliography)
7 DOI; *or* database name and article number; *or* "stable" or "persistent" URL for article

---

EBSCO HOST Research Databases | Basic Search | Advanced Search | Visual Search | Choose Databases

New Search | Keyword | Publications | Subject Terms | Cited References | Index

◀ 2 of 2 ▶   Result List | Refine Search   🖨 Print 📧 E-mail 💾 Save 📤 Export 🖨 Ad

View: 🖼 Citation 📄 PDF Full Text (3.8MB)

Title: **2**	The Promise and Disillusion of Americanization: Sur Terrain of Early-Twentieth-Century *Puerto Rico*.
Authors: **1**	Guerra, Lillian
Source: **3**	Centro Journal; Fall1999, Vol. 11 Issue 1, p8-31, 24p **5** **4** **6**
Document Type:	Article
Subject Terms:	*AMERICANIZATION *COFFEE industry *COLONIZATION *IMPERIALISM
Geographic Terms:	PUERTO Rico UNITED States
NAICS/Industry Codes:	311920 Coffee and Tea Manufacturing
Abstract:	Explores the early impact of U.S. imperialism in *Puerto Rico*. the impact of Americanization; Example of the U.S. colonial p
ISSN:	1538-6279
Accession Number: **7**	10672276
Persistent link to this record:	http://ezp1.harvard.edu/login?url=http://search.ebscohost.com direct=true&db=aph&AN=10672276&site=ehost-live&scope=si
Database **7**	Academic Search Premier
View Links:	FIND IT ⑤ HARVARD

View: 🖼 Citation 📄 PDF Full Text (3.8MB)

◀ 2 of 2 ▶   Result List | Refine Search   🖨 Print 📧 E-mail 💾 Save 📤 Export 🖨 Ad

Top of Page

EBSCO Support Site
Privacy Policy | Terms of Use | Copy
© 2007 EBSCO Industries, Inc. All rights r

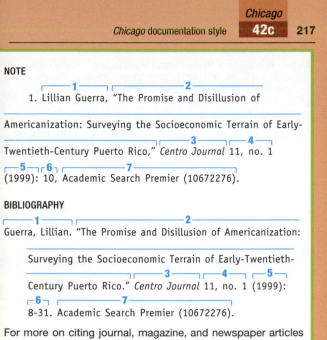

NOTE

1. Lillian Guerra, "The Promise and Disillusion of Americanization: Surveying the Socioeconomic Terrain of Early-Twentieth-Century Puerto Rico," *Centro Journal* 11, no. 1 (1999): 10, Academic Search Premier (10672276).

BIBLIOGRAPHY

Guerra, Lillian. "The Promise and Disillusion of Americanization: Surveying the Socioeconomic Terrain of Early-Twentieth-Century Puerto Rico." *Centro Journal* 11, no. 1 (1999): 8-31. Academic Search Premier (10672276).

For more on citing journal, magazine, and newspaper articles from databases in *Chicago* style, see items 16, 17, and 18.

Journal article from a database

Give whatever identifying information is available in the database listing: a DOI for the article; the name of the database and the number assigned by the database; or a "stable" or "persistent" URL for the article. (For an annotated example, see pp. 216–17.)

16. Constant Leung, "Language and Content in Bilingual Education," *Linguistics and Education* 16, no. 2 (2005): 239, doi:10.1016/j.linged.2006.01.004.

Leung, Constant. "Language and Content in Bilingual Education." *Linguistics and Education* 16, no. 2 (2005): 238-52. doi:10.1016/j.linged.2006.01.004.

Journal article published online

Give the DOI if the article has one; if there is no DOI, give the URL for the article. In a note for an unpaginated article, you may include locators, such as numbered paragraphs or headings, if the article has them.

16. Brian Lennon, "New Media Critical Homologies," *Postmodern Culture* 19, no. 2 (2009), http://pmc.iath.virginia.edu/text-only/issue.109/19.2lennon.txt.

Lennon, Brian. "New Media Critical Homologies." *Postmodern Culture* 19, no. 2 (2009). http://pmc.iath.virginia.edu /text-only/issue.109/19.2lennon.txt.

■ **17. Article in a magazine**   For a print article, provide a page number in the note and a page range in the bibliography.

17. Tom Bissell, "Improvised, Explosive, and Divisive," *Harper's,* January 2006, 42.

Bissell, Tom. "Improvised, Explosive, and Divisive." *Harper's,* January 2006, 41-54.

Magazine article from a database

Give whatever identifying information is available in the database listing: a DOI for the article; the name of the database and the number assigned by the database; or a "stable" or "persistent" URL for the article.

18. "Facing Facts in Afghanistan," *National Review,* November 2, 2009, 14, Expanded Academic ASAP (A209905060).

"Facing Facts in Afghanistan." *National Review,* November 2, 2009, 14. Expanded Academic ASAP (A209905060).

Magazine article published online

17. Fiona Morgan, "Banning the Bullies," *Salon,* March 15, 2001, http://www.salon.com/news/feature/2001/03/15 /bullying/index.html.

Morgan, Fiona. "Banning the Bullies." *Salon,* March 15, 2001. http://www.salon.com/news/feature/2001/03/15/bullying /index.html.

■ **18. Article in a newspaper**   Page numbers are not necessary; a section letter or number, if available, is sufficient.

18. Dan Barry, "A Mill Closes, and a Hamlet Fades to Black," *New York Times,* February 16, 2001, sec. A.

Barry, Dan. "A Mill Closes, and a Hamlet Fades to Black." *New York Times,* February 16, 2001, sec. A.

Newspaper article from a database

Give whatever identifying information is available in the database listing: a DOI for the article; the name of the database and the number assigned by the database; or a "stable" or "persistent" URL for the article.

18. Clifford J. Levy, "In Kyrgyzstan, Failure to Act Adds to Crisis," *New York Times*, June 18, 2010, General OneFile (A229196045).

Levy, Clifford J. "In Kyrgyzstan, Failure to Act Adds to Crisis." *New York Times*, June 18, 2010. General OneFile (A229196045).

Newspaper article published online

Include the URL for the article; if the URL is very long, use the URL for the newspaper's home page. Omit page numbers, even if the source provides them.

18. Doyle McManus, "The Candor War," *Chicago Tribune*, July 29, 2010, http://www.chicagotribune.com/.

McManus, Doyle. "The Candor War." *Chicago Tribune*, July 29, 2010. http://www.chicagotribune.com/.

■ **19. Unsigned newspaper article**   Begin the note with the title of the article; begin the bibliography entry with the name of the periodical.

19. "Renewable Energy Rules," *Boston Globe,* August 11, 2003, sec. A.

Boston Globe. "Renewable Energy Rules." August 11, 2003, sec. A.

■ **20. Book review**

20. Nancy Gabin, review of *The Other Feminists: Activists in the Liberal Establishment,* by Susan M. Hartman, *Journal of Women's History* 12, no. 3 (2000): 230.

Gabin, Nancy. Review of *The Other Feminists: Activists in the Liberal Establishment,* by Susan M. Hartman. *Journal of Women's History* 12, no. 3 (2000): 227-34.

Web sites and postings

For most Web sites, include an author if a site has one, the title of the site, the sponsor, the date of publication or modified date (date of most recent update), and the site's URL. Do not italicize a Web site title unless the site is an online book or periodical. Use quotation marks for the titles of sections or pages in a Web site. If a site does not have a date of publication or modified date, give the date you accessed the site ("accessed January 3, 2010").

Citation at a glance
Primary source from a Web site (*Chicago*)

To cite a primary source (or any other document) from a Web site in *Chicago* style, include as many of the following elements as are available:

1 Author

2 Title of document

3 Title of site

4 Sponsor of site

5 Publication date or modified date; date of access if none

6 URL of document

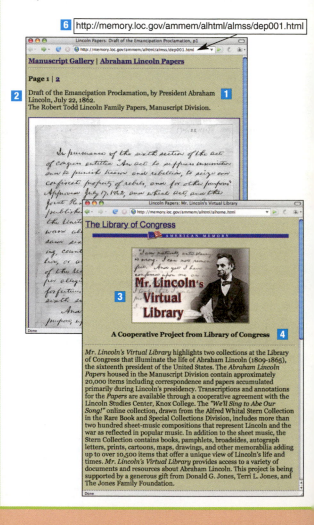

6 http://memory.loc.gov/ammem/alhtml/almss/dep001.html

Lincoln Papers: Draft of the Emancipation Proclamation, p1

Manuscript Gallery | Abraham Lincoln Papers

Page 1 | 2

2 Draft of the Emancipation Proclamation, by President Abraham Lincoln, July 22, 1862. **1**
The Robert Todd Lincoln Family Papers, Manuscript Division.

Lincoln Papers: Mr. Lincoln's Virtual Library

The Library of Congress

AMERICAN MEMORY

3 **Mr. Lincoln's Virtual Library**

A Cooperative Project from Library of Congress **4**

Mr. Lincoln's Virtual Library highlights two collections at the Library of Congress that illuminate the life of Abraham Lincoln (1809–1865), the sixteenth president of the United States. The *Abraham Lincoln Papers* housed in the Manuscript Division contain approximately 20,000 items including correspondence and papers accumulated primarily during Lincoln's presidency. Transcriptions and annotations for the *Papers* are available through a cooperative agreement with the Lincoln Studies Center, Knox College. The *"We'll Sing to Abe Our Song!"* online collection, drawn from the Alfred Whital Stern Collection in the Rare Book and Special Collections Division, includes more than two hundred sheet-music compositions that represent Lincoln and the war as reflected in popular music. In addition to the sheet music, the Stern Collection contains books, pamphlets, broadsides, autograph letters, prints, cartoons, maps, drawings, and other memorabilia adding up to over 10,500 items that offer a unique view of Lincoln's life and times. *Mr. Lincoln's Virtual Library* provides access to a variety of documents and resources about Abraham Lincoln. This project is being supported by a generous gift from Donald G. Jones, Terri L. Jones, and The Jones Family Foundation.

NOTE

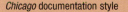

1. Abraham Lincoln, "Draft of the Emancipation Proclamation," Mr. Lincoln's Virtual Library, Library of Congress, accessed July 24, 2010, http://memory.loc.gov/ammem /alhtml/almss/dep001.html.

BIBLIOGRAPHY

Lincoln, Abraham. "Draft of the Emancipation Proclamation." Mr. Lincoln's Virtual Library. Library of Congress. Accessed July 24, 2010. http://memory.loc.gov/ammem/alhtml /almss/dep001.html.

For more on citing documents from Web sites in *Chicago* style, see pages 219–22.

■ 21. Web site

21. Chesapeake and Ohio Canal National Historical Park, National Park Service, last modified April 9, 2010, http:// www.nps.gov/choh/index.htm.

Chesapeake and Ohio Canal National Historical Park. National Park Service. Last modified April 9, 2010. http://www.nps .gov/choh/index.htm.

■ 22. Short document from a Web site

22. George P. Landow, "Victorian and Victorianism," Victorian Web, last modified August 2, 2009, http:// victorianweb.org/vn/victor4.html.

Landow, George P. "Victorian and Victorianism." Victorian Web. Last modified August 2, 2009. http://victorianweb.org /vn/victor4.html.

(For an annotated example, see pp. 220–21.)

■ **23. Blog (Weblog) post**   Treat as a short document from a Web site (item 22). Put the title of the posting in quotation marks; italicize the name of the blog. Insert "blog" in parentheses after the name if the word *blog* is not part of the name.

23. Miland Brown, "The Flawed Montevideo Convention of 1933," *World History Blog*, May 31, 2008, http://www.worldhistoryblog.com/2008/05/flawed-montevideo-convention-of-1933.html.

Brown, Miland. "The Flawed Montevideo Convention of 1933." *World History Blog.* May 31, 2008. http://www.worldhistoryblog.com/2008/05/flawed-montevideo-convention-of-1933.html.

■ **24. Online posting or e-mail**   E-mails that are not part of an online discussion are treated as personal communications (see item 27). Online postings and e-mails are not included in the bibliography.

24. Mary Gray to Copyediting-L discussion list, July 17, 2010, http://listserv.indiana.edu/archives/copyediting-l.html.

Other sources (print, online, multimedia)

■ **25. Government document**

25. U.S. Department of State, *Foreign Relations of the United States: Diplomatic Papers, 1943* (Washington, DC: GPO, 1965), 562.

U.S. Department of State. *Foreign Relations of the United States: Diplomatic Papers, 1943.* Washington, DC: GPO, 1965.

■ **26. Unpublished dissertation**

26. Stephanie Lynn Budin, "The Origins of Aphrodite" (PhD diss., University of Pennsylvania, 2000), 301-2, ProQuest (AAT 9976404).

Budin, Stephanie Lynn. "The Origins of Aphrodite." PhD diss., University of Pennsylvania, 2000. ProQuest (AAT 9976404).

■ **27. Personal communication**

27. Sara Lehman, e-mail message to author, August 13, 2003.

Personal communications are not included in the bibliography.

■ **28. Published or broadcast interview**

28. Robert Downey Jr., interview by Graham Norton, *The Graham Norton Show*, BBC America, December 14, 2009.

How to cite a source without a model

Sometimes you may consult sources for which *Chicago* does not provide citation models. When you encounter such a source, gather the same kinds of information as you do for other sources—author/creator, title, sponsor, date created or modified. Then consult the available models in this section to see which models have features similar to your source. You may need to combine elements from different models, as in items 23 and 29.

Your goal is always to provide readers with enough information to locate the source and to assess its reliability. The following questions may help.

- Is the source originally video, audio, or both? (See items 28–31.)
- Is the source an electronic or audio/video version of a print source? (See the model for the relevant print source.)
- What kinds of sources are similar to this source?
- Does the source list a date on which it was created or modified?

When citing any source without a model, check your work with your instructor.

Downey, Robert, Jr. Interview by Graham Norton. *Graham Norton Show*. BBC America, December 14, 2009.

■ **29. Podcast**   Treat as a short work from a Web site (item 22), including the following, if available: the author's (or speaker's) name; the title of the podcast, in quotation marks; an identifying number, if any; the title of the site on which the podcast appears; the sponsor of the site; and the URL. Before the URL, identify the type of podcast or file format and the date of posting or your date of access.

38. Paul Tiyambe Zeleza, "Africa's Global Past," Episode 40, Africa Past and Present, African Online Digital Library, podcast audio, April 29, 2010, http://afripod.aodl.org/.

Zeleza, Paul Tiyambe. "Africa's Global Past." Episode 40. Africa Past and Present. African Online Digital Library. Podcast audio. April 29, 2010. http://afripod.aodl.org/.

■ **30. Video or DVD**

30. *The Secret of Roan Inish*, directed by John Sayles (1993; Culver City, CA: Columbia TriStar Home Video, 2000), DVD.

The Secret of Roan Inish. Directed by John Sayles. 1993; Culver City, CA: Columbia TriStar Home Video, 2000. DVD.

■ **31. Sound recording**

31. Gustav Holst, *The Planets,* Royal Philharmonic Orchestra, conducted by André Previn, Telarc 80133, compact disc.

Holst, Gustav. *The Planets*. Royal Philharmonic Orchestra. Conducted by André Previn. Telarc 80133. Compact disc.

■ **32. Source quoted in another source**

32. Adam Smith, *The Wealth of Nations* (New York: Random House, 1965), 11, quoted in Mark Skousen, *The Making of Modern Economics: The Lives and the Ideas of the Great Thinkers* (Armonk, NY: M. E. Sharpe, 2001), 15.

Smith, Adam. *The Wealth of Nations*, 11. New York: Random House, 1965. Quoted in Mark Skousen, *The Making of Modern Economics: The Lives and the Ideas of the Great Thinkers* (Armonk, NY: M. E. Sharpe, 2001), 15.

ON THE WEB > **dianahacker.com/pocket** > Research exercises > *Chicago* > E-ex 42–2 to 42–6

---

43 | *Chicago* manuscript format; sample pages

43a *Chicago* manuscript format

The following guidelines for formatting a *Chicago* paper and preparing its endnotes and bibliography are based on *The Chicago Manual of Style,* 16th ed. (Chicago: U of Chicago P, 2010). For pages from a sample paper, see 43b.

Formatting the paper   *Chicago* manuscript guidelines are fairly generic because they were not created with a specific type of writing in mind.

Title page   Include the full title of your paper, your name, the course title, the instructor's name, and the date. Do not number the title page but count it in the manuscript numbering; that is, the first page of the text will be numbered 2. See page 227 for a sample title page.

Pagination   Using arabic numerals, number all pages except the title page in the upper right corner. You may also place your last name to the left of the page number.

Margins and line spacing   Leave margins of at least one inch at the top, bottom, and sides of the page. Double-space the entire manuscript, including long quotations that have been set off from the text. (For line spacing in notes and the bibliography, see p. 226.) Left-align the text.

Long quotations   See page 203 for *Chicago* guidelines for setting off long quotations from the text.

Visuals   *The Chicago Manual* classifies visuals as tables and figures or illustrations (which include drawings, photographs, maps, and charts).

Label each table with an arabic numeral (Table 1, Table 2, and so on) and provide a clear title that identifies the subject. The label and title should appear on separate lines above the table, flush left. Below the table, give its source in a note like this one:

> *Source:* Edna Bonacich and Richard P. Appelbaum, *Behind the Label* (Berkeley: University of California Press, 2000), 145.

For each figure, place a label and a caption below the figure, flush left. The label and caption need not appear on separate lines. The word "Figure" may be abbreviated to "Fig."

Place visuals as close as possible to the sentences that relate to them unless your instructor prefers that visuals appear in an appendix.

URLs (Web addresses)   When a URL must be divided at the end of a line in the notes or bibliography, break the URL after a colon or a double slash or before any other mark of punctuation. If your word processing program automatically turns URLs into links (by underlining them and changing the color), turn off this feature.

Preparing the endnotes   Begin the endnotes on a new page at the end of the paper. Center the title Notes about one inch from the top of the page, and number the pages consecutively with the rest of the manuscript. See page 229 for an example.

Indenting and numbering Indent the first line of each note one-half inch from the left margin; do not indent additional lines in the note. Begin the note with the arabic numeral that corresponds to the number in the text. Put a period after the number.

Line spacing Single-space each note and double-space between notes (unless your instructor prefers double-spacing throughout).

Preparing the bibliography Typically, the notes in *Chicago* papers are followed by a bibliography, an alphabetically arranged list of all the works cited or consulted (see p. 230 for an example). Center the title Bibliography about one inch from the top of the page. Number bibliography pages consecutively with the rest of the paper.

Alphabetizing the list Alphabetize the bibliography by the last names of the authors (or editors); when a work has no author or editor, alphabetize by the first word of the title other than *A, An,* or *The.*

If your list includes two or more works by the same author, use three hyphens instead of the author's name in all entries after the first. Arrange the entries alphabetically by title.

Indenting and line spacing Begin each entry at the left margin, and indent any additional lines one-half inch. Single-space each entry and double-space between entries (unless your instructor prefers double-spacing throughout).

43b Sample pages from a *Chicago* paper

On the following pages is an excerpt from a research paper written for a history class.

ON THE WEB > **dianahacker.com/pocket >** Model papers > *Chicago* paper: Bishop

The Massacre at Fort Pillow: **1**

Holding Nathan Bedford Forrest Accountable

Ned Bishop   **2**

History 214   **3**

Professor Citro

March 22, 2001

1 Paper title, centered. **2** Writer's name. **3** Course title, instructor's name, date.

Annotations indicate CMS-style formatting and effective writing.

Sample *Chicago* page

Bishop 2

Although Northern newspapers of the time no doubt exaggerated some of the Confederate atrocities at Fort Pillow, most modern sources agree that a massacre of Union troops took place there on April 12, 1864. It seems clear that Union soldiers, particularly black soldiers, were killed after they had stopped fighting or had surrendered or were being held prisoner. Less clear is the role played by Major General Nathan Bedford Forrest in leading his troops. Although we will never know whether Forrest directly **1** ordered the massacre, evidence suggests that he was responsible for it.

What happened at Fort Pillow? **2**

Fort Pillow, Tennessee, which sat on a bluff overlooking the Mississippi River, had been held by the Union for two years. It was garrisoned by 580 men, 292 of them from United States Colored Heavy and Light Artillery regiments, 285 from the white Thirteenth Tennessee Cavalry. Nathan Bedford Forrest commanded about 1,500 troops.[1]

The Confederates attacked Fort Pillow on April 12, 1864, and had virtually surrounded the fort by the time Forrest arrived on the battlefield. At 3:30 p.m., Forrest demanded the surrender of the Union forces, sending in a message of the sort he had used before: "The conduct of the officers and men garrisoning Fort Pillow has been such as to entitle them to being treated as prisoners of war. . . . Should my demand be refused, I cannot be responsible for the fate of your command."[2] Union Major William Bradford, who had **3** replaced Major Booth, killed earlier by sharpshooters, asked for an hour to consider the demand. Forrest, worried that vessels in the river were bringing in more troops, "shortened the time to twenty minutes."[3]

1 Writer's thesis. **2** Headings organize paper.
3 Quotation cited with endnote.

Sample *Chicago* endnotes

Notes

1 1. John Cimprich and Robert C. Mainfort Jr., eds., "Fort Pillow Revisited: New Evidence about an Old Controversy," *Civil War History* 28, no. 4 (1982): 293-94.

2 2. Quoted in Brian Steel Wills, *A Battle from the Start: The Life of Nathan Bedford Forrest* (New York: HarperCollins, 1992), 182.

3. Ibid., 183.

4. Shelby Foote, *The Civil War, a Narrative: Red River to Appomattox* (New York: Vintage, 1986), 110.

5. Nathan Bedford Forrest, "Report of Maj. Gen. Nathan B. Forrest, C. S. Army, Commanding Cavalry, of the Capture of Fort Pillow," Shotgun's Home of the American Civil War, accessed March 6, 2001, http://www.civilwarhome.com/forrest.htm.

3 6. Jack Hurst, *Nathan Bedford Forrest: A Biography* (New York: Knopf, 1993), 174.

7. Foote, *Civil War,* 111.

8. Cimprich and Mainfort, "Fort Pillow," 295.   **4**

9. Ibid., 305.

10. Ibid., 299.

11. Foote, *Civil War,* 110.

12. Quoted in Wills, *Battle from the Start,* 187.

13. Albert Castel, "The Fort Pillow Massacre: A Fresh   **5** Examination of the Evidence," *Civil War History* 4, no. 1 (1958): 44-45.

14. Cimprich and Mainfort, "Fort Pillow," 300.

1 First line of note indented ½". **2** Note number not raised, followed by period. **3** Authors' names not inverted. **4** Last names and shortened title refer to earlier note by same authors. **5** Single-space notes, double-space between them.

Sample *Chicago* bibliography

Bishop 10

Bibliography

1 Castel, Albert. "The Fort Pillow Massacre: A Fresh Examination of the Evidence." *Civil War History* 4, no. 1 (1958): 37-50.

Cimprich, John, and Robert C. Mainfort Jr., eds. "Fort Pillow Revisited: New Evidence about an Old Controversy." *Civil War History* 28, no. 4 (1982): 293-306.

2 Cornish, Dudley Taylor. *The Sable Arm: Black Troops in the Union Army, 1861-1865.* Lawrence, KS: University Press of Kansas, 1987.

Foote, Shelby. *The Civil War, a Narrative: Red River to Appomattox.* New York: Vintage, 1986.

Forrest, Nathan Bedford. "Report of Maj. Gen. Nathan Bedford Forrest, C. S. Army, Commanding Cavalry, of the Capture of Fort Pillow." Shotgun's Home of the American Civil War. Accessed March 6, 2001. http://www.civilwarhome.com /forrest.htm.

Hurst, Jack. *Nathan Bedford Forrest: A Biography.* New York: Knopf, **3** 1993.

McPherson, James M. *Battle Cry of Freedom: The Civil War Era.* New York: Oxford University Press, 1988.

Wills, Brian Steel. *A Battle from the Start: The Life of Nathan Bedford Forrest.* New York: HarperCollins, 1992.

1 Alphabetize by authors' last names. **2** First line of each entry at left margin, additional lines indented ½". **3** Single-space entries, double-space between them.

Glossaries

44 Glossary of usage

This glossary includes words commonly confused, words commonly misused, and words that are nonstandard. It also lists colloquialisms that may be appropriate in informal speech but are inappropriate in formal writing.

> **ON THE WEB >** dianahacker.com/pocket **>** Language Debates
> > Absolute concepts such as *unique*
> > *bad* versus *badly*
> > *however* at the beginning of a sentence
> > *lie* versus *lay*
> > *myself*
> > *that* versus *which*
> > *who* versus *which* or *that*
> > *who* versus *whom*
> > *you*

a, an   Use *an* before a vowel sound, *a* before a consonant sound: *an apple, a peach*. Problems sometimes arise with words beginning with *h* or *u*. If the h is silent, the word begins with a vowel sound, so use *an*: *an hour, an heir, an honest senator*. If the *h* is pronounced, the word begins with a consonant sound, so use *a*: *a hospital, a historian, a hotel*. Words such as *university* and *union* begin with a consonant sound, so use *a*: *a union*. Words such as *uncle* and *umbrella* begin with a vowel sound, so use *an*: *an underground well*. When an abbreviation or acronym begins with a vowel sound, use *an*: *an EKG, an MRI*.

accept, except   *Accept* is a verb meaning "to receive." *Except* is usually a preposition meaning "excluding." *I will accept all the packages except that one. Except* is also a verb meaning "to exclude." *Please except that item from the list.*

adapt, adopt   *Adapt* means "to adjust or become accustomed"; it is usually followed by *to. Adopt* means "to take as one's own." *Our family adopted a Vietnamese orphan, who quickly adapted to his new surroundings.*

adverse, averse   *Adverse* means "unfavorable." *Averse* means "opposed" or "reluctant"; it is usually followed by *to. I am averse to your proposal because it could have an adverse impact on the economy.*

advice, advise   *Advice* is a noun, *advise* a verb. *We advise you to follow John's advice.*

affect, effect   *Affect* is usually a verb meaning "to influence." *Effect* is usually a noun meaning "result." *The drug did not affect the disease, and it had adverse side effects. Effect* can also be a verb meaning "to bring about." *Only the president can effect such a change.*

all ready, already   *All ready* means "completely prepared." *Already* means "previously." *Susan was all ready for the concert, but her friends had already left.*

all right   *All right* is correct. *Alright* is nonstandard.

all together, altogether   *All together* means "everyone gathered." *Altogether* means "entirely." *We were not altogether sure that we could bring the family all together.*

allusion, illusion   An *allusion* is an indirect reference; an *illusion* is a misconception or false impression. *Did you catch my allusion to Shakespeare? Mirrors give the room an illusion of depth.*

a lot   *A lot* is two words. Do not write *alot.*

among, between   Ordinarily, use *among* with three or more entities, *between* with two. *The prize was divided among several contestants. You have a choice between carrots and beans.*

amoral, immoral   *Amoral* means "neither moral nor immoral"; it also means "not caring about moral judgments." *Immoral* means "morally wrong." *Many business courses are taught from an amoral perspective. Murder is immoral.*

amount, number   Use *amount* with quantities that cannot be counted; use *number* with those that can. *This recipe calls for a large amount of sugar. We have a large number of toads in our garden.*

an   See *a, an.*

and/or   Avoid *and/or* except in technical or legal documents.

anxious   *Anxious* means "worried" or "apprehensive." In formal writing, avoid using *anxious* to mean "eager." *We are eager* (not *anxious*) *to see your new house.*

anybody, anyone   See pages 22–23 and 32–33.

anyone, any one   *Anyone,* an indefinite pronoun, means "any person at all." *Any one* refers to a particular person or thing in a group. *Anyone in the class may choose any one of the books to read.*

anyways, anywheres   *Anyways* and *anywheres* are nonstandard for *anyway* and *anywhere.*

as   *As* is sometimes used to mean "because." But do not use it if there is any chance of ambiguity. *We canceled the picnic because* (not *as*) *it began raining. As* here could mean "because" or "when."

as, like See *like, as.*

averse See *adverse, averse.*

awful The adjective *awful* and the adverb *awfully* are too colloquial for formal writing.

awhile, a while *Awhile* is an adverb; it can modify a verb, but it cannot be the object of a preposition such as *for.* The two-word form *a while* is a noun preceded by an article and therefore can be the object of a preposition. *Stay awhile. Stay for a while.*

back up, backup *Back up* is a verb phrase. *Back up the car carefully. Be sure to back up your hard drive. Backup* is a noun often meaning "duplicate of electronically stored data." *Keep your backup in a safe place. Backup* can also be used as an adjective. *I regularly create backup disks.*

bad, badly *Bad* is an adjective, *badly* an adverb. *They felt bad about being early and ruining the surprise. Her arm hurt badly after she slid into second.* See section 13.

being as, being that *Being as* and *being that* are nonstandard expressions. Write *because* instead.

beside, besides *Beside* is a preposition meaning "at the side of" or "next to." *Annie Oakley slept with her gun beside her bed. Besides* is a preposition meaning "except" or "in addition to." *No one besides Terrie can have that ice cream. Besides* is also an adverb meaning "in addition." *I'm not hungry; besides, I don't like ice cream.*

between See *among, between.*

bring, take Use *bring* when an object is being transported toward you, *take* when it is being moved away. *Please bring me a glass of water. Please take these magazines to Mr. Scott.*

can, may *Can* is traditionally reserved for ability, *may* for permission. *Can you speak French? May I help you?*

capital, capitol *Capital* refers to a city, *capitol* to a building where lawmakers meet. *The residents of the state capital protested the development plans. The capitol has undergone extensive renovations. Capital* also refers to wealth or resources.

censor, censure *Censor* means "to remove or suppress material considered objectionable." *Censure* means "to criticize severely." *The school's policy of censoring books has been censured by the media.*

cite, site *Cite* means "to quote as an authority or example." *Site* is usually a noun meaning "a particular place." *He cited the zoning law in his argument against the proposed site of the gas station.* Locations on the Internet are usually referred to as *sites.*

coarse, course   *Coarse* means "crude" or "rough in texture." *The hand-knit sweater had a coarse weave. Course* usually refers to a path, a playing field, or a unit of study. *I plan to take a course in car repair this summer.* The expression *of course* means "certainly."

complement, compliment   *Complement* is a verb meaning "to go with or complete" or a noun meaning "something that completes." *Compliment* as a verb means "to flatter"; as a noun it means "a flattering remark." *Her skill at rushing the net complements his skill at volleying. Sheiying's music arrangements receive many compliments.*

conscience, conscious   *Conscience* is a noun meaning "moral principles"; *conscious* is an adjective meaning "aware or alert." *Let your conscience be your guide. Were you conscious of his love for you?*

continual, continuous   *Continual* means "repeated regularly and frequently." *She grew weary of the continual telephone calls. Continuous* means "extended or prolonged without interruption." *The broken siren made a continuous wail.*

could care less   *Could care less* is a nonstandard expression. Write *couldn't care less* instead.

could of   *Could of* is nonstandard for *could have.*

council, counsel   A *council* is a deliberative body, and a *councilor* is a member of such a body. *Counsel* usually means "advice" and can also mean "lawyer"; a *counselor* is one who gives advice or guidance. *The councilors met to draft the council's position paper. The pastor offered wise counsel to the troubled teenager.*

criteria   *Criteria* is the plural of *criterion,* which means "a standard, rule, or test on which a judgment or decision can be based." *The only criterion for the scholarship is ability.*

data   *Data* is a plural noun meaning "facts or propositions." But *data* is increasingly being accepted as a singular noun. *The new data suggest* (or *suggests*) *that our theory is correct.* (The singular *datum* is rarely used.)

different from, different than   Ordinarily, write *different from. Your sense of style is different from Jim's.* However, *different than* is acceptable to avoid an awkward construction. *Please let me know if your plans are different than* (to avoid *from what*) *they were six weeks ago.*

don't   *Don't* is the contraction for *do not. I don't want any. Don't* should not be used as the contraction for *does not,* which is *doesn't. He doesn't* (not *don't*) *want any.*

due to   *Due to* is an adjective phrase and should not be used as a preposition meaning "because of." *The trip was canceled* *because of* (not *due to*) *lack of interest. Due to* is acceptable as a subject complement and usually follows a form of the verb *be*. *His success was due to hard work.*

each See pages 22–23 and 32–33.

effect See *affect, effect.*

either See pages 22–23 and 32–33.

elicit, illicit *Elicit* is a verb meaning "to bring out" or "to evoke." *Illicit* is an adjective meaning "unlawful." *The reporter was unable to elicit any information from the police about illicit drug traffic.*

emigrate from, immigrate to *Emigrate* means "to leave one place to settle in another." *My grandfather emigrated from Russia to escape the religious pogroms. Immigrate* means "to enter another place and reside there." *Many Mexicans immigrate to the United States to find work.*

enthused As an adjective, *enthusiastic* is preferred. *The children were enthusiastic* (not *enthused*) *about going to the circus.*

etc. Avoid ending a list with *etc.* It is more emphatic to end with an example, and usually readers will understand that the list is not exhaustive. When you don't wish to end with an example, *and so on* is more graceful than *etc.*

everybody, everyone See pages 22–23 and 32–33.

everyone, every one *Everyone* is an indefinite pronoun. *Everyone wanted to go. Every one,* the pronoun *one* preceded by the adjective *every,* means "each individual or thing in a particular group." *Every one* is usually followed by *of. Every one of the missing books was found.*

except See *accept, except.*

farther, further *Farther* describes distances. *Further* suggests quantity or degree. *Detroit is farther from Miami than I thought. You extended the curfew further than necessary.*

fewer, less *Fewer* refers to items that can be counted; *less* refers to items that cannot be counted. *Fewer people are living in the city. Please put less sugar in my tea.*

firstly *Firstly* sounds pretentious, and it leads to the ungainly series *firstly, secondly, thirdly, fourthly,* and so on. Write *first, second, third* instead.

further See *farther, further.*

good, well See page 41.

graduate Both of the following uses of *graduate* are standard: *My sister was graduated from UCLA last year. My sister grad-*

uated from UCLA last year. It is nonstandard to drop the word *from*: *My sister graduated UCLA last year*.

grow Phrases such as *to grow a business* are jargon. Usually the verb *grow* is intransitive (it does not take a direct object). *Our business has grown very quickly*. When *grow* is used in a transitive sense, with a direct object, it means "to cultivate" or "to allow to grow." *We plan to grow tomatoes. John is growing a beard.*

hanged, hung *Hanged* is the past-tense and past-participle form of the verb *hang*, meaning "to execute." *The prisoner was hanged at dawn. Hung* is the past-tense and past-participle form of the verb *hang*, meaning "to fasten or suspend." *The stockings were hung by the chimney with care.*

hardly Avoid expressions such as *can't hardly* and *not hardly*, which are considered double negatives. *I can* (not *can't*) *hardly describe my elation at getting the job.*

he At one time *he* was used to mean "he or she." Today such usage is inappropriate. See pages 18–19 and 32–33 for alternative constructions.

hisself *Hisself* is nonstandard. Use *himself*.

hopefully *Hopefully* means "in a hopeful manner." *We looked hopefully to the future.* Some usage experts object to the use of *hopefully* as a sentence adverb, apparently on grounds of clarity. To be safe, avoid using *hopefully* in sentences such as the following: *Hopefully, your son will recover soon.* Instead, indicate who is doing the hoping: *I hope that your son will recover soon.*

however Some writers object to *however* at the beginning of a sentence, but experts advise placing the word according to the meaning and emphasis intended. Any of the following sentences is correct, depending on the intended contrast. *Pam decided, however, to attend Harvard. However, Pam decided to attend Harvard.* (She had been considering other schools.) *Pam, however, decided to attend Harvard.* (Unlike someone else, Pam opted for Harvard.)

hung See *hanged, hung.*

illusion See *allusion, illusion.*

immigrate See *emigrate from, immigrate to.*

immoral See *amoral, immoral.*

imply, infer *Imply* means "to suggest or state indirectly"; *infer* means "to draw a conclusion." *John implied that he knew all about computers, but the interviewer inferred that John was inexperienced.*

in, into   *In* indicates location or condition; *into* indicates movement or a change in condition. *They found the lost letters in a box after moving into the house.*

in regards to   Use either *in regard to* or *as regards*. *In regard to (or As regards) the contract, ignore the first clause.*

irregardless   *Irregardless* is nonstandard. Use *regardless*.

is when, is where   See section 6c.

its, it's   *Its* is a possessive pronoun; *it's* is a contraction for *it is*. *The dog licked its wound whenever its owner walked into the room. It's a perfect day to walk the twenty-mile trail.*

kind of, sort of   Avoid using *kind of* or *sort of* to mean "somewhat." *The movie was a little* (not *kind of*) *boring.* Do not put *a* after either phrase. *That kind of* (not *kind of a*) *salesclerk annoys me.*

lay, lie   See pages 26–27.

lead, led   *Lead* is a metallic element; it is a noun. *Led* is the past tense of the verb *lead. He led me to the treasure.*

learn, teach   *Learn* means "to gain knowledge"; *teach* means "to impart knowledge." *I must teach* (not *learn*) *my sister to read.*

leave, let   Leave means "to exit." Avoid using it with the nonstandard meaning "to permit." *Let* (not *Leave*) *me help you with the dishes.*

less   See *fewer, less*.

let, leave   See *leave, let*.

liable   *Liable* means "obligated" or "responsible." Do not use it to mean "likely." *You're likely* (not *liable*) *to trip if you don't tie your shoelaces.*

lie, lay   See pages 26–27.

like, as   *Like* is a preposition, not a subordinating conjunction. It should be followed only by a noun or a noun phrase. *As* is a subordinating conjunction that introduces a subordinate clause. In casual speech, you may say *She looks like she has not slept.* But in formal writing, use *as. She looks as if she has not slept.*

loose, lose   *Loose* is an adjective meaning "not securely fastened." *Lose* is a verb meaning "to misplace" or "to not win." *Did you lose your only loose pair of work pants?*

may   See *can, may*.

maybe, may be   *Maybe* is an adverb meaning "possibly"; *may be* is a verb phrase. *Maybe the sun will shine tomorrow. Tomorrow may be a brighter day.*

may of, might of   *May of* and *might of* are nonstandard for *may have* and *might have*.

media, medium   *Media* is the plural of *medium*. *Of all the media that cover the Olympics, television is the medium that best captures the spectacle of the events.*

must of   See *may of, might of*.

myself   *Myself* is a reflexive or intensive pronoun. Reflexive: *I cut myself.* Intensive: *I will drive you myself.* Do not use *myself* in place of *I* or *me*: *He gave the plants to Melinda and me* (not *myself*).

neither   See pages 22–23 and 32–33.

none   See pages 22–23 and 32–33.

nowheres   *Nowheres* is nonstandard for *nowhere*.

number   See *amount, number*.

off of   *Off* is sufficient. Omit *of*.

passed, past   *Passed* is the past tense of the verb *pass. Emily passed me a slice of cake. Past* usually means "belonging to a former time" or "beyond a time or place." *Our past president spoke until past 10:00. The hotel is just past the station.*

plus   *Plus* should not be used to join independent clauses. *This raincoat is dirty; moreover* (not *plus*), *it has a hole in it.*

precede, proceed   *Precede* means "to come before." *Proceed* means "to go forward." *As we proceeded up the mountain, we saw evidence that some hikers had preceded us.*

principal, principle   *Principal* is a noun meaning "the head of a school or an organization" or "a sum of money." It is also an adjective meaning "most important." *Principle* is a noun meaning "a basic truth or law." *The principal expelled her for three principal reasons. We believe in the principle of equal justice for all.*

proceed, precede   See *precede, proceed*.

quote, quotation   *Quote* is a verb; *quotation* is a noun. Avoid using *quote* as a shortened form of *quotation. Her quotations* (not *quotes*) *from Shakespeare intrigued us.*

real, really   *Real* is an adjective; *really* is an adverb. *Real* is sometimes used informally as an adverb, but avoid this use in formal writing. *She was really* (not *real*) *angry.* See section 13.

reason . . . is because   See section 6c.

reason why   The expression *reason why* is redundant. *The reason* (not *The reason why*) *Jones lost the election is clear.*

respectfully, respectively   *Respectfully* means "showing or marked by respect." *He respectfully submitted his opinion.* *Respectively* means "each in the order given." *John, Tom, and Larry were a butcher, a baker, and a lawyer, respectively.*

sensual, sensuous   *Sensual* means "gratifying the physical senses," especially those associated with sexual pleasure. *Sensuous* means "pleasing to the senses," especially involving art, music, and nature. *The sensuous music and balmy air led the dancers to more sensual movements.*

set, sit   *Set* means "to put" or "to place"; *sit* means "to be seated." *She set the dough in a warm corner of the kitchen. The cat sits in the warmest part of the room.*

should of   *Should of* is nonstandard for *should have.*

since   Do not use *since* to mean "because" if there is any chance of ambiguity. *Because* (not *Since*) *we won the game, we have been celebrating with a pitcher of root beer. Since* here could mean "because" or "from the time that."

sit   See *set, sit.*

site, cite   See *cite, site.*

somebody, someone, something   See pages 22–23 and 32–33.

suppose to   Write *supposed to.*

sure and   *Sure and* is nonstandard for *sure to.* *Be sure to* (not *sure and*) *bring a gift for the host.*

take   See *bring, take.*

than, then   *Than* is a conjunction used in comparisons; *then* is an adverb denoting time. *That pizza is more than I can eat. Tom laughed, and then we recognized him.*

that   See *who, which, that.*

that, which   Many writers reserve *that* for restrictive clauses, *which* for nonrestrictive clauses. (See pp. 60–61.)

theirselves   *Theirselves* is nonstandard for *themselves.*

them   The use of *them* in place of *those* is nonstandard. *Please send those* (not *them*) *letters to the sponsors.*

then   See *than, then.*

there, their, they're   *There* is an adverb specifying place; it is also an expletive (placeholder). Adverb: *Sylvia is lying there unconscious.* Expletive: *There are two plums left. Their* is a possessive pronoun. *Fred and Jane finally washed their car. They're* is a contraction of *they are. They're late today.*

to, too, two   *To* is a preposition; *too* is an adverb; *two* is a number. *Too many of your shots slice to the left, but the last two were right on the mark.*

toward, towards   *Toward* and *towards* are generally interchangeable, although *toward* is preferred in American English.

try and   *Try and* is nonstandard for *try to*. *I will try to* (not *try and*) *be better about writing to you.*

unique   See page 42.

use to   Write *used to*.

utilize   *Utilize* is often a pretentious substitute for *use*; in most cases, *use* is sufficient. *I used* (not *utilized*) *the best workers to get the job done fast.*

wait for, wait on   *Wait for* means "to be in readiness for" or "await." *Wait on* means "to serve." *We're waiting for* (not *waiting on*) *Ruth before we can leave.*

ways   *Ways* is colloquial when used in place of *way* to mean "distance." *The city is a long way* (not *ways*) *from here.*

weather, whether   The noun *weather* refers to the state of the atmosphere. *Whether* is a conjunction referring to a choice between alternatives. *We wondered whether the weather would clear up in time for our picnic.*

well, good   See page 40.

where   Do not use *where* in place of *that*. *I heard that* (not *where*) *the crime rate is increasing.*

which   See *that, which* and *who, which, that.*

while   Avoid using *while* to mean "although" or "whereas" if there is any chance of ambiguity. *Although* (not *While*) *Gloria lost money in the slot machine, Tom won it at roulette.* Here *While* could mean either "although" or "at the same time that."

who, which, that   Use *who*, not *which*, to refer to persons. Generally, use *that* to refer to things or, occasionally, to a group or class of people. *The player who* (not *that* or *which*) *made the basket at the buzzer was named MVP. The team that scores the most points in this game will win the tournament.*

who, whom   See section 12d.

who's, whose   *Who's* is a contraction of *who is*; *whose* is a possessive pronoun. *Who's ready for more popcorn? Whose coat is this?*

would of   *Would of* is nonstandard for *would have*.

you   See page 35.

your, you're   *Your* is a possessive pronoun; *you're* is a contraction of *you are. Is that your bike? You're in the finals.*

45   Glossary of grammatical terms

This glossary gives definitions for parts of speech, such as nouns; parts of sentences, such as subjects; and types of sentences, clauses, and phrases.

If you are looking up the name of an error (sentence fragment, for example), consult the index or the table of contents instead.

absolute phrase   A word group that modifies a whole clause or sentence, usually consisting of a noun followed by a participle or participial phrase: *His words dipped in honey,* the senator mesmerized the crowd.

active vs. passive voice   When a verb is in the active voice, the subject of the sentence does the action: *Hernando caught* the ball. In the passive voice, the subject receives the action: The *ball was caught* by Hernando. Often the actor does not appear in a passive-voice sentence: The *ball was caught.* Also see section 2.

adjective   A word used to modify (describe) a noun or pronoun: the *lame* dog, *rare old* stamps, *sixteen* candles. Adjectives usually answer one of these questions: Which one? What kind of? How many or how much? Also see section 13.

adjective clause   A subordinate clause that modifies a noun or pronoun. An adjective clause begins with a relative pronoun (*who, whom, whose, which, that*) or a relative adverb (*when, where*) and usually appears right after the word it modifies: The arrow *that has left the bow* never returns.

adverb   A word used to modify a verb, an adjective, or another adverb: rides *smoothly, unusually* attractive, *very* slowly. An adverb usually answers one of these questions: When? Where? How? Why? Under what conditions? To what degree? Also see section 13.

adverb clause   A subordinate clause that modifies a verb (or occasionally an adjective or adverb). An adverb clause begins with a subordinating conjunction such as *although, because, if, unless,* or *when* and usually appears at the beginning or the end of a sentence: *When the well is dry*, we know the worth of water. Don't talk *unless you can improve the silence.* Also see *subordinate clause; subordinating conjunction.*

agreement   See sections 10 and 12.

antecedent   A noun or pronoun to which a pronoun refers: When the *wheel* squeaks, *it* is greased. *Wheel* is the antecedent of the pronoun *it.*

appositive   A noun or noun phrase that renames a nearby noun or pronoun: Politicians, *acrobats at heart,* can lean on both sides of an issue at once.

article   The word *a, an,* or *the,* used to mark a noun. Also see 16b.

case   See sections 12c and 12d.

clause   A word group containing a subject, a verb, and any objects, complements, or modifiers. See *independent clause; subordinate clause.*

collective noun   See sections 10e and 12a.

common noun   See section 22a.

complement   See *subject complement; object complement.*

complex sentence   A sentence consisting of one independent clause and one or more subordinate clauses. In the following example, the subordinate clause is italicized: We walked along the river *until we came to the bridge.*

compound-complex sentence   A sentence consisting of at least two independent clauses and at least one subordinate clause: Jan dictated a story, and the children wrote whatever he said. In the preceding sentence, the subordinate clause is *whatever he said.* The two independent clauses are *Jan dictated a story* and *the children wrote whatever he said.*

compound sentence   A sentence consisting of two independent clauses. The clauses are usually joined with a comma and a coordinating conjunction (*and, but, or, nor, for, so, yet*) or with a semicolon: *One arrow is easily broken,* but *you can't break a bundle of ten. Love is blind; envy has its eyes wide open.*

conjunction   A joining word. See *coordinating conjunction; correlative conjunction; subordinating conjunction; conjunctive adverb.*

conjunctive adverb   An adverb used with a semicolon to connect independent clauses: If an animal does something, we call it instinct; *however,* if we do the same thing, we call it intelligence. The most commonly used conjunctive adverbs are *consequently, furthermore, however, moreover, nevertheless, then, therefore,* and *thus.* See page 66 for a longer list.

coordinating conjunction   One of the following words, used to join elements of equal grammatical rank: *and, but, or, nor, for, so, yet.*

correlative conjunction A pair of conjunctions connecting grammatically equal elements: *either . . . or, neither . . . nor, whether . . . or, not only . . . but also,* and *both . . . and.* Also see 3b.

count noun See page 51.

demonstrative pronoun A pronoun used to identify or point to a noun: *this, that, these, those. This* is my favorite chair.

direct object A word or word group that receives the action of the verb: The little snake studies *the ways of the big serpent.* The complete direct object is *the ways of the big serpent.* The simple direct object is always a noun or a pronoun, in this case *ways.*

expletive The word *there* or *it* when used at the beginning of a sentence to delay the subject: *There* are many paths to the top of the mountain. *It* is not good to wake a sleeping lion. The delayed subjects are the noun *paths* and the infinitive phrase *to wake a sleeping lion.*

gerund A verb form ending in *-ing* used as a noun: *Reading* aloud helps children appreciate language. *Reading* is used as the subject of the verb *helps.*

gerund phrase A gerund and its objects, complements, or modifiers. A gerund phrase always functions as a noun, usually as a subject, a subject complement, or a direct object. In the following example, the phrase functions as a direct object: We tried *planting on the hill.*

helping verb One of the following words, when used with a main verb: *be, am, is, are, was, were, being, been; has, have, had; do, does, did; can, will, shall, should, could, would, may, might, must.* Helping verbs always precede main verbs: *will work, is working, had worked.* Also see *modal verb.*

indefinite pronoun A pronoun that refers to a nonspecific person or thing: *Anyone* who serves God for money will serve the Devil for better wages. The most common indefinite pronouns are *all, another, any, anybody, anyone, anything, both, each, either, everybody, everyone, everything, few, many, neither, nobody, none, no one, nothing, one, some, somebody, someone, something.*

independent clause A word group containing a subject and a verb that can or does stand alone as a sentence. In addition to at least one independent clause, many sentences contain subordinate clauses that function as adjectives, adverbs, or nouns. Also see *clause; subordinate clause.*

indirect object A noun or pronoun that names to whom or for whom the action of a sentence is done: Fate gives *us* our relatives. An indirect object always precedes a direct object, in this case *our relatives*.

infinitive   The word *to* followed by the base form of a verb: *to think, to dream.*

infinitive phrase   An infinitive and its objects, complements, or modifiers. An infinitive phrase can function as a noun, an adjective, or an adverb. Subject: *To side with truth* is noble. Adjective: We do not have the right *to abandon the poor.* Adverb: Do not use a hatchet *to remove a fly from your friend's forehead.*

intensive or reflexive pronoun   A pronoun ending in *-self*: *myself, yourself, himself, herself, itself, ourselves, yourselves, themselves.* An intensive pronoun emphasizes a noun or another pronoun: I *myself* don't understand my moods. A reflexive pronoun names a receiver of an action identical with the doer of the action: Did Paula cut *herself*?

interjection   A word expressing surprise or emotion: *Oh! Wow! Hey! Hooray!*

interrogative pronoun   A pronoun used to introduce a question: *who, whom, whose, which, what. What* does history teach us?

intransitive verb   See *transitive and intransitive verbs.*

irregular verb   See *regular and irregular verbs.* Also see section 11a.

linking verb   A verb that links a subject to a subject complement, a word or word group that renames or describes the subject: Prejudice *is* the child of ignorance. Good medicine sometimes *tastes* bitter. The most common linking verbs are forms of *be*: *be, am, is, are, was, were, being, been.* The following verbs sometimes function as linking verbs: *appear, become, feel, grow, look, make, seem, smell, sound, taste.*

modal verb   A helping verb that cannot be used as a main verb. There are nine modals: *can, could, may, might, must, shall, should, will,* and *would*: We *must* shut the windows before the storm. The verb phrase *ought to* is often classified as a modal as well. Also see *helping verb.*

modifier   A word, phrase, or clause that describes or qualifies the meaning of a word. Modifiers include adjectives, adverbs, prepositional phrases, participial phrases, some infinitive phrases, and adjective and adverb clauses.

mood   See section 11c.

noncount noun   See pages 52–53.

noun The name of a person, place, thing, or concept (*freedom*): The *cat* in *gloves* catches no *mice.*

noun clause A subordinate clause that functions as a noun, usually as a subject, a subject complement, or a direct object. In the following sentence, the italicized noun clauses function as subject and subject complement: *What history teaches us* is *that we have never learned anything from it.* Noun clauses usually begin with *how, who, whom, whoever, that, what, whatever, whether,* or *why.*

noun equivalent A word or word group that functions like a noun: a pronoun, a noun and its modifiers, a gerund phrase, some infinitive phrases, a noun clause.

object See *direct object*; *indirect object.*

object complement A word or word group that renames or describes a direct object. It always appears after the direct object: Our fears do make us *traitors.* Love makes all hard hearts *gentle.*

object of a preposition See *prepositional phrase.*

participial phrase A present or past participle and its objects, complements, or modifiers. A participial phrase always functions as an adjective describing a noun or pronoun. Usually it appears before or after the word it modifies: *Being weak,* foxes are distinguished by superior tact. Truth *kept in the dark* will never save the world.

participle, past A verb form usually ending in *-d, -ed, -n, -en,* or *-t: asked, stolen, fought.* Past participles are used with helping verbs to form perfect tenses (had *spoken*) and the passive voice (were *required*). They are also used as adjectives (the *stolen* car).

participle, present A verb form ending in *-ing.* Present participles are used with helping verbs in progressive forms (is *rising,* has been *walking*). They are also used as adjectives (the *rising* tide).

parts of speech A system for classifying words. Many words can function as more than one part of speech. See *noun, pronoun, verb, adjective, adverb, preposition, conjunction, interjection.*

passive voice See *active vs. passive voice.*

personal pronoun One of the following pronouns, used to refer to a specific person or thing: *I, me, you, she, her, he, him, it, we, us, they, them.* Admonish your friends in private; praise *them* in public. Also see *antecedent.*

phrase   A word group that lacks a subject, a verb, or both. Most phrases function within sentences as adjectives, as adverbs, or as nouns. See *absolute phrase; appositive; gerund phrase; infinitive phrase; participial phrase; prepositional phrase.*

possessive case   See section 19a.

possessive pronoun   A pronoun used to indicate ownership: *my, mine, your, yours, her, hers, his, its, our, ours, your, yours, their, theirs.* A cock has great influence on *his* own dunghill.

predicate   A verb and any objects, complements, and modifiers that go with it: A clean glove *often hides a dirty hand.*

preposition   A word placed before a noun or noun equivalent to form a phrase modifying another word in the sentence. The preposition indicates the relation between the noun (or noun equivalent) and the word the phrase modifies. The most common prepositions are *about, above, across, after, against, along, among, around, at, before, behind, below, beside, besides, between, beyond, by, down, during, except, for, from, in, inside, into, like, near, of, off, on, onto, out, outside, over, past, since, than, through, to, toward, under, unlike, until, up, with, within,* and *without.*

prepositional phrase   A phrase beginning with a preposition and ending with a noun or noun equivalent (called the *object of the preposition*). Most prepositional phrases function as adjectives or adverbs. Adjective phrases usually come right after the noun or pronoun they modify: Variety is the spice *of life.* Adverb phrases usually appear at the beginning or the end of the sentence: *To the ant,* a few drops of rain are a flood. Do not judge a tree *by its bark.*

progressive verb forms   See pages 30 and 49–50.

pronoun   A word used in place of a noun. Usually the pronoun substitutes for a specific noun, known as the pronoun's *antecedent.* In the following example, *elephant* is the antecedent of the pronoun *him:* When an *elephant* is in trouble, even a frog will kick *him.* See also *demonstrative pronoun; indefinite pronoun; intensive or reflexive pronoun; interrogative pronoun; personal pronoun; possessive pronoun; relative pronoun.*

proper noun   See section 22a.

regular and irregular verbs   When a verb is regular, both the past tense and the past participle are formed by adding *-ed* or *-d* to the base form of the verb: *walk, walked, walked.* The past tense and past participle of irregular verbs are formed in a variety of other ways: *ride, rode, ridden; begin, began, begun; go, went, gone;* and so on. Also see 11a.

relative adverb　The word *when* or *where*, when used to introduce an adjective clause. Also see *adjective clause*.

relative pronoun　One of the following words, when used to introduce an adjective clause: *who, whom, whose, which, that.* A fable is a bridge *that* leads to truth.

sentence　A word group consisting of at least one independent clause. Also see *simple sentence; compound sentence; complex sentence; compound-complex sentence.*

simple sentence　A sentence consisting of one independent clause and no subordinate clauses: *The frog in the well knows nothing of the ocean.*

subject　A word or word group that names who or what the sentence is about. In the following example, the complete subject (the simple subject and all of its modifiers) is italicized: *Historical books that contain no lies* are tedious. The simple subject is *books.* Also see *subject after verb; understood subject.*

subject after verb　Although the subject normally precedes the verb, sentences are sometimes inverted. In the following example, the subject *the real tinsel* comes after the verb *lies:* Behind the phony tinsel of Hollywood *lies the real tinsel.* When a sentence begins with the expletive *there* or *it,* the subject always follows the verb. Also see *expletive.*

subject complement　A word or word group that follows a linking verb and either renames or describes the subject of the sentence. If the subject complement renames the subject, it is a noun or a noun equivalent: The handwriting on the wall may be *a forgery.* If it describes the subject, it is an adjective: Love is *blind.*

subjunctive mood　See section 11c.

subordinate clause　A word group containing a subject and verb that cannot stand alone as a sentence. Subordinate clauses function within sentences as adjectives, adverbs, or nouns. They begin with subordinating conjunctions such as *although, because, if,* and *until* or with relative pronouns such as *who, which,* and *that.* See *adjective clause; adverb clause; noun clause.*

subordinating conjunction　A word that introduces a subordinate clause and indicates the relation of the clause to the rest of the sentence. The most common subordinating conjunctions are *after, although, as, as if, because, before, even though, if, since, so that, than, that, though, unless, until, when, where, whether,* and *while.* Note: The relative pronouns *who, whom, whose, which,* and *that* also introduce subordinate clauses.

tenses　See section 11b.

transitive and intransitive verbs   Transitive verbs take direct objects, nouns or noun equivalents that receive the action. In the following example, the transitive verb *loves* takes the direct object *its mother*: A spoiled child never *loves* its mother. Intransitive verbs do not take direct objects: Money *talks*. If any words follow an intransitive verb, they are adverbs or word groups functioning as adverbs: The sun *will set* without your assistance.

understood subject   The subject *you* when it is understood but not actually present in the sentence. Understood subjects occur in sentences that issue commands or advice: [*You*] Hitch your wagon to a star.

verb   A word that expresses action (*jump, think*) or being (*is, was*). A sentence's verb is composed of a main verb possibly preceded by one or more helping verbs: The best fish *swim* near the bottom. A marriage *is* not *built* in a day. Verbs have five forms: the base form, or dictionary form (*walk, ride*); the past-tense form (*walked, rode*); the past participle (*walked, ridden*); the present participle (*walking, riding*); and the *-s* form (*walks, rides*).

verbal phrase   See *gerund phrase*; *infinitive phrase*; *participial phrase*.

A List of Style Manuals

A Pocket Style Manual describes three commonly used systems of documentation: MLA, used in English and the humanities (see section 32); APA, used in psychology and the social sciences (see section 37); and *Chicago,* used primarily in history (see section 42). Following is a list of style manuals used in a variety of disciplines.

BIOLOGY (See <http://dianahacker.com/resdoc> for more information.)

Council of Science Editors. *Scientific Style and Format: The CSE Manual for Authors, Editors, and Publishers.* 7th ed. Reston: Council of Science Eds., 2006. Print.

BUSINESS

American Management Association. *The AMA Style Guide for Business Writing.* New York: AMACOM, 1996. Print.

CHEMISTRY

Coghill, Anne M., and Lorrin R. Garson, eds. *The ACS Style Guide: Effective Communication of Scientific Information.* 3rd ed. Washington: Amer. Chemical Soc., 2006. Print.

ENGINEERING

Institute of Electrical and Electronics Engineers. *IEEE Standards Style Manual.* IEEE, 2007. Web. 9 Feb. 2009.

ENGLISH AND OTHER HUMANITIES (See section 32.)

MLA Handbook for Writers of Research Papers. 7th ed. New York: MLA, 2009. Print.

GEOLOGY

Bates, Robert L., Rex Buchanan, and Marla Adkins-Heljeson, eds. *Geowriting: A Guide to Writing, Editing, and Printing in Earth Science.* 5th ed. Alexandria: Amer. Geological Inst., 1995. Print.

GOVERNMENT DOCUMENTS

Garner, Diane L. *The Complete Guide to Citing Government Information Resources: A Manual for Social Science and Business Research.* 3rd ed. Bethesda: Congressional Information Service, 2002. Print.

United States Government Printing Office. *Style Manual.* Washington: GPO, 2000. Print.

HISTORY (See section 42.)

The Chicago Manual of Style. 16th ed. Chicago: U of Chicago P, 2010. Print.

JOURNALISM

Goldstein, Norm, ed. *Associated Press Stylebook and Briefing on Media Law.* Rev. ed. New York: Associated Press, 2005. Print.

LAW

Harvard Law Review et al. *The Bluebook: A Uniform System of Citation.* 18th ed. Cambridge: Harvard Law Rev. Assn., 2005. Print.

LINGUISTICS

Linguistic Society of America. Language *Style Sheet.* LSA, n.d. Web. 9 Feb. 2009.

MATHEMATICS

American Mathematical Society. *Author Resource Center.* AMS, 2009. Web. 9 Feb. 2009.

MEDICINE

Iverson, Cheryl, et al. *American Medical Association Manual of Style: A Guide for Authors and Editors.* 9th ed. Baltimore: Williams, 1998. Print.

MUSIC

Holoman, D. Kern, ed. *Writing about Music: A Style Sheet from the Editors of* 19th-Century Music. Berkeley: U of California P, 1988. Print.

PHYSICS

American Institute of Physics. *Style Manual: Instructions to Authors and Volume Editors for the Preparation of AIP Book Manuscripts.* 5th ed. New York: AIP, 1995. Print.

POLITICAL SCIENCE

American Political Science Association. *Style Manual for Political Science.* Rev. ed. Washington: APSA, 2001. Print.

PSYCHOLOGY AND OTHER SOCIAL SCIENCES (See section 37.)

American Psychological Association. *Publication Manual of the American Psychological Association.* 6th ed. Washington: APA, 2010. Print.

SCIENCE AND TECHNICAL WRITING

American National Standards Institute. *American National Standard for the Preparation of Scientific Papers for Written or Oral Presentation.* New York: ANSI, 1979. Print.

Microsoft Corporation. *Microsoft Manual of Style for Technical Publications.* 3rd ed. Redmond: Microsoft, 2004. Print.

Rubens, Philip, ed. *Science and Technical Writing: A Manual of Style.* 2nd ed. New York: Routledge, 2001. Print.

SOCIAL WORK

National Association of Social Workers Press. *NASW Press Author Guidelines.* NASW P, 2009. Web. 9 Feb. 2009.

Index

B

Documentation Directory: MLA

For MLA in-text citations, see pages 120–27.

Documentation Directory: APA

For APA in-text citations, see pages 165–70.

Documentation Directory: *Chicago*

Charts and Lists for Quick Reference

Excerpts from Student Papers

MLA

RESEARCH PAPER   151–52

"Online Monitoring: A Threat to Employee Privacy in the Wired Workplace" by Anna Orlov

LITERATURE PAPER   153–54

"The Transformation of Mrs. Peters: An Analysis of 'A Jury of Her Peers'" by Dan Larson

APA

LITERATURE REVIEW   188–90

"Can Medication Cure Obesity in Children? A Review of the Literature" by Luisa Mirano

NURSING PRACTICE PAPER   191–93

"Acute Lymphoblastic Leukemia and Hypertension in One Client: A Nursing Practice Paper" by Julie Riss

BUSINESS PROPOSAL   194–95

"Proposal to Add a Wellness Program" by Kelly Ratajczak

Chicago

RESEARCH PAPER   227–30

"The Massacre at Fort Pillow: Holding Nathan Bedford Forrest Accountable" by Ned Bishop

For full texts of these and other student papers, including annotated bibliographies, visit <**dianahacker.com/ pocket**> and click on Model papers.

Checklist for Global Revision

Focus

► Is the thesis stated clearly enough? Is it placed where readers will notice it?

► Does each idea support the thesis?

Organization

► Can readers easily follow the structure? Would headings help?

► Do topic sentences signal new ideas?

► Are ideas presented in a logical order?

Content

► Is the supporting material persuasive?

► Are important ideas fully developed?

► Is the draft concise enough—free of irrelevant or repetitious material?

► Are the parts proportioned sensibly? Do major ideas receive enough attention?

Style

► Is the voice appropriate—not too stuffy, not too casual?

► Are the sentences clear, emphatic, and varied?

Use of quotations

► Is quoted material introduced with a signal phrase and documented with a citation?

► Is quoted material enclosed within quotation marks (unless it has been set off from the text)?

► Is each quotation word-for-word accurate? If not, do brackets or ellipsis marks indicate the changes or omissions?

Use of other source material

► Is the draft free of plagiarism? Are summaries and paraphrases written in the writer's own words—not copied or half-copied from the source?

► Has source material that is not common knowledge been documented?

Revision Symbols

abbr	abbreviation **23a**	" "	quotation marks **20**
ad	adverb or adjective **13**	.	period **21a**
add	add needed word **4**	?	question mark **21b**
agr	agreement **10, 12a**	!	exclamation point **21c**
appr	inappropriate language **9**	—	dash **21d**
art	article **16b**	( )	parentheses **21e**
awk	awkward	[ ]	brackets **21f**
cap	capital letter **22**	. . .	ellipsis mark **21g**
case	case **12c, 12d**	/	slash **21h**
cs	comma splice **15**	*pass*	ineffective passive **2b**
dm	dangling modifier **7c**	*pn agr*	pronoun agreement **12a**
-ed	*-ed* ending **11a**	*ref*	pronoun reference **12b**
ESL	English as a second language **16**	*run-on*	run-on sentence **15**
frag	sentence fragment **14**	*-s*	*-s* ending on verb **10, 16a**
fs	fused sentence **15**	*sexist*	sexist language **9d, 12a**
hyph	hyphen **24b**	*shift*	confusing shift **5**
irreg	irregular verb **11a**	*sl*	slang **9c**
ital	italics (underlining) **23c**	*sp*	misspelled word **24a**
jarg	jargon **9a**	*sv agr*	subject-verb agreement **10**
lc	use lowercase letter **22**	*t*	verb tense **11b**
mix	mixed construction **6**	*usage*	see glossary of usage
mm	misplaced modifier **7a–b, 7d**	*v*	voice **2**
mood	mood **11c**	*var*	sentence variety **8**
num	numbers **23b**	*vb*	problem with verb **11, 16a**
om	omitted word **4, 16c**	*w*	wordy **1**
p	punctuation	*//*	faulty parallelism **3**
⌃ ,	comma **17a–i**	⌃	insert
no ,	no comma **17j**	✗	obvious error
;	semicolon **18a**	#	insert space
:	colon **18b**	‿	close up space
⌄ '	apostrophe **19**		

Contents